GOLF

THE
MENTAL
GAME

GOLF

THE MENTAL GAME

Thinking
Your Way
Around the
Course

TOM DORSEL, Ph.D.

CUMBERLAND HOUSE

GOLF: THE MENTAL GAME
PUBLISHED BY CUMBERLAND HOUSE PUBLISHING, AN IMPRINT OF SOURCEBOOKS, INC.
P.O. Box 4410
Naperville, Illinois 60567-4410
www.sourcebooks.com

Cover design: Gore Studio, Inc.
Text design: John Mitchell

Library of Congress Cataloging-in-Publication Data

Dorsel, Thomas N.,
  Golf : the mental game : thinking your way around the course / Tom Dorsel.
    p. cm.
  Includes index.
    1. Golf—Psychological aspects. I. Title.

GV979.P75D67 2008
796.35201'9—dc22

2008001384

Printed in the United States of America

RRD 10 9 8 7 6 5 4 3

*To Mom and Dad, who made golf possible for me,
and Uncle Dick, who first took me out to play at age 10.*

CONTENTS

PREFACE

G olf: The Mental Game is a book that has been more than 12 years in the writing. It is composed of articles originally written by the author for *Golf Illustrated*, all with an eye toward being future "lessons" in this present comprehensive work. The organizational structure for the book revolves around three key areas: *Thinking, Emotion* and *Action*. An opening section on "The Basics" and a closing section on "The Strange Game of Golf" and its mental mysteries provide a frame for these core topics.

Many, if not most, golf psychology issues are addressed in these 50 lessons. You can expect minimal repetition, but when it does occur, it is because that point is important enough to mention more than once and/or it applies broadly to more than one area of golf.

As with *physical* lessons, take your time with these *psychological* lessons. Read a little bit at a time and then apply what you have learned. The real advances will occur when you put what you read into practice on the golf course.

ACKNOWLEDGMENTS

Appreciation is extended to the publishing and editorial staff of *Golf Illustrated,* especially editor Jason Sowards, for permission to reprint the articles in this volume. I am also grateful for the expert editing that the staff of *Golf Illustrated* provided over the years.

I would also like to thank the hundreds of golfers who contributed to my articles in ways that most are unaware. Some gave me outright suggestions for topics, but others just did things and said things on the golf course that supplied me with endless ideas to write about. In many ways this book would not have materialized without their stimulating interaction.

I would also like to thank the current publisher, Ron Pitkin, and his able assistant, Stacie Bauerle, as well as editor John Mitchell and the entire staff of Cumberland House Publishing, for taking on this project and answering my many questions from beginning to end. Their creative editing, printing and marketing will most certainly be a critical factor in the success of this work.

Lastly, I could not forget my family. My wife and four children have supported and encouraged me in my world of golf for many years. Even my 97-year-old mother deserves recognition since her recent move to our hometown settled me down long enough to get this job done in a timely fashion.

INTRODUCTION

I can hardly wait for you to read this book, so let me get you off to a head start with a brief overview. The main theme of what you are about to read is that the psychology of golf involves understanding three main areas: *thinking, emotion* and *action.* Indeed, much of psychology, and life in general, revolves around nothing more than these three things.

For example, *psychological disorders* can be organized into categories of thinking, emotion and action. Schizophrenia is a *thinking* disorder—people are confused, disoriented and delusional. Anxiety, on the other hand, is a matter of *emotions* being disturbed—nervousness, fear, even panic attacks. *Action* disorders involve people getting in trouble, as in cases of antisocial behavior—being manipulative, impulsive, aggressive and a con artist.

In the world of *work,* sales might be viewed from a similar perspective. First you have to tap into a prospective client's *emotions*—generate some positive feelings between you and the client and your product. Once you and your product are eliciting positive vibes from the client, then you can get more specific and educate the client about the product. That is, get them *thinking* about the particulars of how this product could be useful and help them. Lastly, you have to exercise your persuasive skills to get them to take *action* and buy the product.

Then there's *life*, more generally. Anytime people say they don't know what is going on in their lives, that all they know is it's something psychological, what they are really saying is that they are having problems somewhere in their *thinking, emotions* and *actions*. Once the area in need of attention is identified, then, and only then, can moves be made to remedy the situation.

And then, *voila*, there are frustrated golfers crying out in agony, "I've got the game, I don't know what's holding me back—it's just something psychological." Again, you know what it is: something to do with their *thinking, emotion* and *action*. Now you just need to learn more about the specifics of each of those areas.

The concepts embodied in *Golf: The Mental Game* are not just theory and principles, but concrete applications that have helped many with their games, to include the author himself. If you want to look ahead to Lesson #40, you will find data that shows how my own game improved through the application of a psychological plan over a five-month period. This stuff works and that is why I am so eager to share it with you in the pages ahead.

Golf has been a major focus of my life since I was 10 years old. Nothing has ever been quite as absorbing for me as the challenges that golf has provided. You might compare it to the unbridled passion expressed by the young assistant pro who lamented, "I just wish I could find a woman that I loved as much as golf."

To take it one step further, I'm reminded of Gen. George Patton, who felt compelled to ask forgiveness for his love of warfare. Perhaps my passion for golf is equally in need of forgiveness, because, by George, I do love it.

GOLF

THE
MENTAL
GAME

PART I

THE BASICS

GETTING STARTED

Lesson #1 addresses a burning question on the minds of many golfers: "What Exactly *Is* the Mental Game?" The answer to this question provides not only a definition of the mental game, but also a useful organizational structure for all of sport psychology. Building on this initial framework, Lesson #2, entitled "The Nine R's of Golf," extends the basic definition above and introduces R's that go well beyond the mere three of the traditional educational system—Reading, 'Riting and 'Rithmetic.

The next two lessons deal with technical aspects of the game. For example, did you know that "Equipment Has a Mental Side, Too" (Lesson #3)? Choose appropriate equipment for your game and you will save a lot of time, money, and frustration. Note, however, that *pride* has no place in your golf bag. "Leave Your Ego in the Locker Room" (Lesson #4) when it comes to choosing the proper tees for each stage of your golfing development. Consider a few suggestions for making the best choice.

Once on the course, it is imperative to keep play moving. "Behavior Modification for Slow Play" (Lesson #5) might be recommended, inasmuch as slow play hurts everyone's game—even yours. Proactively, in this regard, Lesson #6 discusses "Faster Play—Ten Steps to Achieve It." Fast-play is a *skill* along with other areas of expertise in golf.

What Exactly *Is* the Mental Game?

Three Ways to Get Better

BOBBY JONES ONCE SAID, "Competitive golf is played mainly on a $5^1/_2$-inch course—the space between your ears." Raymond Floyd went so far as to suggest that golf is 100 percent mental. Yogi Berra would probably agree that at least 90 percent of golf is half mental.

But what exactly is the mental game? What are the mental skills necessary for becoming an accomplished golfer? Perhaps a basic distinction provides the best starting point for answering these questions.

Physical vs. Psychological

Everything in golf is either physical or psychological, with the physical limited to the mechanics of the swing. If it takes about three seconds from the beginning of the backswing to the completion of the follow-through, then the physical part of a four-hour round with a score in the 90s would be less than five minutes.

That would leave 3 hours and 55 minutes for the psychological side of the game, the part that includes thoughts, emotions and actions leading up to physically swinging the club. Walking down the fairway you think about the factors that enter into the next shot. Upon reaching the ball, emotions kick in depending on the circumstances you find. Then, the action of the pre-shot routine occurs before you begin the actual swing. Only after all this psychological activity comes the three seconds of physically swinging the club.

Notice that the psychological game is more than just the mental game. Mental refers exclusively to thinking, which is only one-third of the psychology in golf. It ignores the other two important psychological components—emotion and action. Therefore, the rest of this article will employ the more accurate terminology—the psychological game—and provide a brief overview of some of the action, emotional and thinking aspects of the psychological side of golf.

Action

Practice—Golf is learned, like everything else, through practice. Psychologists have contributed a lot to making practice more effective and efficient. The key is to arrange practice sessions that are fun and productive so you will spend more time practicing and get more out of it. Some tips for getting started include making practice convenient, creating games out of practice drills, keeping practice scores and records, and quitting while you are still enjoying it.

Pre-shot Routine—A golf shot is a chain of behaviors, or actions, that requires a routine—an automatic sequence for each and every shot. You probably already have some semblance of a routine that you may or may not be aware of. Check yourself out and see just what it is you tend to do before every shot, then tighten it up, concentrate on its useful components and practice the routine so it becomes automatic. A sound psychological game requires the discipline of a consistent routine.

Pre-round Warm-up—Loosening up your muscles and joints has always been viewed as important. Equally important is the loosening up of your psychological game. Think during your warm-up and test your emotions as well. Examples of a sound psychological warm-up include aiming at targets, working through the clubs for the early holes of the round and putting a little pressure on yourself by matching shots with someone else or making so many putts in a row before ending the warm-up.

Pacing Yourself and Time Management—Everyone is concerned about speed of play. The psychological side of this behavioral issue is how to play faster without destroying your game. Walking fast, being ready to play and developing a quick routine might be helpful strategies for speeding up play. The other side of the coin is not getting overly distracted when play is slowed down for reasons beyond your control. Keep yourself busy, rehearse your swing thoughts and enjoy your surroundings as ways of staying in the game while you wait.

Relaxation—Many people think relaxation is something you are either born with or doomed not to enjoy. Actually, relaxation is a behavior that can be learned through practice of psychological techniques. Relaxation techniques range from breathing exercises and muscle-contraction procedures to self-hypnosis and focusing techniques.

Performing Up to **Your** *Potential*—Only when you can hit shots you are capable of at precisely the times you need them is your behavior living up to your potential. Psychology would suggest arranging practice opportunities that mimic the precise situations that give you difficulty. The more times you experience the actual situations, as opposed to something quite removed from reality (as often occurs on the driving range), the more likely you are to become comfortable with the shots and perform up to your potential.

Emotions

Building Confidence—The primary emotion every athlete desires is confidence. This is quite understandable, since true confidence reflects true ability. When it comes to confidence, there are no shortcuts. Skill comes first, and confidence follows, not the other way around. Don't look for quick fixes for confidence. Instead, practice the essential skills that enhance talent and you will develop a feeling of confidence that is truly deserved.

Controlling Emotions—Golf involves the full range of emotions, from joy and excitement to anger and frustration, all of which must be kept in equilibrium lest the emotional side of our psychological make-up overwhelm the thinking and action sides. When overly excited or excessively angry, you will find that it's hard to think clearly or behave in a relaxed manner. Such circumstances lead to poor strategy and tense swings.

One tip for controlling your emotions is to reverse the process. When facing a situation that is stirring your emotions, immediately shift attention to thinking about the next shot and planning your actions for escaping the troublesome situation. Just as emotions can overwhelm thinking and action, the opposite is also true. An intense focus on thinking and action can dampen the impact of a surge of emotions.

Managing Stress and Anxiety—Leftover stress from a recent match and anxiety about an upcoming competition stem from the same source—things you are saying to yourself about those events. The key to controlling these emotional states is to examine what you are saying to yourself and then consider the appropriateness of that internal self-talk.

> *The three psychological components of golf are action, emotions and thoughts.*

For example, you may be unconsciously telling yourself that your best-ever score is mandatory when playing in the club championship, when your average score might be a more reasonable goal or expectation considering the intense stress you are under in this once-a-year tournament. You can't change the event, but you can change what you are saying to yourself about it and thereby reduce your stress and anxiety.

Pressure and Choking—When it comes to handling specific pressurized situations during a round, focus on what you have to do at the moment. A focus on required, immediate behaviors does not allow time for worry about future results. Outcomes, by their very nature, can't be controlled since they are in the future (e.g., the end of the game, or even the final resting place of the current shot). All you can take charge of is your immediate actions over the ball at each stage of the game.

The next time you are standing over a crucial putt on the 18th green, instead of worrying about whether or not it is going to end up in the hole (i.e., the outcome), say to yourself, "I don't know if this putt is going in or not, but I do know that I can stroke the ball with a square putter blade and keep my head perfectly still. That's all I can control and all I'm going to think about."

Motivation—Motivation is the battery that makes behaviors, emotions and thoughts happen. You can know how to do a lot of things, yet have nothing to show for it if motivation is absent.

The main motivation in golf is fun and success. Therefore, be sure golf is fun. Practice only as long as it is enjoyable and productive. Also, play in matches and tournaments that afford you a fair and reasonable chance for success.

Burnout—It's fairly easy to see how golfers can hurt their backs under the continuous strain of the golf swing. Not so readily noted, however, is that the psychological game can also experience injury (i.e., burnout) due to the pressure and concentration involved in consecutive rounds of golf. Top pros play for a series of weeks and then take a few weeks off. They protect both their physical and psychological games from fatigue, thereby allowing themselves to remain top golfers while others grind away into worn-out and burned-out mediocrity.

Thoughts

Goal Setting—It is hard to reach a destination if you don't know the objective and have a road map for getting there. The same holds true with success. It's hard to accomplish anything if you don't know what the goals are and have a plan for achieving them.

The most useful goals tend to be performance goals, as opposed to outcome goals. It's better to think about increasing greens in regulation to 10 per round and lowering your putting average to 30 per round than to entertain goals of shooting certain scores or lowering your handicap to a certain level. Greens in regulation and putts constitute performance goals and provide something specific to work on, while scores and handicaps are outcome goals that don't offer any guidance as to their accomplishment.

Goals are also more useful if they involve a series of short-term steps rather than a single long-term objective. For example, a high-school freshman trying to make the golf team might focus on performance measures for the first few weeks of the current season, then new measures for midseason and still other measures for the end of the season. These relatively short-term goals would be preferable to long-term alternatives such as being captain of the team or winner of the state championship by his senior year.

Swing Keys—The golf swing is triggered by something we say to ourselves or by something we see in our heads. In other words, swing keys involve either words or pictures flowing through our brains. When words are used, we call them swing thoughts. Pictures, on the other hand, involve our imagination and visualization. The trick is to find the most useful swing keys for you.

Swing thoughts might include words that fit into the 1-2-3 rhythm of the golf swing. Examples could be "back and through" or "coil un-coil." Visualization might involve imagining a river flowing over the tee and down the fairway with your body, club and ball being pulled along by the current.

Strategy and Course Management—When you are playing an important match or tournament, strategy is what's planned ahead of time, while course management is what you think about during the round. You should have a strategic plan as to how aggressive your game will be, which clubs to use for various tee shots and how to handle notoriously difficult holes.

Once on the course, manage mistakes wisely if your plan goes awry. When in trouble, get the ball back into play so as to minimize the damage. Make wise decisions regarding lay-up shots versus the risk/reward of going for it. Make your opponent beat you rather than you beating yourself.

Concentration and Focus—Perhaps the biggest mental challenge in golf is concentrating over four consecutive hours. The key to concentration is restricting focus to a limited number of factors at any one time. In other words, you don't have to play the entire 18 holes on the first tee.

Break up the task into comfortable segments. Perhaps you are comfortable concentrating on two nine-hole segments, three six-hole groupings or even six three-hole chunks. Maybe your focus won't be on results at all, but rather on your routine and swing keys for each individual shot. If you diligently take care of the immediate business before you, the four-hour, 18-hole result will take care of itself.

Self-talk and Imagery—Self-talk and imagery pervade life on and off the golf course. Their involvement in swing keys has already been mentioned, but they go far beyond that. Humans are constantly talking to themselves and picturing things as their way of thinking throughout the day.

Our self-talk and imagery about golf begin as soon as we start thinking about playing. While it is not advisable to be Pollyannaish, you can still make those mental processes as positive as possible.

Talk to yourself like a winner. Remind yourself of your strengths instead of your weaknesses. When it comes to pictures, entertain vivid images of great shots that you have recently hit. Cultivate images of rhythm and smoothness or of being on cruise control. Visualize playing with the power and grace of a smooth-running machine, one that is moving effortlessly down the fairways with automatic efficiency. Or imagine you're Iron Byron, properly positioned beside the ball and pumping out automatic shots with the unemotional precision of a perfectly calibrated robot.

Whatever the self-talk or imagery you find useful, it is important to rehearse it and maintain it throughout the round. This type of thinking can keep a good round going or help you recover from a bad one. It should become a part of you, something that is automatic.

Commitment and Responsibility—The good thing about golf is that it can be played over a lifetime. The bad thing about golf is that it may take a lifetime to get any good at it. Commitment will determine how far you get in the process.

Those who think they can get by with never practicing, playing only a few times a year or laying off for an extended period of time are setting themselves up for frustration and disappointment. Blaming will become their main defense for poor play: "I need new clubs," or "Who can play a course like this?"

To become proficient at anything requires responsibility. If you haven't committed yourself to improvement yet, then the responsible thing is to admit it: "I'm playing at just the level you would expect for someone who doesn't practice and play regularly." Of course, it would be better if you could say, "I'm ready to responsibly commit to the hard work required for becoming a truly skilled and confident golfer."

THE NINE R'S
OF GOLF

I T DOESN'T TAKE LONG to realize that golf is harder than school. After all, millions of college graduates and thousands of Ph.D.'s populate the planet, while only a relative handful of scratch golfers exist, and even fewer professional tour players.

So, it's not surprising that multiple R's are required to succeed in golf, compared to just the three (Reading, 'Riting and 'Rithmetic) considered important in academic circles. By honoring the Nine R's described below, you will enhance your chances of graduating *summa cum laude* in golf.

Realism

Realism refers to setting appropriate challenges for your age and abilities. A 10-year-old just beginning to play must be realistic about the distance the ball will travel and the scores he or she can shoot. Appropriate tees should be selected, and all strokes counted so that a realistic assessment of developing abilities can be determined.

For the senior golfer, care must be taken not to let pride stand in the way of making adjustments that will allow achievement of realistic goals. Moving forward on the tees is totally appropriate, and breaking 100 instead of 80 may still be an admirable accomplishment for someone no longer in his prime.

Both junior and senior players should take appropriate handicap strokes when competing with players whose age and ability allow them to play at a superior level. A fair, realistic game will result in greater motivation and persistence as well as continued development or maintenance of each player's abilities.

Responsibility

Elite athletes have been known to resist taking the blame for a loss, attributing unfavorable outcomes to circumstances beyond their control. Such an attitude may be useful for the stars in maintaining motivation when they are members of a weak team or when environmental conditions mitigate against a good performance. In addition, elite players may be able to afford to make excuses, because they already have developed tremendous ability.

However, for the rest of us, the wiser reaction to unfavorable outcomes is to check ourselves for an explanation of what went wrong. In other words, we need to take responsibility for our miscues. Most golfers still have a lot of work to do to become elite performers. If time is spent blaming and making excuses for everything that goes wrong, identification of mistakes and practice of skills needed to remedy the situation are delayed.

Certainly, there is plenty of bad luck to go around. But it won't do the average player much good to bemoan his fate when the only thing that will lead to improvement is taking responsibility for mistakes and then taking corrective action.

Regularity

Everyone knows the benefits of regularity for our bodies, but regularity is also important for golf. In developing a successful golf game, it is much better to practice or play a little bit every day than to spend all day Saturday trying to remember and resurrect what you were doing a week ago.

Psychologists determined long ago that distributed practice is more effective than massed practice. Teachers have also encouraged regular study as opposed to cramming for exams. Applied to golf, this simply means to do a little something on a regular basis, as opposed to doing a lot every once in a while.

While you may not be able to practice and play 18 holes every day, you might be able to stop by the range or putting green for a half-hour on the way home from work. On a day when that is not possible, perhaps you could swing a club in the backyard or putt a little on the carpet before dinner. When time doesn't allow for even minimal practice, at least review your swing thoughts to keep them fresh in your mind for the next opportunity to play.

Relaxation

A relaxed body is key to the fluid action required in golf. You may think that some people are simply born relaxed, while others are doomed to be tense. Not so! Relaxation is a skill, and anyone can learn to be more relaxed than they currently are.

You want to learn to relax without props and in any situation no matter how pressurized or chaotic it may be. For starters, here are a few tips that you might try on your own, remembering that they are no substitute for complete, supervised relaxation training:

Abdominal Breathing—A simple beginning relaxation technique is to put your hand on your abdomen and feel it expand and contract as you slowly inhale and exhale.

Let the Air Breathe You—Once you experience the expansion and contraction of your abdomen, sport psychologist Dan Kirschenbaum suggests thinking of the air as breathing you, rather than you breathing the air. Become more passive than active in the process, letting go of some of the tension that goes along with being actively in control of everything.

Let the Club Swing You—Similar thinking might be applied to swinging a long, heavy club like the driver. Indeed, with today's lightweight materials, you might do well to put a warm-up weight out on the end of the driver so you can truly feel the clubhead. Then, let the heavy clubhead simply swing you. Go with it, not trying to guide the club or totally control your balance. Just swing the club along its natural plane, comfortably extending the orbit of the clubhead around your body and letting it swing you, while stretching and relaxing your muscles.

Contract and Release Your Muscles—If certain muscle groups still feel tight or tense, voluntarily contract them even more and then let them go. For example, if your arms feel tight and are resisting fluid action, intentionally clench your fists and squeeze your arm muscles tighter. After holding the tension for several seconds, let this self-created tension go quickly, as if you were just dropping it out of your arms. The resulting limpness and tingling in your arms will indicate the desired relaxation level.

Routine

A routine refers to the repetitious preparatory behavior that every accomplished golfer employs in playing a shot. This standard sequence of steps puts your game on automatic and tends to run off without much thought or emotion once the sequence is begun.

Everyone has his or her own unique routine that may vary in the number of steps and amount of time necessary to implement. Consider starting from a position with the ball between you and the target, in an effort to get proper alignment. Next, determine how and when to take your grip and stance. Then, waggle and attend to the swing thought or image that triggers the swing. Do all this in a standard sequence that runs off in about the same number of seconds every time. Curiously, it was noted that the timing of Greg Norman's routine was off by a mere second or two during his fabled collapse on the back nine at the 1996 Masters.

When you first start using a routine, make it your sole goal to execute the routine. You will be aware of the successful completion of the routine even before you look to see the outcome of the shot. You can just sense it that quickly. If you can say that you did what you were trying to do, then even if the result isn't perfect, consider the shot a success because you properly executed your routine. Rest assured that successful outcomes will soon follow from successful routines.

A routine is particularly helpful under pressure. As you move through the routine's steps in a timely fashion, distracting thoughts and emotions have minimal opportunity to intrude and interfere. Routines are also helpful when you are overconfident and, therefore, at risk of neglecting important steps in the execution of a shot. For example, you may have had a series of good holes and now be thinking that the next drive is going to be easy. Such thinking should be a cue to pause and make sure you don't forget your routine. After all, that solid routine is what got you to this favorable point in the round in the first place.

Other times when a routine can be helpful are when you are tired and fading, or conversely, excited and pumped up. Again, these are times when you might overlook something important in your game. Stay in touch with your routine, and it will keep your thoughts focused and your emotions in balance.

Repeatability

Repeatability is the essence of science. Ben Hogan might have also called it the essence of golf. Hogan's goal was to have a swing that could be repeated under the intense pressure of tournament play. He wasn't content with a swing that worked beautifully under typical playing conditions but let him down when he really needed it.

The fastest way to repeatability is a simple one-piece swing that allows for good balance and precision. You might call this a swing with minimal moving parts. While Hogan struggled to achieve such a swing, Sam Snead seems to have been born with it. You'll probably never see a swing more simple, natural and easy than that of the Slammer.

Rationality

Rationality refers to the use of reason, in contrast to reacting emotionally or impulsively. You may have noticed that the majority of tour players exhibit steady emotions. When they exit a green, it's hard to tell whether a birdie or a bogey is going to be recorded on their cards.

Besides having steady emotions, rationality also calls for having a reason for the way you play each shot. Don't just grab a club and hit it. Think about placement of the shot on a given side of the fairway or green. Play the percentages that are favorable for you, rather than taking a lot of risks. Just because you are on the tee doesn't mean you have to use the driver any more than being in the sand dictates the absolute choice of a sand wedge. Many factors can tempt us to make poor decisions, but calm, cool reasoning will ultimately win the day.

Reinforcement

Don't forget to give yourself credit for the things you are doing well. Even if you are not yet performing at the level you intend, you are making progress and should reward yourself for that accomplishment. Keep records of your scores and various statistics (e.g., number of putts, number of greens in regulation, number of pars or birdies) so you can occasionally take inventory and note your progress. Reflection on records can add fun to your game and enhance your motivation to keep practicing and playing.

Reliability

Once you have done all the above, consider yourself a reliable performer and depend on your own good judgment. Trust your swing and decision-making, abide by your strengths and weaknesses, and resist being swayed by the advice of others who know less about your game than you do. This is not to suggest that you should avoid taking lessons and learning from the experts. The caution is simply to beware of experimenting too much based on every new thing you see or hear from your peers.

Reliability further extends to the attitude of the golfer. An enjoyable playing companion is one who shows consistency in demeanor and dependability in behavior. Show up on time for the match. It is quite disconcerting to deal with players rushing to make their tee time, not to mention wondering if they are going to show up at all. Always play hard and finish the round, no matter how poorly you might be playing. Playing carelessly, giving up or walking off the course violates the basic tenets of the gentlemanly game of golf.

The Nine R's of Golf

Realism	Responsibility	Regularity
Relaxation	Routine	Repeatability
Rationality	Reinforcement	Reliability

EQUIPMENT HAS A MENTAL SIDE, TOO!

M ANY ATHLETES, AS WELL as the general public, have a narrow view of sport psychology. A common belief is that sport psychology is nothing more than relaxation training. Others limit the discipline to visualization techniques. The worst misconception is that sport psychology is only for troubled athletes.

While sport psychology is, indeed, useful regarding the above topics, it also can offer much more to the athlete. It can help in building confidence, focusing concentration, handling pressure, thinking strategically, managing motivation and, perhaps most importantly, learning how to practice efficiently and effectively.

But did you ever think that sport psychology even might be a factor in choosing equipment? That's right, even equipment has a mental side. Check out the five points below to see how.

1. Be Scientific in Choosing Equipment

When you are about to invest half your life savings in a new, high-tech driver or the latest set of space-age irons, you want to make sure that you are rational, rather than merely emotional, in the decision-making process.

Rationality requires objectively testing equipment options, as opposed to simply hitting a few unmeasured shots on the range or even worse waggling the club in the pro shop and then making a very subjective decision that "this club feels great, so I'll buy it."

Staying with the example of choosing a driver, objective testing involves selecting several drivers, including your current one, and taking them to an open, flat driving hole on the course where you can air out repeated shots with such variables as wind and roll held constant. In addition to the drivers, take a half dozen new balls to the test site so all the clubs get an equal chance to perform well.

As you test the drivers, work through them in different orders so no club is always the first or the last one hit in case there is any advantage or disadvantage to a given position in the sequence of shots. Pick targets to check for accuracy and step off distances to objectively check whether you actually are hitting any of these new, expensive pieces of equipment any better than your trusty old driving weapon. Be sure to mark the balls distinctively so that after you've walked 250 yards down the fairway, you know for sure which ball was hit with which club. If you happen to use balls that aren't new, particularly ones with varying distance characteristics, be sure to rotate the balls that you hit with the various drivers.

This may seem like a laborious process, but it actually can be fun to get out on the course in the evening with no one around and collect a little data on yourself and your clubs. An additional benefit is that you also are practicing making good swings, which are the only ones that allow for a fair test of the equipment.

2. Look and Feel Can Inspire Confidence

Once you have rationally chosen the club or clubs that perform best for you, emotional aspects such as look and feel might contribute to making the final decision. That is, if one set of high-performing clubs looks better to you than another set of equally high-performing clubs, that look may actually help you relax and inspire confidence, giving you yet another edge when it comes to performance.

The feel of the club can have the same effect. Some clubs just feel solid or provide a special sensation all the way from the clubface into your hands, thereby providing important feedback that is sure to lead to better performance and pleasure from the golf swing.

3. Get Fitted for
"No Excuse" Golf

Once you have chosen your clubs based on their objective performance as well as their subjective look and feel, it's time to eliminate any possible excuses based on equipment by having the clubs adjusted and set personally for you.

It may come as a surprise, but sometimes mass-produced clubs are not accurately set to specifications for loft. That is, a 6- and a 7-iron might be expected to have 4 degrees difference in loft, while in reality a given set might have them only 2 degrees apart. That means that one or the other of those clubs is not going to serve you well in providing the variety of distances you need to shoot your best score.

Furthermore, mass-produced clubs can't be set for a golfer's personal requirements for length and lie (i.e., the angle between the club shaft and the clubhead) since these factors depend on the physical stature and swing characteristics unique to each individual golfer.

Therefore, take your clubs to a reputable clubfitter and have the lie, loft and length set in a tailor-made fashion for you and your swing characteristics. Then, you'll know for sure you've got the right clubs in your hands and that the rest is up to you.

4. Dress for Success

Yes, even the clothes you wear are part of your equipment and can have a psychological impact. Consider how teams pick uniform styles, patterns and colors that send opponents a psychological message that "we're a team to be reckoned with." This impression comes simply from the team's appearance before the competition even has begun.

Furthermore, there are essential elements of clothing, such as pads for football players, outerwear for skiers and light material for runners, that would be considered part of those athletes' equipment arsenal. So why shouldn't golfers consider clothing part of their equipment, and what might be the psychological impact of that wardrobe?

Gary Player is a good example of someone who chose his attire with a purpose in mind. By wearing all black, he was easily recognizable on the course when fan support and TV coverage were quickly becoming major parts of the game. More importantly, he felt black was a color that exuded strength, and being of small stature, he probably wanted to draw all the strength he could from the physical resources available to him.

I think one other element of his attire could have had a psychological effect. Wearing one solid color, whatever that color might be, provides a unified look to the body—a look that may translate into the unified feel of a simple, one-piece swing.

One other example of dressing for success might be that of Bernhard Langer wearing colors that would match the green jacket he was hoping to be awarded after the final round of what turned out to be his second Masters victory. Might those colors and the associated anticipation of victory have given Langer the additional motivation he needed to play his best?

5. Maintain Your Equipment for a Sustained Mental Edge

Once you are set, from clubs to clothes, keeping your equipment maintained can give you a renewed psychological lift, even after the honeymoon with that equipment is over.

For example, there is nothing like the soft, tacky feeling of clean grips to make you anticipate a firm hold on the club as you swing through the ball. Clean grooves on your clubs also inspire confidence that the ball will do what is expected when it comes off the clubface. New spikes (soft or metal) give you the assurance that you are anchored to the ground while making a balanced swing. And clean shoes, as well as nicely pressed pants and shirts, can give you the feeling of a professional, which might be beneficial in your efforts to play like one.

Lesson #4

LEAVE YOUR EGO
IN THE LOCKER ROOM

ONCE A FOURSOME GETS the handicaps straight and the game in place, the next issue is which tees to play. This is not necessarily the simplest of the above considerations.

After all, handicaps are merely a matter of math and honesty, and the competitive format involves nothing other than knowledge and creativity. But the tees, now that's a different matter—a matter of ego.

The selection of tees will decide the degree of challenge the foursome will be facing that day, how well the group is going to keep up with the pace of play, the level of scores the players will take away from the round, how fair the competition will be and how much fun everyone is going to have. These are no small considerations for the fragile human ego.

Tradition

Over the years the customary labeling of tees has been based on gender, age and skill level. The most common of these has been the gender distinction that has led to men's and women's tees. Age enters in when junior or senior tees are designated. Skill level is highlighted when the course provides championship or professional tees.

The naming of tees in this fashion may have been appropriate in a bygone era, but in the present day of high-tech equipment, physical fitness and a burgeoning number of participants in the game, I'm not sure what gender, age or skill level have to do with the selection of tees.

How would you like to compete against Laura Davies from the women's tees, or from any tees for that matter? Consider going up against a 71-year-old Arnold Palmer from the senior tees, while you play the regular men's tees. You might be the club champion, but does that mean you should be relegated to the championship tees against some long-hitter who claims the right to play the regular men's tees because his handicap is a few strokes higher than yours?

Tees Should Fit

Ultimately, tees have nothing to do with gender, age or skill level. Tees have strictly to do with how far a player can hit the ball. The choice of tees should be based solely on each golfer's distance statistics. In effect, each golfer needs to select the tees that fit him or her.

Consider going into a department store looking for a suit and being measured for a size 40 pair of pants. You protest, saying "I've been wearing pants for 52 years, and I'll have you know that I should be able to wear a size 34 after all this experience wearing clothes. I don't care what I measure. I'm going to take the size 34s because that's what I belong in— whether they're comfortable or not!"

Of course, that would be ridiculous, but it's not too far from what happens on the golf course. Regardless of the status of a player's game, he might be heard to say, "I'm a man, I've been playing for 30 years and I should be playing the championship tees. So, damn the torpedoes, I'm going back there!" While that may be the macho approach, it's not a very smart or enjoyable one.

Finding the Proper Tees

The proper tees for a golfer are those that provide the player with a chance to reach the green in regulation using a variety of clubs, ranging from fairway woods to short irons. The average club used for approach should be a 5- or 6-iron. Some holes would call for a 9-iron or pitching wedge, while others might demand as much as a 3-wood. Such a layout should provide challenge without inducing considerable frustration.

Many golfers think playing the back tees allows them to compare themselves with the pros. However, consider that if the pro drives the ball 50 yards farther than the amateur and hits a 7-iron from the same distance the amateur has to hit a 4-iron, then a 430-yard hole will likely require a 9-iron second shot for the pro, while the amateur has to pull out a fairway wood. Does that sound like a meaningful comparison?

If you want to compare yourself to the pros, make the comparison between the 150-yard marker and the green. Even though the pro will still have the advantage of hitting a shorter iron into the green, the amateur will at least have a shot of reasonable distance to the green. Furthermore, from the 150-yard marker on in, about 80 percent of the shots on the hole remain—approach shots, sand shots, pitches, chips and putts. If you play the back tees, the drive is the only point of comparison. Allow each player a well-struck drive to the 150-yard marker and multiple comparisons still lie ahead.

If you are a tournament golfer, another consideration in choosing tees might be the set that would be used in a tournament at your level of competition. For example, most club championships seem to be played from an intermediate set of tees, suggesting that the best preparation for such competition would be from the regular men's tees.

Senior tournaments are played from shorter tees. So, if you are a competitive senior, you might want to get yourself up to the tees that you are going to be tested from in competition.

On the other hand, women who aspire to regional and national competition might want to prepare from the regular men's tees, which offer a better comparison with the lengths of courses advanced competition presents. Similarly, juniors might be advised to progressively match the tees that their advancing age groups demand.

Alternatives to the
Traditional Naming of Tees

Until the naming of tees is changed from the traditional nomenclature of gender, age and skill level, it's going to be hard to get golfers to change their ways in choosing tees. The naming of tees needs to become less evaluative and more neutral or descriptive.

One alternative would be to name the tees like ski runs—beginner, intermediate, advanced, expert and professional. Such a label would remove gender and age, but include skill level in the terminology. Furthermore, there is no reference to the primary thing that the tees are meant to reflect—the ability to hit the ball varying distances.

A better alternative would be to use neutral labels such as A, B, C, D, E or I, II, III, IV, V. This manner of labeling removes gender and age along with any references to skill level. It merely indicates that the further you go down the series of letters or numbers, the farther you are starting from the green.

> *The choice of tees should be based solely on each golfer's needs to select the tees that fit him or her.*

Perhaps the best way to distinguish the tees is in a blatantly descriptive manner that lists the distance you hit your typical drive along with the club you normally hit from 150 yards. For example, if you hit your drive 220 yards and a 6-iron from 150 yards, you would play the 220/6i tees. A set of five tees might progress as follows: 1) 170/3w, 2) 195/4i, 3) 220/6i, 4) 245/8i and 5) 270/pw.

A very short tee might also be included for those who are unable to hit their drives 150 yards. This additional tee might be labeled the 100/D tee, referring to the fact that the driver is hit about 100 yards and a driver would still have to be hit from 150 yards. These tees, however, should rarely be more than a couple hundred yards from the green, leaving the golfer with few approach shots of more than 150 yards.

Tee designations such as those described above would apply to males and females of any age and various skill levels. Golfers who know their games would have an easy time identifying appropriate tees, and those who are new to the game could easily be helped by a pro or the starter.

Benefiting from All the Tees

With the stigma of gender, age and skill level removed from the nomenclature, the various teeing grounds can become useful resources in the enjoyment and development of your game. Playing occasionally from different tees allows you to enjoy variety on the course you play regularly. When you find yourself hitting approach shots from new distances and different angles than those with which you are familiar, your same old course will provide you with new and interesting challenges.

If you want to stretch your game out a bit, move back to some longer tees and see if you can get a little more distance out of your game. On the other hand, if you want to assess the weaknesses in your game, move up to the shortest tees for a few rounds. What you may find is that if the long game is holding you back, you will score better from the shorter tees. However, if your short irons, pitching and/or putting are the culprits, your score may be no better from the shorter tees than from the tees you play regularly. With the information from such an assessment, you should know better which parts of your game to work on.

Another advantage of playing the shorter tees occasionally is to acquaint yourself with the feeling of lower scoring. That may sound strange, but sometimes we need a catalyst to move us out of our comfort zone. If you can shoot a low number from the shortest tees, it may strike you that it shouldn't be too hard to achieve the same score from the next longer set of tees. If successful from these tees, why not the same score from the next set of tees? Before you know it, you're back to your designated tees with a new mindset for lower scoring.

Aside from experimenting with the various tees as described previously for the purpose of game development, the bottom line in everyday tee selection is to give yourself a fair chance to play a productive and enjoyable game. Young children are not asked to play with a 10-foot rim in basketball. Women are not expected to roll a 16-pound bowling ball. Men 45 years of age enjoy slow-pitch softball rather than fast-pitch hardball. Why shouldn't golfers of varying physical qualities and stages of development benefit from adjustments in their conditions of play?

Rarely do inquisitors ask you what tees you played. They are usually interested in what you shot, or more importantly, how you played and whether you enjoyed yourself. Pick the appropriate tees and you will be more likely to provide positive answers to these questions.

BEHAVIOR MODIFICATION FOR SLOW PLAY

HUMORIST DAVE BARRY RECENTLY wrote about tons of space dust inundating the Earth and leading to everything getting heavier and slower. He calculated that "at the current rate of gravity buildup, by the year 2038, an ordinary golf ball will weigh the equivalent, in today's pounds, of Rush Limbaugh. Even a professional golfer, using graphite clubs, would need dozens of strokes to make such a ball move a single foot." Barry calculated that the average round of golf under such conditions "would take four months—nearly TWICE as long as today."

Golf is too slow. Playing golf is wonderful, but there are still other things to do in life—like going home and telling your wife about every shot in your round; or getting on the computer and calculating the stats on each of those shots; or watching three different tournaments simultaneously on TV. But you can't get to any of those other worthwhile activities if you're stuck for five hours behind a group of malingerers.

Slow play not only drives everybody on the golf course crazy, it also has the potential to hurt the games of slow players themselves for the following reasons:

Concentration—Concentrating for an hour can be tiring. Intensely concentrating for 18 holes takes an even greater toll. But when the 18-hole concentration task is stretched out over five hours, it can be downright exhausting. Any reduction in time spent concentrating should limit the price paid, as well as enhance performance.

Distraction—When preparing to hit a shot, it's difficult to hold a positive thought for very long. Once having captured a positive image or swing key in your mind, act on it quickly before a negative thought creeps in and competes for your attention. The negative thoughts will win out over the positive ones if you stand over the ball too long.

Stress—Another distraction for the slow golfer is the inescapable realization that other players are getting impatient. Instead of thinking about putting, the slow golfer begins to think about everybody else's reactions to his pace of play. He may even berate himself with negative self-talk: "Everybody is waiting on me. Why can't I hit the thing? I don't even know what I am doing now, but I can't stop and start over again because I've already taken too much time. Oh, just go ahead and hit it."

This is not a frame of mind conducive to hitting good shots.

Tension—Think about a shot too long, and spontaneity is replaced by tension. Swing thoughts get over-rehearsed, and the swing becomes stiff. Compare this scenario to a public speaking engagement where you have to wait behind several other speakers before you take your turn at the podium. You sit there not listening, rehearsing your speech, all the time getting more and more tense. When you finally approach the podium, you're stiff as a board with all spontaneity left behind. You would have been much more relaxed and natural if you had not had to wait so long to take action.

Rhythm—A golf shot involves a chain of responses similar to many of our daily activities. For example, walking down the stairs involves (a) lifting one foot, (b) lowering it to the first step, (c) simultaneously unweighting the other foot, and proceeding in such a fashion until you are safely at the bottom of the stairs.

When chains of responses are practiced repeatedly, they tend to run off automatically with little conscious effort. However, too much attention paid to one of these automatic chains can disrupt the smooth execution of the activity. Think too much about the precise moves, and you are liable to fall flat on your face. Think too much about the golf swing, and you are likely to meet with similar embarrassment.

How to Speed Up Play

1. Make Easy Changes—Certain adjustments in game management can make play faster without making you feel rushed. For example, walking or riding faster allows you to spend more time preparing your shot. Being the first to the green—quickly repairing your ball mark, clearing debris from your line and gauging your speed and alignment—permits you to spend a little extra time over the ball, if that's your style.

> *Another distraction for the slow golfer is the inescapable realization that other players are getting impatient.*

Other minor adjustments include cart parking so as to require the fewest number of steps and paying attention to your own game instead of worrying about everybody else's.

2. Take the Leap—Once you have captured a positive swing thought and have addressed the ball, don't waste time executing the shot. The internal dialogue at address might go like this: "OK, I'm set. I've got the image. Now, swing."

3. Talk to Yourself—Putting out more frequently, without marking and waiting, has the potential to speed up play over the course of a round. However, golfers often talk themselves out of putting out by saying, "I know if I putt out I'm going to miss it."

But what if one were to say, "This putt is no different now than later, and I can make it now or later. Sure, I can miss it, too, but that won't be due to when I putt—it will be due to how I putt. The putt is my responsibility to make, with no excuses, now or later." This is not to say that golfers should always putt out. The suggestion is merely that players can putt out more often.

4. Pre-shot Routine—John Daly shocked a lot of people in his inaugural PGA victory by putting out frequently—often from 5 or 6 feet, even when the putt was very important. How could he do this when he was on the brink of winning not only his first PGA Tour event, but a major? Putting out was most likely part of his usual routine, and he wasn't going to change it just because the pressure was on.

Develop a pre-shot routine that you get used to and call on it for every shot. Turn to it especially under pressure so that the response chain of the golf shot runs off automatically without delay. A pre-shot routine also will keep play moving at a steady pace.

Dealing with Slow Play

Consider these defensive techniques to protect yourself from the deleterious effects of slow play from others.

1. Stay Away from Your Equipment Until Ready to Play—Instead of selecting a club, triple checking the wind and alignment, and taking 38 practice swings, stay away from your clubs. When it is your turn to play, approach the shot with your normal rhythm and go through your normal pre-shot routine, making the pace of your shot the same as it would be if you were playing on an empty course.

2. Appreciate Your Surroundings—Golf courses are beautiful places, and you pay a considerable amount for your time on those exquisite pieces of real estate. Therefore, what's the rush? When a slow round is unavoidable, look around and smell the roses.

3. Excuse Slow Players—Instead of privately berating the slowpoke ahead of you, can you think of any big-hearted reason why the poor guy is slower than molasses? For example, maybe it's some old fellow who hasn't played for years, who was very nervous about playing today, but his son finally got him out—and the old guy is struggling. Do you really want to ruin this elderly gentleman's day with an obnoxious display of impatience? Sure you do! But consider that you may screw up your round more than his. By thinking in an altruistic fashion, you will calm yourself instead of huffing and puffing and ruining your day.

4. Be Assertive—When the course is open ahead, don't hesitate to ask the slow group in front if you can play through. The key is to ask assertively rather than aggressively. Don't get sarcastic or put down the slow players in any way.

One last reminder when playing through the slow group: Be sure not to rush your shots. Whether playing through or not, you have the right to take the time necessary to hit good shots. Besides, nothing will speed up play more than taking as few strokes as possible.

Lesson #6

Faster Play

10 Steps to Achieve It

Most would agree that fast play is good for the general popularity of golf. But up until now, about all that has been issued are complaints about the opposite—slow play. What is needed are some concrete suggestions on how to play faster.

Pace-of-play consultant Bill Yates of Pace Manager Systems has suggested that one of the main culprits preventing faster play is player behavior. Since psychology is the science of behavior, consider the following behavioral changes for quicker, more efficient play.

1. Walk or Ride Quickly—If you can walk a mile (1,760 yards) in 20 minutes, then you should be able to walk a 350-yard hole in about one-fifth of that time (about 4 minutes). Allowing for an average of 13 minutes per hole (which would constitute a sub-4-hour round), you have an average of 9 minutes remaining to execute the shots on each hole. Even if you require six shots per hole, this allotment of time allows $1^1/_2$ minutes per shot, which should be ample time, even taking into account waiting on other players and looking for an occasional lost ball. Of course, if you ride in a cart, the 4 minutes in transit might be cut in half, allowing even more time for each shot.

An added benefit of walking or riding quickly is that getting to the ball faster will help alleviate the mental distraction of having to rush your shots.

2. Be Ready to Play—Readiness means more than just having arrived at your ball. It means having checked the lie, the distance and the wind, as well as having cleared any loose impediments, made a final club selection and positioned yourself behind the ball to align the shot. Then, the only thing remaining when your turn arrives is to address the ball and swing. Readiness is what is accomplished during the $1^1/_2$ minutes allotted for each shot, a time span that often coincides with other players executing their shots. Remember, readiness involves being organized, which in turn gives a player the feeling of greater control over his game.

3. Prepare to Putt—Just like getting ready in the fairway, once on the green you do not have to wait for your turn to putt to begin the process of preparing your putt. For example, if you get to the green ahead of your playing companions, or even while they are assessing their putts, start clearing debris from your line, checking the distance and determining the line so you are ready to putt when it is your turn. Save only the last elements of your pre-putt routine for the moments before you stroke the ball. Putting, above all, benefits from a feeling of being prepared and unhurried. Save yourself from any opposing feelings by optimizing your use of time on the green.

4. Putting Out—Once your ball gets within a few feet of the hole, consider finishing out the hole. Marking the ball and waiting each time you putt add considerable time to an 18-hole round. For example, if every golfer in a foursome routinely marked and waited, thereby extending each hole 30 seconds per golfer, a foursome could easily add an extra half hour to the round.

Putting out does not mean rushing or doing anything casually or carelessly. On the contrary, you should line up the putt just like any other putt and go through your normal routine. Create additional focus by saying to yourself, "This putt is no different now than it would be after I marked it. Making the putt is not so much a matter of when I putt, but rather how well I execute my routine."

It might actually be better to putt out early than to later feel rushed or in the spotlight with the next foursome staring you down from back in the fairway. Putting out can become a comfortable habit if you do it regularly.

5. Don't Let Carts Slow You Down—It sounds ironic, but carts can actually slow you down under certain circumstances. For example, progress is delayed by cleaning your club and reinserting it into your bag before getting back in the cart, rather than getting directly into the cart with club in hand and waiting to do your clean-up and replacement chores until after arriving at your partner's ball.

How about the impact of parking carts inefficiently? Parking 20 yards in front of the green leaves you with a 20-yard return walk upon leaving the green, often backward and into the face of the following foursome. In contrast, parking on the side of the green by the next tee leaves you a shorter walk in the direction of the next hole when you finish putting.

If wet conditions require you to keep your cart on the path, consider walking the course, which allows you to go directly to your ball and to the green instead of back and forth from the cart path.

Carts have the potential to speed up play. Don't let them become a liability or a distraction. Anything that draws attention away from your game is likely to be a detriment to your score.

6. Scorekeepers Beware—The green is not the place to be collecting data regarding scores. Instead, wait until the next tee. If you have the honor, hit your drive before recording the scores. You'll have plenty of time to do the pencil work while the others follow your lead-off drive. Conversely, if your score on the previous hole put you at the back of the bus, do your scorecard work before you hit, while those with the honor keep play moving.

As mentioned earlier in regard to being ready to play, organization and efficiency can give you a feeling of greater control and allow you to make better use of your time.

7. Take Responsibility for Your Game . . . Not Everyone Else's—If you keep on top of your own game, you will be doing more for your playing companions than all the help and attention you might otherwise offer them. A round of golf is no time for giving lessons. Save that for the 19th hole.

Once down the fairway, look for your own ball and let your playing companions look for theirs. When you locate your ball, hit it. If another player is still lost, then help them out. To help unnecessarily beforehand and then be unable to find your own ball is going to benefit no one and actually slow down play.

Even compliments can be a nuisance. If you watch the complete flight of every ball and comment profusely on everyone's shots, time is wasted that could have been spent preparing and hitting your own shot. Of course, an occasional well-deserved accolade is part of the game. However, indiscriminate banter after every shot is uncalled for, time consuming and actually annoying.

Responsibility is perhaps the overriding psychological issue in life. If everyone would just take care of their own duties, mind their own business and allow others to do the same, the world and a round of golf would run a lot smoother.

8. Playing Through—There is an inefficient and an efficient way to let a group play through. The inefficient way involves putting out and waiting on the next tee. Considerable time passes with no progress on your part while waiting for the faster group to hit their approach shots and putt before catching up with you.

The more efficient way to let a group through is to begin the process while your foursome is still on the green. Before you begin putting, step aside to a safe location and invite the group behind you to hit their approach shots to the green. While they are walking up to the green, your group can finish the hole and perhaps even move to the next tee and hit drives before the group behind catches up and moves through. With this procedure, both groups keep moving and making progress while merely exchanging positions on the course.

A complete halt in play for several minutes while waiting is likely to hurt the rhythm of your round. Any disruption in the flow of the game can be both physically and psychologically detrimental to your performance.

9. Experienced Players Must Monitor Inexperienced Players—While most players are hesitant to do so, the responsibility sometimes falls to the knowledgeable veteran to say, "We are going to have to pick up the pace a bit." One way to pick up the pace is to agree to play ready golf—hitting when ready, no matter who is farthest from the hole. Another option is the 10-shot rule—picking up and recording a 10 after that many shots have been executed.

The sad result of not picking up the pace is that the veteran player will pay the price by rushing his shots to make up for others' slow play. Even though golf is an individual sport, leadership still has its place. Who better to take on that role than the knowledgeable veteran?

10. Last Resort—If slow play continues to plague you, consider this last-resort technique as the sun goes down and all the slowpokes are heading home. Put on your jogging shoes and run, using a single club for all shots (sand shots and putts included). I've shot a 97 with nothing other than a 3-iron, and I did it in 57 minutes. A more challenging 1-iron run produced a 99 in 59 minutes. The best combination I've had involved carrying five clubs for an 86 in 67 minutes.

This exercise not only relieves the frustration of slow play but also offers the additional benefits of vigorous activity, focused practice with selected clubs, creative shotmaking and not worrying about your score.

Admittedly, golf isn't a race, but neither is it a funeral procession. These behavioral changes should help you get moving, make golf more fun and improve your scores.

THE SCORE

Love it or hate it, the score is the bottom line in golf—and the foundation of the rest of the game. Scorekeeping is more complex and has a greater impact on the game than might seem to be the case at first glance. For example, consider "The Four Things in Every Round that Determine Your Scores" (Lesson #7).

We all know that golf is a game of honor. But, believe it or not, some among us have been known to massage scores and handicaps to the point that the numbers risk being inaccurate. While I say this tongue-in-cheek, it is no laughing matter that these folks are truly cheating themselves. Lesson #8 encourages golfers to "Count *All* Your Strokes" in order to legitimately become better players. Lesson #9 goes even further in explaining "How to Determine Your True Handicap."

Even though you can't hide from the traditional scoring system, you can still "Measure Your Progress with Alternative Scores" (Lesson #10). These measures might be used to enhance your enjoyment, maintain motivation and monitor game improvement when *old man par* is getting the better of you.

And, then, "The Scoreboard—Should You Look?" (Lesson #11). Or is it better to just play the game and find out when it's over how it all turned out?

Lesson #12 concludes this section on the score by considering "The Case for Serious Golf." I mean, *really*—how seriously should this game be taken?

FOUR THINGS IN EVERY ROUND THAT DETERMINE YOUR SCORES

TOUR PLAYERS TALK ABOUT putting a number on the scoreboard. That is, they want to produce a score that will set a standard and put them in contention at the end of the day.

But that score is no simple number. A golf score is a complex, elusive entity that's the net result of four determining factors—what the course giveth, what the course taketh away, what the player giveth and what the player taketh away. Before being too hard on yourself for not producing the numbers you intend, consider each of the above factors and see how many variables enter into a golf score.

The Course Giveth

Gifts received from the course come in the form of good luck—the bounce off the tree into the fairway, the skip across the lake, the skulled pitch shot that rolls through heavy fringe and stops next to the hole, the pulled putt that catches the lip and goes in anyway. None of these results are deserved, but the course grants the blessings nonetheless along with the question "What does one do with good luck?"

Don't Forget It—When the tables turn and misfortune rears its ugly head, keep in mind the good luck you had earlier. Students are renowned for complaining about the "tricky" test items gotten wrong when they felt they knew the material, totally disregarding the items they guessed at and got right when they didn't know the material. Similarly, golfers tend to forget all the good luck they've had when the bad luck finally strikes.

No Apologies—A contrasting reaction might involve a twinge of guilt or embarrassment when opponents start complaining about how lucky you are. You may feel undeserving of the good fortune and compelled to give it back in some way. Resist this compulsion! Take the good luck and run with it. Rest assured that your opponents will get their share of good luck and will make no apologies for it. Furthermore, your current run of good luck is payback for all the bad luck you've had in the past. You don't owe anything to your opponents, the course or the golf gods. It will be a long time before the good luck catches up with the bad luck. Whether this line of thought is accurate or not, it is a good angle to take in holding onto good luck.

Create Good Luck—Many a talented golfer when taunted about being lucky has offered this rejoinder: "The more I practice, the luckier I get." How true! Skill produces luck. Sure, your ball skipped across the lake, but you also hit it crisply enough that it had the force behind it to skip like that. Crisp hits, even crisp mishits, come from some degree of developing skill. Similarly, a pulled putt may have slid into the hole, but that was only because your head was kept still enough that the ball stayed on line and caught the lip. You didn't learn to keep your head still without practice.

The Course Taketh Away

For everything the course gives in good luck, it never hesitates to take back in bad luck. You may get through a round with seemingly all good breaks, but over time you will pay the price. It all balances out in the long run. So, the issue becomes, "What do you do with bad luck? How do you handle it? Can you possibly turn bad luck around in your favor?"

Stay Positive—What hasn't gone wrong? OK, you're behind a tree, but you're not wedged between two roots. You're in the water, but you're also 160 yards closer to the green. In either case, all is not lost. These are situations you can still salvage with solid play from this point forward. Even though you can't deny the negatives of the situation, make an effort to look for the hidden positives. Trouble is merely opportunity in work clothes.

Develop Mental Toughness—Every time trouble arises, a golfer has a chance to practice overcoming adversity. Struggling through adversity is the only way to develop mental toughness. No one gets mentally tough when everything is going your way. Those who have never had to struggle are prime candidates to crumble when adversity ultimately strikes.

The Joy of Recovering—The greatest thrills in sports are come-from-behind victories. No one gets a kick out of watching someone overpower an opponent, but everyone loves to see the underdog who is being stomped suddenly rise from the ashes and claw his way to victory.

Comebacks, however, can't occur unless adversity first sets the stage. Just think, if all the teams and individuals who faced adversity had given up instead of persevering, none of the great comebacks in sports history would have occurred. All those wonderful memories and stories would be lost. Similarly, if you give up every time trouble arises, you may be cheating yourself of a place in your own personal history of achievements. You never know when your time will come, but if you don't take advantage of every chance to make it happen, you may not be around when the time finally does arrive.

Empower Yourself—The next time you find your ball in a divot after a perfect tee shot, say to yourself, "Good thing this didn't happen to a lesser player than me. Someone not as mentally tough as me would fall apart right now, while I can handle this situation. This is a chance to show myself and everyone else just how capable I am."

In contrast, you've seen players stomp around and point at their bad luck, as if to say, "I'm not responsible for the bad shot I'm about to hit." Of course, they now have to hit the bad shot just to prove how unlucky they were. Not Jack Nicklaus, however. One time at Doral, Nicklaus found himself in a divot in the middle of the 18th fairway on the final hole of the tournament. He paid not the slightest homage to his misfortune. He simply stepped off the yardage and smacked the ball out of the divot and onto the green for victory. There were no excuses, no moaning and groaning—just part of the game. He showed himself and everybody else what a great player could do. I wouldn't be surprised if Nicklaus occasionally thought to himself, *Good thing I have some bad luck every once in a while, just to make it fair for the rest of the field. Imagine how bad I'd beat them otherwise.*

The Player Giveth

Once the course is done with its contributions to the score, then the player takes over. Good shots constitute how a player contributes favorably to the score. But where do those good shots come from and how do you maintain them as a favorable factor over an entire 18-hole round?

The Primary Sources—It's no mystery that good shots come from the teaching of experts followed by endless practice on the part of the learner. However, learning doesn't occur during the lessons themselves. Learning occurs from the extensive practice that takes place after the relatively brief lessons.

Don't Waste Your Time—A corollary to the above is that good shots do not come from shared tips and observations among incompetent playing companions. Such sharing of non-expert information merely leads to a contagion of errors with poor technique merely being traded and imitated ad infinitum.

In addition, good shots do not emerge simply with the passage of time. If something different isn't done with the swing or the practice regimen, nothing is going to change miraculously. Consider all the 25-handicappers you know today who were 25-handicappers 25 years ago. Nothing has changed in them or their games because they haven't done anything different to create a change.

Another waste of time is expecting gimmicks (physical or psychological) to bail you out. There are no shortcuts to a proficient game of golf. Extensive practice of physical and mental fundamentals is the only way to expertise.

Keep Good Shots Coming—It's one thing to hit a series of good shots on the driving range and quite another to hit them consistently over an 18-hole round. Here are a few thoughts to keep you on cruise control.

First, maintain even-keel emotions. Don't get too excited over a good shot or hole any more than you would get overly dejected over a bad shot or hole. No one should be able to tell from your demeanor whether you just birdied or double-bogeyed the last hole.

Second, focus on what you have been doing (your swing thoughts or images) to create the good shots, as opposed to attending to the immediate results. The only thing you have control over is technique. Little can be done to directly control any result. Once the ball is struck, it's on its own, sometimes with a will of its own.

Also, segment your round so that it doesn't seem like such an overwhelming task. Thinking in terms of an 18-hole score or even a nine-hole score is not required. A running tally of three-hole scores, for example, might be more useful in maintaining focus and making the task seem more manageable.

Tom Wargo used a contrasting approach to his advantage. He thought of the entire round as a single hole. Birdies or double-bogeys didn't exist—just a series of equal shots around this linkage of tees, fairways and greens that added up to a giant one-hole score in the final accounting. No one shot was any more important than any other.

The Player Taketh Away

Finally, bad shots are what players contribute to the detriment of their scores. Bad shots are different than bad luck. Bad luck comes from the course, while bad shots come from players as a result of deficiencies in practice, skill, physical prowess and a host of other sources. Whatever the case, something has to be done with bad shots. Something favorable has to be drawn even from bad shots.

Recognize What You Can and Can't Change—For example, there's not a lot you can do about being built low to the ground (as soccer players refer to shortness), being a 98-pound weakling or having two left feet when it comes to coordination. These are things you simply recognize, accept and cope with. Fortunately, golf affords numerous ways to overcome limitations as evidenced by players who have made it to the professional tours with considerable handicaps.

While you can't do much about physical limitations, you can do something about skill development via lessons, reading and diligent practice. Something can also be done about managing the time and efficiency of your practice. To paraphrase the famous Serenity Prayer, accept what you can't change about your golf game, change what you can and exercise wisdom in knowing the difference.

Great Shots Are Rare—The legendary Ben Hogan felt he hit only one or two great shots in a typical round of golf. Most of his shots were imperfect, but they still allowed him to shoot reasonable scores, which for Hogan were likely par or better. The message for the average golfer is that even bad shots can be part of a good score. Keep the less-than-perfect shots in perspective. Let them blend in with the good shots en route to an acceptable 18-hole round.

Don't Panic—Good advice in golf is, "Don't try to follow a bad shot with a great shot. Just make a good shot." That is, don't try to get it all back at once. If you've missed your drive and now can't make it over the lake in two, just hit a solid layup and put yourself in position to maybe stick a third shot close for a one-putt par. If you try to hit some gargantuan 3-wood over the lake, you are likely to compound your problems. Be patient and control the damage. Plenty of holes remain to get back the botched drive.

The same type of thinking applies to bad holes. If you've just had back-to-back double bogeys and your game seems to be falling apart, just try to make a solid bogey on the next hole or maybe a scrambling par. Then go for a routine par. Once you have settled down, think about going for some birdies.

Make Adjustments—Many great golfers, Nicklaus and Tiger Woods to name two, have the ability to make adjustments in the middle of a round. When they find themselves hitting bad shots, they look for the cause and make necessary changes in order to survive the round. Then it's off to the practice tee for a more thorough assessment of what has gone wrong.

The golfer who can make the quickest and most effective adjustments in the heat of the action is the one whose score is going to be least impacted by bad shots. Again, perfection is not necessary—only the ability to deal quickly and effectively with imperfection.

So, there you have it—the equation for a golf score. Both you and the course giveth and taketh away. Indeed, blessed are players and courses that giveth more than they taketh away.

Lesson #8

COUNT ALL YOUR STROKES

Keeping Accurate Score Improves Your Game

D ID YOU KNOW THAT the first time Arnold Palmer played St. Andrews he shot an 86? In fact, last year The King recorded another 86 in the PGA Seniors Championship—under ideal conditions. If Palmer would allow for one more painful anecdote, he scored 85 twice at his own Bay Hill Classic on a layout that might be considered his home course.

In a similar vein, one of the worst-kept secrets during the Ryder Cup at Kiawah's Ocean Course was that if the pros had been playing medal play, most of them would have shot in the 80s.

Now, if subscratch handicappers who play golf for a living can shoot scores such as these, why can't average amateurs shoot high scores without falling all over themselves making excuses, offering apologies and otherwise engaging in verbal gymnastics aimed at avoiding embarrassment?

Perhaps one reason is that the typical amateur golfer doesn't appreciate the difficulty of the game. Consider the following factors that on any given day can easily contribute to a high score:

Course Difficulty—Many new courses are built to challenge the great professionals of our time. These same courses, therefore, are extremely difficult for the amateur. The holes are often of unbearable length, some carries over water are next to impossible and hazards are everywhere.

I would say that playing a 140 slope-rated course, compared to your more typical 125 slope-rated course, has the potential of adding 10 strokes to a player's score.

Course Unfamiliarity—It's one thing to play a difficult course, but if the course is also unfamiliar, prepare for a double whammy. On an unfamiliar layout, shotmaking tends to be tentative, distances are uncertain, and hidden hazards jump up and grab you—sometimes even on good shots. Unfamiliar green surfaces (e.g., Bermuda vs. bent grass) can easily affect your confidence on putts. It seems reasonable to estimate that the unsettling aspects of an unfamiliar course can contribute an additional five strokes to your score.

Choice of Tees—Play the back tees on one of these unfamiliar, difficult courses and you can add another seven or eight shots for all the trouble you'll get into on your drives, not to mention the reduced number of greens you'll hit in regulation.

Weather—Cold, rain and wind are likely to add still more strokes, depending on your experience and preparation regarding these conditions. I've heard pros say they don't mind the rain, but they can't stand the cold. Nonetheless, for the average golfer, cold, rain and wind are likely to add several strokes to one's expected score.

Playing Companions—Most golfers have experienced their scores fluctuating with the level of competition. Tee it up with a few guys where you feel in over your head, and all of a sudden you concentrate a little harder and score better than you might have expected. On the other hand, play a social round with hackers from work, and before you know it your score lackadaisically drifts toward the high side. Not only is motivation lacking, but playing with less-than-serious golfers can add distractions that will certainly cost a few strokes.

Playing By the Rules—If you are accustomed to routinely taking two off the first tee, playing the root rule and picking up putts inside the leather, you'll add another six or seven shots when you play by the bona fide rules of golf. Don't forget that the rules require you to go back to the tee and add two strokes for a drive out of bounds, rather than just drop a second ball somewhere out in the fairway and count one stroke.

In defense of some of the above infractions, modern golf doesn't promote enforcement of some standard rules of the game. For example, most of the time you can't return to the tee as the rules might require, or even take time to finish out a hole that has gotten away from you, because to do so would interfere with the expected pace of play. Similarly, even putting everything out is frowned upon at some courses because it slows play. Unfortunately, the logical extension of this rationale is to not hit any shots because they are all time-consuming.

Being a Little Off On One Part of Your Game—Did you ever think that if you were remiss on all your short putts on a given day, even if you played perfectly from tee to green, you could shoot 90 instead of 72. And the only flaw in your game would have been a lapse in ability to make short putts. Poor driving can similarly add to a golfer's scoring woes. Eighteen pitch outs from the woods add up to a considerable chunk of extra score.

Unrealistic Expectations—After watching the pros on TV, particularly those leading the tournaments and therefore playing at the top of their games, it is understandable that golfers might harbor unrealistic expectations about how easy the game might be. To distort expectations further, viewers are sheltered from seeing the players who didn't make the cut, the ones who struggled all day with many of the same frustrations amateurs face regularly. The resulting unrealistic frame of reference partially explains the limited frustration tolerance of amateurs, which in turn lends itself to higher scores due to giving up when rounds become tedious. Result: add four or five more strokes for loss of intensity.

With all the pitfalls described above, it should be no surprise that high scores, even very high scores, are inevitable on occasion for even the best of golfers. And while that is some consolation, it is still a long way from making those painful scores enjoyable. So what do you do about them?

I would suggest that when it happens to you, rather than running and hiding, just matter-of-factly state your score without apology or excuse. Any true golfer will understand.

If you happen to meet with condemnation by your questioners and feel compelled to respond, ask them if they would like to hear a blow-by-blow account of your round, along with all the disasters you encountered, before they pass sentence. If playing conditions were particularly tough that day, encourage them to go out and play a few holes and see what they shoot. If your high score is still deemed unacceptable, explain that you are only human and sometimes you play less than perfect. But above all, don't ever let the reactions of others make you afraid to keep a true and honest score.

And that leads to perhaps the most important issue of all. Why is it so important to keep score? If the game is so difficult, and high scores make golfers so uneasy, why not refuse to keep score and just hit balls?

The simplest answer is that we have to keep score because golf is a game, and games have scores. Of course, golf involves exercise and beautiful surroundings, but those benefits are similarly available from a hike in the woods, snow skiing or jogging. When you come in from a round, the guys around the pro shop don't ask you how you feel, how much exercise you got or did you enjoy all that beauty. No, they ask you what you shot! No score, no game, no golf.

A second reason for keeping score is that a consistent, accurate history of your score is a measure of your development as a golfer. All golfers, no matter at what level they play or how seriously they take the game, want to improve over time. Score is the bottom line when it comes to improvement. You can talk all you want about how you are hitting the ball better or that you've got this or that figured out, but if your scores aren't improving, you don't have a lot to show for it.

A related point is that keeping score allows players to get in touch with their weaknesses. Only after a round in which every stroke is counted can a legitimate game review reveal the golfer's strengths and weaknesses. From such a debriefing evolves the prescription for what has to be practiced for improvement.

Perhaps the most important reason to keep score is that it makes you play the game differently. Consider the volleys that are fired back and forth when you warm up for a tennis match. During warm-up, little concern is entertained for each shot's outcome. But then the match is engaged and scorekeeping begins. Suddenly the result of each shot becomes of paramount importance, and you start playing an entirely different game.

Well, it's the same in golf. No scorekeeping means no overall strategy for the round, no planning for the next shot and no assessment of risks involved in various decisions. Something as fundamental as aiming shots takes on less importance because who really cares where exactly the shot goes—it's not going to add up to anything. When score is irrelevant, you can avoid difficult shots. Just throw the ball out where you can hit it, you might say. The result: no practice at hitting difficult or unusual shots.

> *Score is the bottom line when it comes to improvement . . . if your scores aren't improving, you don't have a lot to show for it.*

Keeping score, on the other hand, requires you to plan ahead, cut losses when necessary, calculate distances and direction precisely and hit unusually difficult shots from time to time. Your strengths and weaknesses hit you between the eyes in a way that you can't avoid them, but which in turn direct you regarding improvement. Lastly, keeping score and publicly reporting it at the end of your round mean that you are playing the real game of golf, you aren't afraid to face the difficult challenges of the game, and you are mentally and emotionally prepared to play any other golfer who is willing to play the real game of golf with you.

Many fine articles have been written on how to lower your score. But before you can benefit from them, you have to start keeping it. Keeping score is not just for scorekeeping's sake. Scorekeeping contributes to the development of the golfer's entire game, not to mention his integrity.

Play the real game of golf, keep a genuinely accurate score and refuse to be embarrassed or apologetic about it. Do this and you can count yourself among a special class of golfers who proudly play golf the way it was supposed to be played.

How to Determine Your True Handicap

G OLFERS OFTEN JOIN UP with other golfers whom they have just met or whom they know only in passing. Subsequent to exchanging pleasantries, the following conversation frequently occurs as a round is planned with a new golfing companion.

"Why don't we see if we can get up a little game (wager, that is)?" Pete Putter asks. Receiving a tentative, but affirmative nod from Willie Wedge, his new acquaintance, Pete then asks, "What is your handicap?"

Willie clears his throat, avoids eye contact and begins working the tee box like a used car salesman. "Well," he says, "officially my handicap is 9—at least that's what it says in the pro shop—but I've been trying to break in a new set of clubs, and I'm actually playing around a 13. Now, if I were playing with my old clubs, I'd probably be around 11 or 12, but there is no way I should ever be a 9."

Pete replies, "Yeah, I know what you mean. My handicap is 14, but I've had a bad back and been busy at work, so I'm playing so bad I haven't broken 90 in two months. If I were healthy and playing regularly, I still should only be around a 17. But right now, realistically, my handicap has to be 20."

Willie, feeling a sense of kinship in that he is playing with another used car salesman, suggests that he give Pete three strokes on the front side, and that they adjust on the back. And so on and so on . . .

Ladies and gentlemen, this is not the way the handicap system was designed to work. Your posted handicap is your handicap. If you are playing regularly and posting all your scores, then your handicap should be accurate. If your handicap is accurate and your playing companion's handicap is accurate, then there should be no need for adjustment after nine. Indeed, this is why the handicap system was designed—to allow players of differing abilities who may not even know each other to appeal to a universally accepted standard that enables them to compete fairly and to compare their scores on an equitable basis without any special provisions.

Unfortunately, the handicap system is an imperfect system open to considerable abuse. Everyone knows golfers with artificially low handicaps that they can't live up to. Everyone also knows golfers with artificially high handicaps that make them instant winners in handicapped events. Everyone knows it, yet these individuals and the handicap system are protected behind an open shield of secrecy.

One's handicap can, of course, be manipulated. If a high handicap is desired, just turn in nothing but high scores. If a low handicap is the objective, then turn in only low scores.

It's easy to understand the desire for an artificially high handicap. It ensures winning, even if at the cost of honesty. The only problem is that people talk about you behind your back, they don't trust you and you have to live with the knowledge that you are cheating in a game that is otherwise a model for honor and honesty.

However, the more curious phenomenon is the golfer who engineers an artificially low handicap and the methods used to achieve this status.

The first technique in artificially lowering one's handicap is to accept all 3-foot putts ("inside the leather") as gimmes. I would venture to say this device is worth three or four strokes toward a lower handicap.

A second way to achieve an unrealistically low handicap is to engage in match play while posting a score as if medal play were the format. The scenario is as follows: The hole is already won by your opponent(s). You still have a 15-foot putt for par. It's meaningless as far as the match goes, so what happens? You pick up your putt and give yourself a par on the hole. The result is that your handicap stays artificially low.

The third way is more subtle. A golfer might unwittingly maintain an unreasonably low handicap by coming back the next day to finish a good round that was ended prematurely the day before because of rain or darkness. This is permissible according to the handicap system, and I do not take issue with this practice. The problem is that golfers rarely go out of their way to come back the next day to finish up rounds in which they were playing poorly. Again, the result is an artificial lowering of the handicap.

> *There is nothing like an honest handicap. Other players respect you for it, you can play comfortably with anyone and you can be proud of yourself when you shoot a score that matches or improves your handicap.*

The last technique is another subtle one to which even the well-intentioned player might fall victim en route to artificially lowering his or her handicap. A little background is necessary for understanding this one. Handicaps are calculated every month. They are based on the best 10 scores out of the last 20 reported. Handicap lists also indicate how current the handicap is by listing the day and the month of the last score entered.

Naturally, the more current the handicap, the more valid it is since it reflects how one is playing at the present time. If 20 scores have been entered over the past two or three months, then the handicap might be considered current.

But isn't it interesting that some very low handicap golfers report only one or two scores per month, stretching out their 20 posted scores over a 10- or 15-month period? Can a score submitted a year ago be a valid reflection of how one is playing at the present time? Furthermore, how could a scratch-handicap golfer maintain such a low handicap by playing only once or twice a month?

One way they could "honestly" achieve this low handicap on only a few scores is by doing the following. Every time a bad front nine is played, quit and don't play the back nine so a high score isn't turned in. Or if the back nine is already under way and the score is getting out of hand, then find an excuse to quit, start messing around or take out a few extra balls and start practicing. Any of these maneuvers will result in an incomplete round and provide a "legitimate" excuse for not turning in a higher than desirable score.

This subtle manipulation of the handicap system even might happen quite innocently. When one is playing poorly, one often gets tired a bit sooner and or loses interest in the game for the moment. It's quite easy to succumb to the temptation to quit, go home and come back tomorrow for another go at it. It may not even occur to the golfer that he has avoided posting a score that would be less than flattering to his "low" handicap.

The handicap system is a wonderful idea. It is a way to make all golfers comparable when it comes to competitive events in which such comparability is desired. But the system will work only when handicaps are valid.

As stated earlier, it's easy to understand why golfers seek unduly high handicaps—in order to win at all costs. But why would golfers want an artificially low handicap?

Enter the mental game. Golfers in pursuit of unrealistic low handicaps are, in truth, in pursuit of appearing to be better golfers than they actually are. They are afraid they can't shoot scores consistent with their handicaps so as to present a more favorable picture of themselves than is actually the case. Such golfers settle for appearing to be skilled instead of accepting their current level of play and working toward bona fide improvement.

What a shame. Golf is a difficult game. Very low, valid handicaps are hard to come by. Few players should expect this of themselves. Artificially lowering one's handicap only puts added pressure on the golfer and makes it difficult for him or her to compete in events involving handicaps. Indeed, it even makes it uncomfortable for the golfer to participate in congenial weekend matches without feeling self-conscious about throwing the friendly competition out of whack.

There is nothing like an honest handicap. Other players respect you for it, you can play comfortably with anyone and you can be proud of yourself when you shoot a score that matches or improves your handicap. The way the handicap calculation is done, you shouldn't expect to score lower than your handicap more than 25 percent of the time. Think about that. If your handicap is a true 8 (which puts you in very good standing), you can expect to shoot scores in the 80s 75 percent of the time.

Come on! Take it easy on yourself. Golf's a tough game. The next time you are confronted on the first tee with someone who is trying to maneuver around his posted handicap, consider the following reply: "My handicap is 10. It is based on scores over the past three moths ranging from 74 to 90. Therefore, my score today can be expected to fall somewhere in that range. My handicap is accurate and honest, and assuming you have a similar handicap, we can have a fair and enjoyable game."

MEASURE YOUR PROGRESS WITH ALTERNATIVE SCORES

T HE 18-HOLE SCORE IS the basic currency of golf, the commodity that is exchanged in expressing how one performed on the golf course on a given day. When a golfer walks into the locker room, the first question that is likely to be asked is, "What did you shoot," as opposed to, "How many good shots did you have," or "How was your ball striking today," or even "How much money did you win?" The bottom line is the 18-hole score.

Now, it wasn't always that way. Golf began with match play where the overall score was immaterial. You either won a given hole, tied it or lost it, and it didn't matter by how much or how little. The objective was simply to win more holes than the other guy, no matter how many shots it took.

It must have been quite a shock when the first Scotsman suggested that an overall score be kept. Imagine someone today suggesting that tennis, which has historically been played with a format similar to match play in golf, shift to a total score measure in place of games and sets. I suspect there would be quite an uproar.

Another exception to the emphasis on overall score can be seen in the way professional golfers communicate with one an other after the day's round. Touring pros tend to ask each other how they played, focusing more on the execution of shots as opposed to whether or not the ball found the hole as often as one might have liked. The thrust of the conversation is toward good shotmaking, which eventually will lead to lower scores. They talk about the cause rather than the result.

Similarly, a club pro will tend to ask members how they played, rather than going for the jugular with the ever sensitive score issue. Indeed, the club pro is truly interested in how you are striking the ball, since that is the main thing he or she teaches in golf lessons.

So, while the 18-hole score remains important, it is clearly not the only measure in golf. Nor is it the only score that might be interesting to keep. Consider some of the following alternative scores that may prove useful in measuring your progress, maintaining your motivation and keeping you focused even when the almighty 18-hole score is letting you down.

1. *Match Play Against the Course*—Most amateur golfers with limited time to practice and play tend to have a few bad holes that are out of character with their actual skill level. If they were playing more frequently, many of these bad holes wouldn't occur.

If you are an occasional golfer, a more accurate measure of your potential may come from playing match play against the course. If you are a single-digit handicapper, give yourself a win for any hole that you par, while the course wins for bogey or higher. Give yourself a double win for a birdie.

If you are a higher handicapper or a beginner, the standard for winning could be adjusted so that you are a winner against the course if you make a double bogey, for example. The course wins on anything higher. The objective is to win more holes than the course does, with the assurance that those inevitable bad holes won't wipe you out.

2. *Performance Points*—A good product is a combination of its components. For example, low scores in golf are the result of hitting fairways, hitting greens and making putts. To encourage focus on these components, another motivating alternative score would involve giving yourself a point for each fairway hit, each green hit in regulation and each one-putt. You also could throw in points for other golfing skills such as successful sand shots, pitch shots to within 10 feet and chips to within 3 feet. The objective is simply to accumulate as many points as you can, increas-

ing your total with every round. An added benefit is that no matter how the 18-hole score is going, you can always earn more points with the shots remaining in the round.

3. Swing-Key Percentage—Awarding points for the outcome of various shots is one thing, but the process of striking the ball is also important. For example, each time you play, you probably have something you are trying to do. It might be keeping your head still or making some move to initiate the backswing or the forward move into the ball. It might be to visualize the shot through impact or some tempo device to encourage a rhythmic swing. Whatever it is, consider counting the percentage of shots on which you actually do what you are trying to do.

In other words, in the split second before you look to see where the ball is flying, you know whether or not you have kept your head down. If your assessment is that your head was down, give yourself a point toward your swing-key percentage. When the round is over, take the number of shots where you successfully performed your swing key and divide by your overall score, the result being your swing-key percentage.

With this measure, the actual outcome of shots is unimportant. The only thing that matters is how often you actually do what you are trying to do.

4. Great-shot Score—If you are an expert golfer and want to raise the bar a bit, consider this alternative score that combines both process and result. It may also change your focus from mediocrity to greatness.

Each time you play a round, make it your objective to hit some great—and I mean GREAT—shots. That is, intend to knock in at least one shot from the fairway, hole-out at least two pitch or sand shots, sink a minimum of three chip shots and roll in upwards of four putts more than 20 feet in length. Give yourself a point each time you hole-out one of these great shots.

Chances are you won't accomplish many of these objectives, and a score in the 5 to 10 range would be magnificent. But think what this strategy will do for your focus. Instead of trying to survive out there or just get it close, you will be intent on knocking down the flagstick on every shot. You will have to be precise with your calculations and your setup, and your swing will have to be pure. As a bonus, if the 18-hole score gets out of hand, you will still have opportunities for great shots in the holes remaining.

Whichever alternative score you decide to keep, be sure to maintain a record of your performance over time. At a minimum jot down an alternative score along with each of your 18-hole scores, both serving as references for what your best-ever scores have been. Better yet, graph the scores so that your highs and lows, and the progress you are making, can be seen at a glance.

The important thing to remember is that while the 18-hole score may be the bottom line, there are still many other measures that can also pay dividends on the golf course. Furthermore, if you make progress with the various alternative scores, improvement in the 18-hole score is sure to follow.

THE SCOREBOARD

Should You Look?

T HE 1999 HONDA CLASSIC saw Vijay Singh come from behind in the final round to post victory over a field battered by windy conditions so fierce that a driver was required by some of the pros to reach the par-3 15th hole. During a post-round interview, Singh revealed that he had been watching the scoreboard closely. When he saw that Eric Booker—the current leader playing behind him at the time—had double-bogeyed the 16th, Singh said that it motivated him. When he learned from the scoreboard that Payne Stewart had bogeyed the 18th up ahead, it relaxed him.

Interestingly, no one questioned Singh's wisdom in attending to the scoreboard during the round. A few years ago that might not have been the case, as debate raged over whether or not players should stay in touch with the scoreboard.

Flashback to the 1994 British Open. Jesper Parnevik has a one-shot lead going down the 72nd fairway. He's unaware of his lead because he decided before the round not to look at the scoreboard. He goes for birdie on the last hole, ends up with a bogey and loses the tournament. Parnevik is criticized for not checking the scoreboard during his round.

Now, move ahead to the 1995 Western Open. Bob Estes has a one-shot lead on the 70th hole. He's watching the scoreboard, which has not yet been updated to reflect his one-shot lead. Estes thinks he is tied for the lead. He goes for birdie, makes double bogey and loses the tournament. Estes is criticized for looking at the scoreboard.

Meanwhile, in the same Western Open, Billy Mayfair, like Parnevik the year before, isn't watching the scoreboard. Mayfair sticks one stiff for birdie on the 72nd hole and faces a slippery, downhill 4-footer for victory. He actually thinks the putt is for a share of the lead because he hasn't been watching the scoreboard and doesn't even know his own score. He makes the putt and wins the tournament. Everyone applauds. As with Singh more recently, nobody seemed to care whether or not Mayfair was paying attention to the scoreboard.

> *What golfers need to do is get used to scoreboards, just like players in other sports.*

So, just what is the wisest approach for dealing with the scoreboard? From the examples above, the correct approach seems to depend more on whether you win or lose than anything else. Parnevik didn't look, lost and was criticized for not looking. Estes looked, lost and was criticized for looking. Mayfair, didn't look, had the actual situation all fouled up, but won. Scoreboard, snoreboard! As long as he won, nobody cared. The same goes for Singh—victory muted all criticism.

Indeed, it seems that looking or not looking at the scoreboard may not be the real issue. The more important consideration is what scoreboard watching or the lack thereof does to your game plan. You should always stick with your game plan, playing to your strengths and not allowing yourself to be influenced by outside agents such as the particular tournament, course, competition or scoreboard.

In the 1995 U.S. Open, Corey Pavin didn't come out with a new game plan just because it was the national championship. He didn't suddenly try to play long ball against a lengthy Shinnecock Hills layout. Pavin didn't try to match the bravado of his primary competition, Greg Norman. And he didn't let the scoreboard change his steady game down the stretch, even though he knew very well where he stood at each point in the tournament. Pavin just kept the ball in play, hitting fairways and greens, and ultimately won the tournament.

If forced to choose on the issue of looking or not looking at the scoreboard, I would favor looking. Scoreboards are an integral part of golf and should be from the first hole to the last. What golfers need to do is to get used to scoreboards, just like players in other sports.

Imagine a football game where the players didn't know the score until they got into the locker room, or a baseball game where nobody looked at the scoreboard until after the ninth inning. How about this from a basketball coach to his players after the final buzzer: "OK, guys, this may come as a surprise to you, but we're in overtime. Too bad you didn't take that easy layup instead of going for that wild three-pointer. But that's basketball without a scoreboard!"

With all the technology available to the PGA Tour, there is no reason not to have updated scoreboards for the players and fans to see on every hole. The score is the bottom line, the fun of the game and, in reality, not the problem. The problem lies in golfers' management of their emotions, decision-making and performance in the face of information about the score.

That this is a problem for players is understandable, considering that scoreboards have never been as prevalent in golf as they have been in other sports from the earliest stages of a player's development. Indeed, golfers even at the highest levels of amateur golf rarely have the opportunity to know how the field is playing until they have finished their round. It's little wonder that when they hit the professional circuit, it comes as a bit of a shock to see scoreboards with increased frequency.

A general recommendation for getting used to scoreboard shock is to stay with your game plan and play to your strengths, no matter what's on the scoreboard. If putting is your forte, you are much more likely to move up the scoreboard by getting yourself into positions to make longish putts, rather than all of a sudden starting to fire at the pin with approach shots you don't have in your bag.

Of course, there will be situations, based on the information on the scoreboard, where you may have to take a little more risk than your game plan called for, such as needing to birdie the last hole in order to win. But even here, build your risks around your strengths. Instead of trying to reach the par-5 over water in two—a strategy that confronts your weakness in the length department—lay up and take the risk with your strong wedge game, leaving yourself a reasonable length birdie putt for the win.

The bottom line is that golfers need to get used to scoreboards. More expansive use of scoreboards should be encouraged in local tournaments from the junior level to city championships. More opportunities are needed to post scores so that golfers can get used to the visibility of their performance and that of others.

There is nothing to worry about regarding the scoreboard as long as you stick with your game plan and play to your strengths. Do that and you will enhance your chances of finding your name at the top of the scoreboard when the competition has ended.

Lesson #12

THE CASE FOR SERIOUS GOLF

WHATEVER HAPPENED TO THE serious golfer—the one who used to tee the ball up and not touch it again until it was in the hole? The one who actually used to putt the ball into the cup 18 times every round? The one who played a simple game of golf, where winning was based on who shot the lowest score for 18 holes, not on who had the most greenies, sandies, chippies, poleys or bingo-bango-bongos?

Back in the late '50s and early '60s, people played a serious game of golf. I don't necessarily mean expert golf, just serious. Many people shot in the 80s or 90s, but they played serious golf.

By that I mean a pure and simple game played by a standard set of rules. They completed all the holes, counted all their shots, recorded all their scores and generated accurate and reasonable handicaps. When I was a junior golfer in the '50s and '60s I played serious golf, and I assumed that as I grew older I would continue to be able to play serious golf. But here it is two decades later, and I look around and there's nobody to play with.

I realize I'm overstating it. I occasionally run into other serious golfers, and I jump at the chance to play with them. But in general, golfers nowadays are making a mockery of the game.

For example, many golfers today are afraid to keep their score. "Let's play match play." "Give me an 'X' on that hole." "I'll just drop a ball here instead of going back to the tee." "Anything inside the length of the flagpole is a gimme." Why do you think scores soar in the club championship? Because finally you're seeing something that resembles an accurate score.

This, of course, assumes that you can get someone to play in the club championship. Many golfers won't play competitively unless they can disguise their scores in a best-ball event or a captain's-choice scramble, where some ridiculously low team score goes on the board and saves the golfer from revealing how he really played.

Golf, in the more serious sense, was meant to be a game where the individual puts himself on the line and stands or falls based on his own talent or lack thereof. So why are there so few serious golfers left in the world? It may be because expectations have become unrealistic. People think they should play better than they do, and they're embarrassed when they shoot what should really be considered a very respectable score.

And why do they think they should play better than they do? Probably because their main frame of reference is what they see on television—the best golfers in the world, all warmed up, playing the final holes of a round, at a time when, as they've already proved by making the cut, they're on their game. This level of play isn't representative of even the typical touring professional.

If only we could see some of the stars when they are missing cuts, struggling on the early holes of a round, blowing three-foot putts—then, maybe, modern golfers would develop more realistic expectations for their own play.

Beyond this, the amateur golfer needs more opportunities to compete seriously. Having one's score posted would then be less of a shock, and seeing what everyone else was really shooting would provide a realistic frame of reference.

Opportunities to compete might include old-fashioned president's and governor's cup tournaments, along with the traditional club championship. The latter event, in fact, might be elevated to a position of special honor, as it used to be. I sometimes fantasize that every golfer at a golf club should be required, as a stipulation of his membership, to play in the club championship. The true champion would then be given the recognition that such an accomplishment deserves.

Clubs could also hold less formal monthly tournaments—just for the sake of competing, rather than for costly prizes. Or a challenge ladder might be set up, giving golfers a way to seek out whatever level of competition they want.

> *Most golfers won't play competitively unless they can disguise their scores.*

There are, of course, those who will say, "Hey, I just want to have fun, socialize, drink a few beers. What's all this seriousness stuff about? Are you trying to take all the fun out of golf?"

I refer this person to a statement by the late Adolph Rupp, the famed basketball coach at the University of Kentucky, who was frequently criticized for being too hard on his players. His rejoinder was: "My boys get their fun out of winning national championships."

And I get my fun out of playing serious golf. If I want to have a social gathering with food and drink, I have a party. If I want to get some exercise, test my developing skills, compete and win, I play golf. Naturally I accept other folks' desires to have a social event—to ride around in golf carts, drink beer and call it an afternoon of golf. That's fun for them. But as for me, I like to work at the game, feel the turf under my feet, compete individually and win or lose based on my ability.

Golf is a grand old game. It rests on its own merits. It doesn't need gimmicks to jazz it up. It has its rules, it has its standards, it has its traditions. And there's no tradition greater than using your own talent and posting your own score, for better or worse.

After all, the bottom line for success in golf is the score—your individual score on a given day, not your team's best, scrambled, handicapped score from a randomly chosen nine holes drawn from rounds played over the past three months.

PART II

CLEAR THINKING

CONCENTRATION

To "Maintain Focus—A Can't-miss State of Mind" (Lesson #13)—is one of the greatest challenges in golf. Here are some techniques you can use to improve your concentration.

A question, however, may still remain regarding "Just What *Do* You Focus on During the Swing?" (Lesson # 14). Explore in this lesson some useful things to focus on and how to do it.

One consideration is to "Isolate Yourself to Improve Your Focus" (Lesson #15). That is, retreat into your own personal cocoon to protect yourself from extraneous things going on around you. How do you enter this cocoon? Ben Hogan knew how, and you can learn, too.

Ultimately, negative thoughts are the biggest obstacle to concentration during a round of golf. Lesson #16 explores specific situations where such distractions are likely to occur and offers "Tips for Eliminating Negative Thoughts."

Maintain Focus

A Can't-miss State of Mind

Whenever you play a round of golf, you are somewhere on a continuum of concentration between total distraction and "the zone."

At the total distraction end of the continuum, your mind is racing, your nerves are frazzled, and your performance is quite unpredictable. Conversely, at the zone end of the continuum, you're not thinking about much of anything, confidence replaces nervousness, and your performance is not only predictable but almost effortless with a "how-can-I-miss" air about it.

Somewhere in the middle of those extremes of concentration is a state of focus that requires considerable effort on your part. You have to hone in on what you want to think about, work at staying calm and thereby create a situation in which your body can perform like you want it to.

No one has yet determined a method for propelling oneself into the zone. However, focus is something we can control.

The Foundation of Focus

Cultivate Even-keel Emotions—Being on an emotional roller coaster can distract you from thinking clearly, while emotional control affords you a much better opportunity to focus. To say it more bluntly, if you are using all your energy controlling (or losing) your temper, you haven't got much energy left for thinking clearly about the next shot.

Become Aware Of Details—Focus involves an awareness of minute details—picking up on a lot of little things that are necessary for success. Indeed, part of being in "the zone" involves enjoying sharper sensations that reflect the slightest details in the situation (e.g., you don't just see grass, you see individual blades of grass; you don't just see the ball, you see the individual dimples on the ball).

So, in learning to focus, practice identifying details in situations in which you find yourself. Look at the trees and notice the different colors or shades of green. Feel the golf ball and notice its texture. Waggle the club and sense the weight of the clubhead. This awareness of detail prepares you for focusing on the important subtleties of situations that are the object of successful concentration.

Set Short-term Goals—In entertaining long-term goals such as becoming a star player, cutting your handicap in half or winning the current match, you really have nothing concrete or immediate on which to focus. On the other hand, if you think about the hole at hand, the shot at hand or even better, each step in making the shot at hand, you have something very concrete and immediate on which to focus. Then, the concentration task becomes much more manageable.

What Specifically Do You Focus On?

Basically, you focus on the step-by-step details of the shortest-term goal possible, zeroing in on the precise action you have to take at the moment. Distracting emotions have to be set aside so you can focus on the immediate action at hand. Consider focusing on one or more of the following:

Routine—This is the sequence of steps used in executing a shot. These are the step-by-step details that precede a successful shot. There is no single correct routine. Everyone has his or her own unique way of beginning the shot process. The important thing is that you settle on an effective routine for you, and then do it every time.

Swing Thoughts—These are the self instructions golfers entertain in their heads that they hope will make their way to the rest of the body on the way to hitting a shot. Swing thoughts are tricky things. First, it is easy to take them for granted, to think you are doing them and actually be doing something quite different than you intended. Second, if you reveal your swing thoughts to someone else during a round, those thoughts quickly can lose their beneficial effect. So, if you have some successful swing thoughts working for you, you would be well advised to check the details of them regularly and keep them to yourself until the round is over.

Images—If a picture is worth a thousand words, then a good image might be worth a thousand swing thoughts. A single image can pull together a number of separate elements of a situation, making the concentration task easier since you have to focus on only the single image rather than each of the separate elements.

For example, Jack Nicklaus reportedly imagined his putter shaft as being made of delicate glass. If the shaft were indeed made of delicate glass, he would have to hold it very lightly and swing it very smoothly, lest the fragile material snap in his hands. So, with one image (i.e., a delicate glass shaft), Nicklaus was able to generate a light grip and a smooth stroke without having to think of those two things separately.

Target—A popular point of focus among expert golfers is the target. And why not? It is the target that we are trying to reach. But concentrating on the target is more than just "looking" at it. Target golf refers to proper alignment in relation to the target, body posture oriented toward the target and ultimately locking in your visualization on the successful flight of the ball toward the target before you ever check to see what actually has happened. Indeed, your visualization of the ball soaring toward the target should be so vivid that when you finally do look to see the outcome, it is a total shock if the result you visualized hasn't really happened.

Concentration Techniques

Two basic techniques for concentration have been alluded to above. Let's be totally clear about what they are and how to execute them.

Visualization—This right-brain activity is the basis of imagery. If you picture things easily in your imagination, you probably are right-brain dominant and already should be quite skilled at visualization. Nonetheless, it is important to fully understand the steps in the visualization process:

1. Begin by standing with the ball between you and the target, and look down the target line visualizing the swing you are about to make and the beautiful flight of the ball (or roll, in the case of a putt) to its target.

2. Address the ball, precisely aligning your feet, hips and shoulders with the target line.

3. Now, execute the beautiful swing that is part of the overall visualization and vividly see the flight or roll of the ball before you look up to find out the actual result. This last step in the visualization process may be the most important because it contributes the added dimension of keeping you down on the shot and completing the move through the ball before you look to check on the outcome.

> *Concentrating on the target involves more than just looking at it. It's also important to visualize the successful flight of the ball toward the target.*

Self-talk—This left-brain activity follows from pre-planned swing thoughts. Left-brain thinkers are much better at talking to themselves and thinking in terms of words and numbers than they are at conjuring up mental pictures. They concentrate by giving themselves self-instruction based on their swing thoughts just prior to or even during the swing. Once again, a few considerations are in order regarding the most efficient way to talk to yourself in putting swing thoughts into action:

1. Keep it simple. The fewer things you say to yourself, the more likely you will be able to focus on them. Three swing thoughts should be the limit. They will fit nicely into the three-count, back-and-through tempo of the swing. However, there is nothing wrong with limiting your self-instruction to one or two swing thoughts. Under pressure, such limitations might be necessary.

2. Consolidate swing thoughts whenever possible. Anytime one swing thought does the work of two, you have less on which to concentrate. For example, if keeping your head still prevents you from swaying and encourages you to hit through the ball, then you only have to say one thing ("head still") to yourself. The other two ("don't sway" and "hit through") will follow automatically.

3. Expect to change your swing thoughts periodically. Swing

thoughts seem to have a limited half-life, if you remember that concept from Chemistry 101. That is, swing thoughts, like chemicals, retain their potency for only a limited period of time. Even though the important elements of your swing probably don't change, it seems you have to constantly come up with new ways of talking to yourself to get your swing to do the same thing.

Special Situations
Requiring Concentration

Maintaining Concentration for an Entire Round—If focusing for 18 holes is a problem, break up the round into smaller segments. The segments don't have to be of the traditional nine-hole variety. If you mess up one segment, focus on the next one, with the goal of seeing how many small segments you can handle. Try to improve that number in each successive round.

Maintaining Concentration After Success in the Early Going—When you find yourself starting to think that this is your day to set the course record, that maybe just the time to slow down and review the routine or swing thoughts that have gotten you off to this fast start. Make a special effort at this moment to focus on the details of what you are doing so well, so that you are sure to keep doing those important things on the upcoming holes.

If you are thinking in terms of small segments of the round as discussed above, success in the first segment means nothing regarding success in the second segment. So, don't rest on your early success. You have to refocus with each new segment.

Maintaining Concentration During Breaks in the Action—If play slows down or there is a pause between nines, stay to yourself and avoid yucking it up with your playing companions. Periodically review your routine, swing keys or images so that you stay in some kind of action just as if play had not been disrupted.

Maintaining Concentration in the Face of Distractions—The answer here is simply to practice in the face of distractions so you get used to concentrating despite distractions. Think of what the pros go through on tour with all the spectators moving around and with the noise from action at other holes. They get used to it, and you can, too. When you are practicing and the lawnmower is passing by or people are moving or talking in the background, go ahead and hit anyway, viewing the situation as an opportunity to practice focusing in the face of distraction. And if you flub the shot, there are no excuses. It is your responsibility to focus even when distractions are present.

Maintaining Concentration When You Are Physically Tired—Fatigue is just another distraction. You now are focusing on your body instead of on your game. When fatigue occurs, give yourself a pep talk. Pick up the pace a bit and walk spiritedly toward your ball as if you were full of energy. Fool yourself. When your mind sees your body operating energetically, it will say, "This guy must not be as fatigued as I thought." As a last resort, talk yourself into focusing for just one more shot, then one more shot and one more shot, until you collapse in the clubhouse.

Additional Tips for Improving Concentration

Slow Down—If your mind is racing with anxiety and distraction, it is likely that your body will follow by rushing, also. Conversely, if you slow your body down a bit, it is possible that your mind may also stop racing, giving you the opportunity to relax and refocus.

Focus Your Eyes—Don't let your eyes wander from the task at hand. They didn't call Ben Hogan "The Hawk" because he had wings. No, his eyes were piercing, like those of a bird of prey. You've also seen that intense gaze in the eyes of Raymond Floyd and Tiger Woods, as if they were on a mission. And when that gaze appears, what do we say? "Whoa, they are really focused!" So, next time you are trying to concentrate, don't look for the answer in your surroundings. Keep your gaze down the middle of the fairway, rehearsing your swing thoughts or visualizing the beautiful trajectory of your next shot.

Stay in the Present—It's been said that the present is what is happening when you are either worrying about the past or planning for the future. How true this is in the case of golf! How can you concentrate on the present shot when you are still brooding over the misfortunes of the previous hole or worrying about how you are going to keep this good round going in the upcoming holes. The past is over, and the future is yet to come. All you truly have is the shot that is before you. So, why not give it your full focus and immerse yourself in it as if it were the last shot of your life. Make it a good one!

JUST WHAT *DO* YOU FOCUS ON DURING THE SWING?

THINKING ABOUT NOTHING IS actually thinking about something—it's thinking about nothing. I've always been intrigued by those who say they don't think about anything while they are swinging a golf club. They tend to immediately follow with, "The only thing I think about is . . ."

To suggest that during the swing golfers shouldn't think because they might get confused is like suggesting that during the swing golfers should not breathe or use their muscles because they might get tense. Imagine the following advice: "Since your breathing becomes irregular under pressure, quit breathing during the final holes of a tight match." Or how about: "Everybody knows muscles get tense when you have to produce, so avoid using your muscles when you swing the club."

Ridiculous, you say. A golfer can't eliminate his body from the game, or he won't have anything to play with. The same applies to the brain. Golfers are stuck with brains; they can't stop using their brains merely because they are playing golf. Just like golfers have to learn to control their breathing and relax their muscles, they also have to learn to control their thinking when swinging the club.

A successful golfer who asserts that he doesn't think is most likely thinking one important thought that automatically unifies his swing into a productive ball-striking machine. An analogy might be a cyclist focusing on pedaling efficiently. The turning of the pedals puts the rest of the cycling mechanism into synchronous action without any additional attention from the cyclist. Or consider starting a car. All the driver focuses on is the key in the ignition. But that one little spark generated by turning the key ignites a whole chain of events that runs off without any extra attention from the driver. In a similar fashion, the golfer has to find the key that puts his swing on automatic.

An additional benefit of focusing on one key thought is that the thought serves to block out all other distractions for the moment. To extend the earlier analogies, people who are pedaling or turning ignition keys don't think about much else beyond getting the machine going. Other thoughts can wait for when they are coasting down the road, or, in the case of golfers, down the fairway.

As alluded to above, the important thought in the golf swing may be one swing key that pulls together several mechanics of the swing to produce an integrated, total swing. For example, relaxing over the shot may allow a number of swing mechanics to fluidly fall into place. The experienced golfer with a grooved swing might think of nothing other than relaxing in order to produce a smooth, unified swing.

Another potential important thought might be some image that draws out the player's swing in the direction of a productive result. For example, Frank Ford, a contemporary of Bobby Jones and winner of many prestigious amateur tournaments in his day, once told me that when he was playing his best he thought of nothing other than "knocking down the flagstick." This image may have helped him keep still over the ball as well as propel his follow-through straight down the target line toward the flagstick.

In both cases above, the player's concentration is focused on one key thought, the swing is unified in a productive manner, and the player is blocking out other distracting thoughts that might otherwise intrude. Indeed, the mistaken suggestion to not think about anything could have just the opposite effect of allowing plenty of room for distracting thoughts and not doing anything to encourage a swing that hangs together.

The challenge, therefore, is to forget about not thinking and devote your energies to finding the most useful thing to focus on during the swing. Here are a few candidates to consider.

The Target—Harvey Penick, in his *Little Red Book*, stressed the notion of "taking dead aim." This is certainly what Frank Ford was doing when he was "knocking down the flagstick." Any image that encourages your body movement to extend down the target line is likely to contribute to an overall productive swing.

Flight of Ball—Jack Nicklaus has been known to envision the entire flight of the ball before making his swing. You've probably noticed the Bear standing behind the ball, or even during his pre-shot waggle, gazing down the target line with a trance-like stare, no doubt seeing the perfect shot even before he hits it. Once again, that perfectly envisioned scenario has the tendency to draw out the perfect swing that most of us have the potential to produce.

> *The important thought in the golf swing may be one swing key that pulls together several mechanics of the swing to produce an integrated total swing.*

Steadiness Over the Ball—If images aren't your forte, then a unifying swing key to focus on might be staying steady over the ball. If the axis of the swing is kept in a fairly constant position during the coiling action of the hips, shoulders and arms, then the chances of the club returning to its point of origin to make crisp contact with the ball are enhanced. Golfers may produce steadiness over the ball in various ways such as staying down on the shot, keeping the swing on plane or keeping the head down or eye on the ball.

Slow or Big—Nicklaus offered another bit of advice when he said the one thought he kept in reserve for critical situations was a slow back-swing. While Jack was thinking about slowness, that slowness probably encouraged a proper swing plane, steadiness and acceleration through the ball without any additional effort in thinking about those factors.

To extend the slowness idea a bit further, consider making the entire swing in slow motion. Focus on a slow-motion swing that "looks good," and that picture-perfect swing may become a reality.

Similar to focusing on slowness, when Tom Watson wants to hit the ball hard, he thinks of "big," rather than "hard." For Tom, bigness is the key that creates the hardness he is striving for.

Imitation of a Good Player—While the slow-motion swing just suggested involves a slow version of your own best swing, an alternative would be to put into slow motion some other golfer's swing. Of course, this other golfer should be a skilled golfer—perhaps a touring pro, your club pro or some accomplished amateur in the area. Whoever it is, the golfer you imitate should be someone similar to you in stature and basic swing technique. Once you have observed that model golfer sufficiently, simply think the unifying thought that you are him or her when you swing. That fluid image might prove to be a relaxing and productive thought in pulling together the various components of your swing.

Focused Energy at Impact—Boxers, kickers and tennis players forcefully exhale (grunt) at impact. There is no reason golfers can't do the same thing. Don't worry about embarrassing yourself in this gentlemanly game of golf. Exhaling, even forcefully, can be accomplished in a barely audible fashion.

Before beginning the swing, take a deep cleansing breath and exhale about 90 percent of it. Then, during the swing, think of nothing else but exhaling the final 10 percent toward the ball at impact. This simple thought will help you concentrate on the ball, focus power at the precise point of impact, eliminate other distractions and create an element of abandon in the swing that counteracts any tentativeness or holding back that might otherwise intrude.

Pre-shot Routine—A routine is admittedly more than one thought. It is a sequence of thoughts. However, this chain of thoughts ultimately leads to one key thought for making the swing.

Lee Janzen has been said to have a whole checklist of maneuvers he goes through leading up to the swing. That checklist, most assuredly, converges on one important thought that allows Janzen to pull the trigger. You may not want a checklist, but some consistent routine is essential to manage the thinking task in golf, to eliminate distractions and narrow the focus to the key thought that will put your swing on automatic.

The "stream of consciousness," which yogis immerse themselves in when they meditate, allows unwanted thoughts to simply flow downstream and out of awareness. Immersion in the stream of consciousness is probably as close as one can come to "not thinking." Such meditational skill requires a lot of practice, and even if you're a skilled yogi, it just isn't going to happen on the golf course. There's too much going on, too much to attend to and too much to think about for you to enter a meditational state for each shot during a round.

Let me say it one more time: It's impossible to "not think" when playing golf. So, commit yourself to finding something constructive to think about and focus intently on that key thought during the swing.

Lesson #15

ISOLATE YOURSELF TO IMPROVE YOUR FOCUS

MANY SUCCESSFUL GOLFERS RETREAT into their own personal cocoon before they begin a round. Remember the story about Ben Hogan telling the lady who was asking him for an autograph as he was warming up for his round, "Excuse me, madam, but I am already playing my round." Hogan was entering his cocoon, and he did not want to be disturbed in the process.

When watching the touring pros play, particularly in the flesh at a tournament site, one can sense an almost eerie quietness about their movements. Everything seems to be in slow motion, methodical, deliberate. The pros are seldom off balance, never seem to rush, and physical exertion appears to be absent. A gentle rhythm pervades their every move. Phil Mickelson is a classic example as he glides down the fairway with a silky smoothness that readily spreads to his entire game. As close as spectators are to the action, the players seem to be in another world, in their own personal cocoons.

So, how does a golfer enter this cocoon? What was Hogan doing on the practice tee that allowed him entry into this private world? We can only speculate, but I would bet that he was doing some of the following, all of which might be good advice for any golfer:

Practice a Routine—Before you can practice a routine, you must identify one. A routine begins with the walk toward the next shot and the assessments being made regarding the elements, the terrain and club selection. The routine continues as you review your swing keys, pick a target and address the ball in the same manner every time. The routine is complete only after the waggle has been standardized and the trigger that puts the swing on automatic has been identified.

Once a routine is established, it must be practiced regularly and focused on during warm-up for a round. The walk to the first tee is no time to be fiddling with your routine. It must already be firmly set in your mind from many repetitions during warm-up, repetitions that are the fibers of your personal cocoon.

Rehearse the Game Plan—To get a head start on the round, start simulating holes right there on the practice tee. Imagine fairways, aim at targets, vary the clubs you use just as will be the case in a few more minutes on the course. If there is a tree line down the right side of the practice range and you are worried about similar wooded areas out on the course, physically move your bag of balls to the right side of the practice tee and rehearse those shots. You are beginning the thought processes that are about to transpire during your round and, at the same time, strengthening your cocoon.

Review Self-Talk and Imagery—What are you going to say to yourself before each shot? What positive images can you entertain during the round? What are you going to say to yourself when you face a challenging situation? What calming image can be used in the face of potential disaster? If these mental tools are not readily available as you begin your round, don't expect to discover them in the heat of the action. These items must be stored away in the cocoon during preparation for the round.

So now, with your cocoon ready and constructed of routine, game plan, self-talk and imagery, how do you remain in the cocoon? How do you keep the fragile membrane intact when it is surrounded by hostile forces?

The answer lies in choosing the proper focus for your attention. That is, attention must be defocused from outcome and focused instead on what has to be done to achieve that outcome. The outcome of a shot resides outside the cocoon and can quickly destroy the cocoon if it becomes the object of attention. In contrast, what you do with your mind, body and golf clubs to produce that outcome is the territory inside the cocoon, and to the extent that you maintain a focus on those matters, you are maintaining the integrity of your cocoon.

Consider what happens when a golfer looks up to see the outcome of a shot before having completed the task of crisply striking the ball. By looking up, the golfer breaks the peaceful cocoon and makes himself available to the turmoil of the shot's disastrous results. He is distracted from his routine and game plan and now focused outside instead of inside the cocoon.

But, you say, I've got to watch for the ball so I can find it for my next shot. Agreed, but watch it with a certain detachment for the sole purpose of knowing its location. Don't stand there and evaluate the result, berate yourself and pass judgment on your game. To do so will destroy the cocoon. Each shot is a neutral event that just is and must not be allowed to disturb the peaceful, methodical rhythm of your private cocoon.

Watch the touring pros again if you want an example of defocusing from outcome. I find it particularly evident on chip shots where the players seem to stay down on the shot forever just watching the action between the clubhead, the ball and the turf. Outcome seems to be of only secondary concern. It's as if the pros were saying, "All I have to do is my job over the ball, and everything will work out as planned. I don't have to see it. I know what is happening even before I look for the result." And, incidentally, whatever the result, the most successful players keep their reactions inside the cocoon.

Other steps that might help you remain in your cocoon are to practice with distractions present so that you get used to them. Remember positive self-talk and imagery when outside events threaten the cocoon. Stick with your routine no matter what the circumstances. Immerse yourself in your swing thoughts and avoid talking to others or making eye contact with anyone or anything that might distract you from the task at hand. If your personal space is unavoidably intruded upon, move politely by and re-enter the cocoon via the use of some cue word like "calm" or "return" or simply "cocoon." As you maintain the normal pace of play, you might entertain a feeling of being in slow motion in this inner sanctuary that only you control. The world around you may be going crazy, but you are in quiet control of this peaceful, private world that is your cocoon.

TIPS FOR ELIMINATING NEGATIVE THOUGHTS

FOR ALL THE FUN golf is supposed to be, why does it scare us half to death? Gary McCord claims golf isn't brain surgery, but that doesn't rule out ulcers, atrial fibrillations or nervous disorders. Anyone who has ever felt queasy approaching the first tee, heart palpitations before a crucial approach shot or shaky knees over a pressure putt knows what I'm talking about.

Charlie Brown once lamented in response to Lucy's sport-psychology consultation, "My mind and my body hate each other." How true that is sometimes, but not absolutely necessary.

Consider the following situations that lend themselves to anxiety and negative thoughts, and then reflect on how each might be viewed differently, thereby reducing the conflict between your mind and body.

Playing a New Course

Anytime you confront unfamiliar circumstances, uneasiness is to be expected. A new course may introduce negative thoughts related to unforeseen trouble, illusions regarding distances or unfamiliar turf and green conditions. The result is you're nervous and expecting difficulty even before you begin to play.

Learn to be more realistic. When you play a new course, allow for the fact that your score is likely to be a little higher than usual. It might help to realize Arnold Palmer shot 86 the first time he played St. Andrews, and that occurred in his prime.

Play the percentages in order to keep your score as low as possible. Don't take foolish chances cutting doglegs or trying to clear hazards. Position your ball strategically around the course, thereby providing percentage shots into greens and taking big numbers out of the equation.

Relate unfamiliar holes at the new course to familiar holes at your home course. For example, when facing a long hole over water, consider how you negotiate a similar long hole over water back home. Then play the new hole with the same cautious game plan that has helped you survive the similar hole on your home course.

Jinx Holes

Certain holes conjure up thoughts of disaster. It might be the woods to the right of the tee at the 15th or the second shot from a downhill lie over the lake at the 10th. It might even be that little creek directly in front of the first tee that drives you crazy on the first shot of the day. These are your jinx holes, the ones you have to conquer in order to have a successful round.

Develop a routine that puts you on automatic and doesn't allow a given circumstance to dictate your behavior. As you stand on the 15th tee, look at a target down the fairway, address the ball and swing in the same timely fashion as you do on any other tee shot. Just because it is the dreaded 15th doesn't mean you have to suddenly change your routine and start gazing at the woods, taking more time to hit the shot than usual and quickly looking up to see if it went in the woods—which will probably happen if you change your routine.

Another remedy involves taking several balls out to the jinx hole and hitting the shot of concern repeatedly until you see that not every shot will be disastrous. After you hit enough good shots in the situation, you can take a more realistic perspective toward the hole and recognize that success may be just as possible as disaster. It may still be a difficult shot, but not one to be considered totally doomed.

Competition

Unless you play competition regularly, feelings of panic in the face of "real golf" should come as no surprise. Casual games with friends are fun, but they often lend themselves to the deception that you are playing better than you actually are. In contrast, tournaments tend to accurately display your true level of play. This introduces that old nemesis, ego, the ever-sensitive dimension of our personality open to anxiety and negative thoughts.

Try exposing yourself to milder forms of competition on a regular basis so you get used to facing the competitive situation. Challenge friends to medal-play matches where you actually play by the rules and count all your strokes. Develop a challenge ladder at your club so you can learn to compete with relative strangers, which is similar to the playing conditions found in tournaments. Play club tournaments and one-day state events to ease into larger scale competition. Observe what you shoot under these conditions and develop a realistic measure of your ability.

Once you know how you truly perform under competitive conditions, you can be realistic about how good you should play in a given tournament. Hopefully that level of play will place you among the leaders. Even if it doesn't, give yourself credit simply for being willing to put yourself on the line. Remember that those who might be critical of your performance are likely to be the same timid souls standing coldly on the sidelines and knowing neither victory nor defeat.

Lastly, look for gradual improvement in your competitive performance. I once knew a lady golfer who couldn't wait to get into the competitive game. In her haste, she shot 186 for her first 18 holes in the club championship. However, in doing so, she established a true reference point for her beginning ability. After a year or two of hard work and gradual improvement, this lady shot 86 in the same club championship, knocking 100 strokes off her score.

Partner Golf

Golf is typically an individual sport with well-known individual challenges. Inject a partner into the situation and a whole new set of difficulties arises. What does my partner expect of me? What if I let my partner down? Will he distract me or apply extra pressure? What if our playing styles or personalities don't mesh?

Despite all his ability and cockiness, Sam Snead must have experienced some of these same anxieties. On the first tee, Snead reportedly would say to his partner that he was going to be playing as hard as he could today, even if it may not always look like it. Then he would add that he was going to apologize up front for all the mistakes he might make today, and that no more apologies would be forthcoming for the rest of the round.

Both of these statements are profound. When someone studies a shot, focuses intently and swings with all the energy and purpose he can muster, how can anyone think for a moment that the player wasn't trying, even if the shot goes awry? No one wants or tries to hit a bad shot. Golf courses are comprised of nothing but motivated people who for one reason or another can't always produce. For that, no apologies are needed.

In fact, if any apology is in order, it should be for endless apologies. Forget the whining, moping and self-deprecation. Simply move on and try just as hard on the next shot. If you do, you will represent yourself admirably on the golf course.

When playing with a partner, it is helpful to discuss beforehand each of your particular styles of play and the conditions under which you perform best. For example, if given the choice, would you rather hit first or second? Do you want to share opinions in lining up putts or decide on your own? If such issues and others are clarified beforehand, a lot of anxiety and confusion might be avoided.

Above all, you should never make a partner feel like he or she let you down. Whatever a partner does should be excused, be viewed as positive in some way or simply be considered as some unavoidable misfortune. To do otherwise risks losing the effectiveness of your partner for the remainder of the round. Once a player feels that he has let his partner down, the pressure mounts to contribute and further letdowns become more likely.

Tips for Eliminating
Negative Thoughts

1. Close the Gate to Negativity—If you think of your brain as having a gate that allows only so much into the brain for attention, then anything that competes with negativity for access to the gate will be useful in blocking out negativity. When negative thoughts start calling for attention, clog up the gate with other competitive thoughts, such as your game plan, images of previous success, even your Christmas list. Anything that denies negative thoughts access to the brain can only be beneficial.

2. Keep Things Simple—As is the case with swing mechanics, positive thinking may also benefit from simplicity. If positive thinking involves too many mental gymnastics, then all those positives might add up to one big negative—confusion. Identify a few positive thoughts or actions that reliably work for you, and then put them into action at the first signs of negativity.

> *Develop a routine that puts you on automatic and doesn't allow a given circumstance to dictate your behavior.*

3. Be Patient—Jack Nicklaus had the rare ability to stand over a putt and let the negative thoughts flow by until a positive image appeared on his radar screen. Only then would he promptly stroke the putt. We might learn from Nicklaus' approach that we don't have to run from negative thoughts. Instead, we can just go ahead and experience them until we get, in effect, bored with them, leaving nothing to attend to but positive thoughts.

4. Hit It Quickly—As an alternative to Nicklaus' patient approach, consider hitting the ball quickly. This is not to suggest rushing your shot or abandoning your routine. Just develop an efficient routine that doesn't waste any time or allow negative thoughts to creep in. Remember, it only takes an extra half-second for a negative thought to gain your attention and throw off an otherwise successful swing.

Positive thoughts and images are powerful, but they won't last forever. Once you have the positive thought in your mind, execute! Even Nicklaus pulled the trigger promptly once he settled on a positive image he liked. Lee Trevino used to say it took him only 5 seconds to tap his foot and hit the shot, but that was a very serious 5 seconds. Trevino had a quick, intense, focused routine that did not allow time or space for negativity to get involved.

5. Talk to Yourself—Much of what is called positive thinking is actually positive self-talk. The challenge is coming up with positive things to say to yourself. To meet this challenge, make a list of negative things you regularly say to yourself. Then make a parallel list of positive things you could say that counter each of those negative items. The positive things have to be realistic and believable, the positive truth that is always hidden within every situation. Write the list of positive thoughts on a note card and carry it with you, rehearsing the items and using them when you get in tight situations. One or two of the positive thoughts will emerge as faithful friends to help you when the going gets tough and negativity starts crying for attention.

6. Focus on Where to Hit the Ball, Rather than Where **Not** *to Hit It*—In truth, there is usually more fairway than rough. For example, the fairway on a given hole might be 30 yards across with only 7 or 8 yards of rough on either side. That's twice as much fairway as rough. Yet we tend to fixate on that lesser amount of rough and neglect all that beautiful short grass in between.

Go ahead and look at the rough, the woods and the lakes. Enjoy them, appreciate them and admire them. But when it comes to addressing the ball, look at nothing but the target down the fairway, initiate your routine and fire.

SWING KEYS
AND VISUALIZATION

In the previous section on concentration, *swing keys* and *visualization* were identified as prime candidates for focus during a round. But which one is best for you? Lesson #17 addresses this question and contends that one or the other, "Swing Keys and Mental Images Can Lower Your Scores."

If it turns out to be swing keys for you, then important considerations arise: When do you use them, how do you choose them, what are some examples, how can I maximize their effectiveness? Lesson #18 explores "How to Use Swing Keys More Effectively."

If, on the other hand, visualization emerges as the method of choice for you, other considerations are important: Why is visualization advantageous, how does it work, what exactly do you visualize, how do you put it into practice? Lesson #19 seeks to clarify how one can "Visualize Success—Every Shot Pretty as a Picture."

Curiously, everything seems to work better in golf if you slow it down. You'll hit the ball farther and straighter, achieve better balance, be more relaxed and think more clearly, as explained in Lesson #20, "Play Slow-motion Golf for Better Results."

Lastly, the overriding mantra in golf is to *keep your head down*. The precise moment of contact between clubhead and ball that is being referred to by this directive is certainly "The Most Important Millisecond in Golf" (Lesson #21). But what exactly does it mean to *keep your head down*, why is it important, and how do you get yourself to do it? This lesson offers some insight into these matters.

Lesson#17

SWING KEYS AND MENTAL IMAGES CAN LOWER YOUR SCORES

ALL GOLFERS CAN BE divided into basically two groups—visualizers and verbalizers. The former tend to picture things quite clearly when they are playing, while the latter are better at talking themselves through a round.

Visualizers tend to be dominated by the right hemisphere of their brain, which controls artistic and creative thought, thinking by means of images or pictures, and integrating things rather than taking them apart. The result of this integrative activity is often the development of the big picture without a lot of distraction from details. Visualization is a major part of what has been referred to as target golf.

Verbalizers, on the other hand, tend to be dominated by the left hemisphere of their brain, which controls logical and analytical thought, thinking by means of words and numbers, and taking things apart as opposed to putting them together. The result of this analytical activity is often a set of verbal self-instructions regarding how to proceed. Verbalizing is at the heart of the use of swing keys.

Since being a visualizer or a verbalizer seems to involve inborn hemispheric dominance of the brain, there may not be too much you can do about whichever you are. So don't fight your natural tendency. Go with your strength and just become the best visualizer or verbalizer you can be.

Keys to Visualization

Visualization is a three-step process. Let's take the tee shot, for example. Standing at the back of the tee box looking down the target line with the ball between you and the target, vividly imagine the swinging of the club and the flight of the ball to its landing and bounding down the fairway to a premier location for your second shot.

Next, walk toward the ball and address it from the side, all the while entertaining the image you just generated at the back of the tee box. You might narrow the image down a bit at this time to include only the components of the swing and the flight of the ball.

Lastly, and perhaps most importantly, hang onto that image just after impact with the ball and before you look to determine the result. While you are still looking at the plot of ground that the ball just vacated, you should be seeing in your mind's eye the ball doing exactly what you had envisioned before the swing. The image should be so vivid and real that you are truly shocked if it hasn't actually happened when you do ultimately check to see the result.

Of course, this same sequence of events can be applied to chipping, where the central image might be of the ball landing on a spot on the green and then rolling gently to the hole. Or, the image could involve a putt rolling at the appropriate speed, taking the break and falling into the hole. Whatever the shot, begin the visualization behind the ball, continue it over the ball and then hang onto the image immediately after impact before you look to see the result.

Keys to Verbalization

The key to being an effective verbalizer is in generating the minimum number of things to say to yourself in order to produce an effective swing. The things you say to yourself are swing keys—the key moves that, in effect, open the door to a beautiful swing.

The most swing keys you can probably entertain are three—a number that corresponds to the 1–2–3, back-and-through tempo of the golf swing. So, you might self-instruct yourself to take the club back slowly, pause at the top and fire the right side. During the swing, you might simply say to yourself, "Slow, pause, fire."

If three swing keys are cumbersome, try two—one for the backswing and one for the move through the ball. For example, "Coil, uncoil."

If you want to try the minimum, use one swing key. This number is ideal, especially in pressure situations when you are lucky if you can successfully attend to just one thing. When I am particularly worried about a shot, I think of nothing but staying down on the shot—keeping a proper spine angle and my eye on the ball. I'm down at address, down on the backswing and screaming "DOWN" in my mind at the point of impact with the ball. Indeed, after the ball is gone, I'm still looking down at the divot, not at where the ball has gone. That one self-instruction can simultaneously pull together a lot of important swing mechanics.

The only goal for verbalizers is to produce the moves associated with their swing keys, and this accomplishment is their sole measure of success. While results are important, those results are beyond a golfer's control and not something to be distracted by. The only things verbalizers consider under their control are the swing keys that produce solid contact between the club and the ball, and those are the only things they think about. It is as if the verbalizer is saying, "I'll do my job over the ball, and the rest will depend on physics and the golf gods."

Other Visualization Considerations

1. Visualization Can Be Internal or External—When you visualize, you can either be on the inside looking out (as if your eyes were camera lenses) or you can be on the outside looking in (as if the camera were aimed at you from a tripod). Interestingly, Jack Nicklaus once said, "Before every shot, I go to the movies inside my head."

When you're on the inside looking out, the focus is likely to be more narrow and directed toward feel or mechanics. You may see your swing flowing down stream or your arms and club as components of a big spinning wheel. You might even imagine yourself to be a flawless robot like Iron Byron. Whatever the image, you will see it through the camera lenses of your eyes.

When the camera is outside and you are in the movies, a broader focus is likely to paint a big picture of the action. Now you see not only the picture-perfect swing, but also the dynamic flight of the ball and a beautiful result. All of this is seen from the vantage point of something like a golfing out-of-body experience.

Some evidence exists that internal visualization as opposed to external visualization might yield better results. However, most elite athletes who visualize report using both approaches. The most important thing is that you get a clear, useful image that works for you.

2. Images Must Be Vivid—Images must be clear, detailed and use more senses than just the eyes. A truly vivid image is not only seen in your mind but is also heard, felt, smelled and tasted, if all those happen to apply.

For example, in imagining the perfect drive, your image certainly will contain the marvelous sight of the ball flying through the air. But right along with that visual image is the explosive sound and feel of the ball propelling off the clubface, as well as the unique smell of the golf course grass that surrounds you as you experience the fullness of this event.

The more sensations you can reconstruct from previously successful experiences with the driver, the more likely you are to produce effective images for future tee shots.

3. Employ Integrative Images—The old axiom that a picture is worth a thousand words applies to visualization as much as to painting or photography. Images that incorporate a number of aspects of the golf swing into the same picture are likely to be the simplest and most effective.

For example, entertaining an image of the golf swing as being like baseball's submarine pitch integrates three important swing components into one image. That is, the combined sidearm/underhand action of this pitch incorporates the golf swing's weight shift to the back leg on the backswing (baseball's windup), the weight transfer to the forward leg on the forward swing (baseball's pitch), and the energy flow directly toward the target on the follow-through (both in golf and baseball). All of these components are accomplished by thinking of only one image—the submarine pitch—rather than each of the components individually.

4. Visualization Is More Effective When You Are Relaxed—Having a relaxed body and mind is conducive to producing your best images. Consider how easily your mind wanders when you are listening to relaxing music or taking in a beautiful, calming scene. So practice relaxation techniques in conjunction with your visualization. Furthermore, before playing, get yourself relaxed in preparation for producing your most effective images on the course.

5. Visualize in Real Time—Practicing visualization may not be the most exciting thing you ever do, so you may find yourself impatiently speeding through practice sessions. Don't do it! Practice in real time. If the action you are visualizing actually takes 20 seconds to perform, then devote 20 seconds to practicing the visualization of that action. This rule applies to whether you are practicing the image at home or implementing it on the golf course. Completely visualize the image in real time.

Other Verbalization Considerations

1. Keep Swing Keys Simple—Avoid unnecessary self-instructions. You might be saying to yourself, "Slow down the backswing," when you could simply be saying, "Slow." You know it applies to the backswing so you don't have to say that part. Or you might be saying, "Stay down and watch the ball," when either of these directives alone would accomplish the same thing.

Make the thinking and memory task as simple as possible. The golf swing occurs too fast to be able to concentrate on too much.

2. Consolidate Swing Keys as Much as Possible—Similar to the above consideration, if one swing key will pull together two or more necessary ingredients of the swing, it is like getting a bargain. For example, if thinking about your upper body simply coiling around your properly angled spine results in you simultaneously keeping the club on plane and staying over the ball, you are getting three swing ingredients for the price of one swing thought. All you have to say to yourself is, "Coil."

3. Do What You Say—Make sure you are actually doing what you are saying to yourself. Sometimes you find an effective swing key, say it to yourself and implement it admirably. But then, before you know it, you are merely saying it, not actually doing it—and you may not even realize it. So, if you are instructing yourself to move forward into the shot, monitor yourself to make sure you are actually moving forward and that you continue to do it.

4. Write Down Your Swing Keys—There is nothing more frustrating than to spend the first six holes of a round trying to remember what worked so well the last time out. Write down your swing keys and review them before you begin each round. Also, a good form of mental practice on the days you cannot play would be to get out your notes and rehearse your swing keys, at least in your mind.

Can You Visualize and Verbalize?

Just as some people are ambidextrous, there may be those who can visualize and verbalize. For such lucky folks, there is no reason why both tools shouldn't be employed. A good blend might be to talk yourself through the shot up to the address position, then allow some useful image to kick in as you initiate your swing.

You might also try to develop the component that doesn't come naturally for you. For example, if you tend to be a visualizer, a little of the self-instruction of a verbalizer might make you a more disciplined player.

As an example, Tiger Woods seems to indicate that he naturally entertains strong images of success in the process of hitting great shots. However, you will notice that he also has become a very disciplined and methodical player, which may reflect the additional use of self-instruction in managing his game.

If you are a die-hard verbalizer, powerful images may still occasionally pop into your head. Sometimes you can perfectly see the line of a putt and have a wonderful feeling that you are going to make it. Don't fight these favorable images when they come along. Go with the visualization while it lasts.

Visualization also can be practiced off the course. Close your eyes and try to vividly picture things that tax all your senses. Most people can visualize what it's like to be by the ocean with all its sights, sounds, feelings, tastes and smells. Try this exercise with phenomena that get closer to the golf course. You may find that you can learn to construct some images that will help the creative side of your game.

Remember, most switch hitters in baseball didn't start out being switch hitters. They worked at it. Maybe you too can become a switch hitter when it comes to visualizing and verbalizing, employing useful mental images and swing keys to effectively combine discipline and creativity on the golf course.

Lesson #18

HOW TO USE SWING KEYS MORE EFFECTIVELY

H ARDLY ENOUGH CAN BE said about the importance of swing keys—the triggers that fire the golf swing. A lifelong challenge in golf is finding the simplest keys that will do the job for you.

What Are Swing Keys?

Swing keys come in two varieties—images you entertain during the swing and words you say to yourself during the swing. In other words, you can picture the swing or you can talk yourself through the swing. Whichever the case, the simpler the picture or the fewer the words the better. Little room exists for gabbiness or flamboyance when it comes to an efficient and effective golf swing.

When to Use Swing Keys

Swing keys can be entertained almost anytime, but primarily during the pre-shot routine. As you stand behind the ball looking at the target and preparing to take your stance, the swing-key process begins by rehearsing either what you are going to picture or say to yourself during the swing. A second swing-key rehearsal takes place as you address the

123

ball, waggle and take a final look at the target. Then, the rehearsals end, the trigger is pulled and you kick the swing keys into action as you take a swipe at the ball.

The traditional phrase "keep your head down" is often used to help maintain a certain stability of the golfer's head in the center of the circle that is figuratively drawn by the full swing of the golf club.

However, the usefulness of swing keys extends beyond their implementation during the golf swing. For example, the rehearsal of what you picture or say to yourself during the swing is an effective form of mental practice, even when you are away from the course. Swing keys can be mentally rehearsed at any time—during boring business meetings when you are not at the podium, at cocktail parties when the conversation bogs down or even during romantic encounters that are going nowhere. (Reminds me of the assistant pro who once lamented not finding someone of the opposite sex who was more stimulating than golf!)

Perhaps the most important time to rehearse your swing keys is in the car on the way to the golf course. Prepare your mind for the round before you arrive, because you never know what kind of distractions might interfere with mental preparation once you step out of the car.

Where Swing Keys Come From

Swing keys emanate from such things as instructional books, articles, videos, lessons and watching others, as well as from personal experience and knowledge of your own particular golf swing. Have you ever obtained some new insight into the golf swing while watching a televised golf tournament? Something strikes you about a move a player makes or something an analyst says and immediately you want to dash out to the course and try what you are mentally imagining. You have a new swing key that will surely make a difference in your game—and sometimes it does!

Another fertile source of swing keys comes from a periodic review of the fundamentals of the swing. Either on your own or with the assistance of a professional teacher, check your grip, stance, posture, alignment, swing plane, position at follow-through, etc. Frequently you will discover something important you have been overlooking that might serve as an effective swing key for the future.

Tips from fellow golfers might also prove useful in developing swing keys, but too many tips from too many sources may complicate the picture and be counterproductive. Ultimately, after playing for a while, you will generate a repertoire of swing keys that will serve as the best source of alternatives for your particular swing.

Examples of Swing Keys

Swing keys are so idiosyncratic that there are probably as many swing keys as there are individual golfers. Consider further that many golfers use more than one swing key, revising them over and over during a career, and the number of possible swing keys begins to stretch to astronomical values. However, all these swing keys will tend to factor down to some fairly common denominators that can serve as broadly generic examples.

One common denominator of any effective golf swing is maintaining a fairly stable hub for the arms and club to rotate around. The traditional phrase that golfers have said to themselves in trying to accomplish this stability is the ever familiar "keep your head down." What this refers to is maintaining a certain stability of the golfer's head in the center of the circle that is figuratively drawn by the full swing of the golf club.

While "keeping your head down" is the most common mantra among golfers, a similar stability of the hub of the golf swing can be accomplished with the reminder to "keep your eyes on the ball." Other stabilizing points of focus include the sternum, torso or spine. Indeed, the swing more accurately rotates around these latter body parts than it does around the head. Therefore, thinking of the spine as a rod that the upper body rotates around, or the torso as a spring that coils and uncoils, or the entire upper body turning as if in a slanted barrel might be very useful as swing keys for achieving stability.

Golfers have also struggled for years to find swing keys that will provide a smooth transition between the top of the backswing and the forward move into the ball. Such actions as turning one's belt buckle toward the target or (in the context of right-handed golfers) slamming down the left heel, driving the right knee or firing the right hip toward the target have all been suggested as potential swing keys for initiating the forward swing.

Another common denominator of a good golf swing is the flow of the body on the follow-through to an upright position facing the target. Swing keys that encourage this result might include images of throwing the clubhead at the target (figuratively speaking), pointing the sternum or naval at the target as you follow through, or picturing the entire swing as caught up in the current of a powerful stream that is flowing directly at the target.

All of the above are very basic swing keys that might be refined in various ways by individual golfers. Personally, I try to combine swing keys so that I don't have to think of two or three things at once. For example, a simple and effective swing key for me is to focus on "hitting the ball with my torso." Admittedly, I can't actually hit the ball with my torso. However, when I concentrate on nothing but the torso turning as if to hit the ball, I accomplish three things at once: 1) I coil with stability around the torso on the backswing; 2) I provide a key for transition into the forward swing by simply uncoiling the same thing I have coiled; and 3) I thrust my body toward the target on the follow-through since it is hard to restrain the forward movement of this uncoiling major body part. Said another way, I create a stable backswing, smooth transition and solid follow-through all with one swing key—"hitting the ball with my torso."

The Half-life of Swing Keys

It is the dream of every golfer to find that one key that will put his or her swing on automatic and never have to be changed again. Forget it! Swing keys do not last forever.

While the fundamentals of an effective swing are fairly constant, the swing keys necessary to elicit those fundamentals seem to change over time. That is, a mental picture or something you say to yourself may work for a week or two, but then it gradually loses its effectiveness. It's kind of like medicine or chemicals on a shelf—their potency diminishes by half after established periods of time. The potency of swing keys seems to have a half-life, too.

Two possible reasons for the short-lived effectiveness of swing keys might be as follows:

Satiation—Any time you experience or do something repeatedly, it tends to lose its effectiveness. If you eat nothing but ice cream, eventually ice cream doesn't taste particularly good anymore. If you watch nothing but the same movie over and over again, boredom eventually sets in and you find yourself no longer paying any attention to the movie. Similarly, if you repeat the same swing key shot after shot for a number of rounds, after a period of time you may find yourself not paying any attention to that swing key anymore.

> *Remembering to "keep your eyes on the ball" can provide another stabilizing point of focus.*

Overconfidence—You may become so comfortable with your swing key that you begin taking it for granted. You may even assume you are implementing the swing key when, in fact, you are ignoring it. It is so easy to tell yourself to "swing smoothly," while unwittingly still jumping at the ball without your awareness.

So prepare to be constantly tampering with your swing keys. Each round may lead to changing one swing key here, refining another one there or even returning to an earlier, effective one that is stored away in your memory bank.

How to Extend the Potency of Swing Keys

Swing Key Secrecy—Refrain from talking to others about your swing keys during a round. Anytime something is working, there is considerable temptation to tell others about it. However, as soon as you tell someone, you run the risk of becoming self-conscious about the very keys that have been working for you. Your playing companions will start watching to see if it works. You will be trying to show them how well it works, and the result of this demonstration mentality is distracting from doing the very thing that has been working so well for you. So, keep your swing keys to yourself, at least until the round is over.

Swing Key Notes—Write your swing keys on a note card (the back of an old business card works well in this regard) and carry it around in your wallet for review at any time. Once you write down your swing keys, don't take them for granted. You might find yourself saying, "I know what I wrote on the card—I don't have to bother getting it out and reviewing it." On the contrary, get it out! It is amazing how quickly you can forget a small element you wrote down just a few days ago. Review the card thoroughly before each round, and if your game starts heading south in the middle of a round, get the note card out again and do a step-by-step recheck to make sure you are not inadvertently neglecting some aspect of your swing keys.

Because of the half-life of swing keys described previously, write your notes in pencil so you can easily erase and make minor revisions after each round. Indeed, keep a stack of cards handy because the revisions will eventually become so numerous that you won't even be able to read your notes because of all the erasures.

> *Thinking of the entire body turning as if in a slanted barrel also can be a very useful swing key for achieving stability.*

Finally, don't show your note card to anyone. It won't make any sense to them because of the idiosyncratic nature of swing keys, and it may even open you up to ridicule. For example, my swing key about hitting the ball with my torso makes perfectly good sense to me, but it may do nothing for someone else or even seem humorous to others. The last thing I need when I am trying to concentrate on my game is for someone to be needling me along the lines of, "Well, are you getting the old torso into it today, big boy?" or even worse, "Looks like the torso didn't do the trick on that one, did it?"

Swing keys are the triggers of the golf swing. When you identify useful ones, write them down, store them away, refer to them regularly and keep them to yourself. Above all, don't take them for granted. Treat your swing keys with respect, and they will serve you well, as you gradually discover the ones that work best for you.

Lesson #19

VISUALIZE SUCCESS

Every Shot Pretty as a Picture

ISUALIZERS ARE THE LUCKIEST and most misunderstood people in golf. They are lucky because they seem to have a distinct advantage. They're misunderstood because non-visualizers don't have a clue as to what visualizers are talking about.

I've heard non-visualizers say sarcastically, "What's this visualization thing all about?" Non-visualizers identify with swing keys, triggers, swing thoughts and things like that. They talk themselves through the shot. Non-visualizers just don't get "this visualization thing."

Indeed, some people do seem to be more adept at visualizing than others. Perhaps it is those with dominant right-brain hemispheres, where processing is done in an integrated, picturesque fashion. But, nonetheless, all golfers could enhance their ability with visualization if they only understood it a little better. So let's begin with the obvious question . . .

What Exactly *Is* Visualization?

Visualization, simply described, involves picturing shots before they are executed. For example, picture in your head the house in which you grew up. If you are not in proximity to that house but can still imagine it, then you are visualizing. As Dennis the Menace said, "Close your eyes, Joey, and if you can still see anything, you're thinking." Joey was visualizing, which is one form of thinking.

Why Does Visualization Offer a Distinct Advantage?

Golf has so many variables operating at the same time that it is difficult, if not impossible, to micromanage them in your brain. Take a breaking putt, for example. You have to simultaneously consider the break and the speed while making the proper stroke and keeping your head still. In addition, all this has to be done within the two-second span of a putting stroke.

Now, while your brain would have a hard time talking you through this process in two seconds, employing a unifying picture that integrates all the factors might be considerably more manageable. For instance, if you visualize the ball rolling smoothly around the curve like a stock car at Daytona, your stroke might be drawn right down the lane (to extend the analogy) so as to produce the proper combination of speed and break for a successful outcome. And it's all done in one picture as opposed to a thousand words.

The above example is pretty simple compared to the complexity of the full swing, ball flight, bounce, spin and roll of the ball when hitting a drive or approach shot. Try to process all those factors by talking to yourself rather than using one unifying visualization to pull it all neatly together.

How Does Visualization Move from the Mind to the Body?

Visualization may have an impact in various ways. For example, neuromuscular activity has been detected in the legs of athletes as they simply visualized using their legs in an athletic event. Although they weren't actually moving their legs, simply imagining that they were moving them produced some portion of the underlying neural and muscular activity that would have occurred if they had been physically moving them. This phenomenon suggests that repeated visualizations of the perfect golf swing might offer some actual physical warm-up of the underlying neuromuscular components of the swing.

Another way that visualization may aid your swing is that it may establish a mental blueprint of the activity you want to perform. Through repeated visualizations, a reference image is stamped into your head that can then be modeled physically later on. An example of building this blueprint might come from watching the pros on TV as they perform beautiful swings, one right after the other. After a weekend of such viewing, you want to run out to the course with the feeling that you can swing just like the pros do. The blueprint has been set in your mind, and that image begs to be duplicated in reality.

One final way visualization might help is that in the process of visualizing, you are concurrently doing some other important things. You may find yourself relaxing a bit, focusing your attention on certain things and concentrating for a period of time. Therefore, while visualizing you are actually practicing relaxation, focus and concentration. Any or all of these would be useful adjuncts to the other benefits of visualization described previously.

What Exactly Do You Visualize?

When Frank Ford, multiple winner of the South Carolina Amateur and contemporary of Bobby Jones, was nearly 90 years old, I asked him what he thought about during the golf swing. He replied that he didn't think of anything other than knocking down the flagstick. All he visualized during the shot was the ball banging into the flagstick and knocking it on the ground. What a wonderful thought to entertain, particularly if you could do it like Canadian golfers Moe Norman and George Knudson who used to make a game out of who could hit the most flagsticks during a round.

Now, hitting flagsticks is an end result similar to the image U.S. Olympic softball pitcher Lisa Fernandez uses when she visualizes the ball already being past the hitter and in the catcher's glove before she even throws it. Other athletes, however, focus more on the process than on the end result. Arnold Palmer described, in somewhat poetic fashion, the flight of the ball rising against the blue sky on its way to its appointed destination. How about imagining the current of a river flowing down the fairway and just letting your swing flow with the current irresistibly toward the target downstream?

You might visualize the action at impact like Amy Alcott, who had "Oompah" written on the shaft of her driver to remind her of the rhythm of the swing as she took the club back slowly ("Oom") and then exploded into the impact of the shot ("pah"). Similarly, Nicklaus used to visualize his putter as having a glass shaft, which encouraged him to hold it lightly and make a gentle, smooth stroke through the ball. To do otherwise would snap the "glass" shaft.

Clearly, there is no end to the ideas for use regarding visualization during the golf swing. Each person must find his own idiosyncratic images that help him produce important things like confidence over the ball, smoothness to the swing, power, control, relaxation and favorable results.

Visualizing During the Swing

In providing an example of a three-step process for implementing visualization during a round, let's assume the focus of the visualization is the flight of the ball.

Step 1—The visualization process begins with the player standing behind the ball, with the ball positioned between the player and the target. From this position, the player assesses the landscape ahead and looks for what seems to be the friendliest flight of the ball. You have seen this performed by Phil Mickelson, Jack Nicklaus, Tiger Woods and a myriad of other professional golfers as they stare down the fairway before addressing the ball. Their glassy stares absorb everything before them and implant powerful images into their brains.

During this initial stage of visualization, the golfer is assessing what the situation requires. That is, what does the ball really want to do here? For example, the hole may be a dogleg right with the fairway banked from left to right. Everything about this situation is screaming for a fade. Don't fight it. Go with that image since that is what your body, brain and the ball all want to do. The alternative of trying to draw the ball into the slope requires going against all your natural tendencies in this situation. Go with the friendliest image.

Once that friendly image is settled upon and while you are still behind the ball, turn your body so you can take some smooth practice swings down the envisioned line of flight, still visualizing the friendly ball flight you have just imagined.

Step 2—Now you are ready to address the ball and assume the precise alignment you determined from behind the ball. As you waggle through the pre-shot routine, continue to entertain the beautiful image of the flight of the ball. The key consideration at this stage is that favorable images don't last forever, even friendly, natural ones. If you stand and waggle too long or refuse to swing until the image is perfect, you will soon find yourself fighting negative images that will begin to creep in. Develop a tight, relatively quick routine that allows enough time to recapture the image you visualized behind the ball but also moves right into the swing before favorable images dissipate into thin air or something worse.

Step 3—As you swing and make contact with the ball, make one last intense visualization of the ball flight before you actually look to see the result. Grab onto that image with a vengeance. It should be so vivid that you are surprised if it hasn't happened when you ultimately check to see the actual result. Indeed, that final image should be so real that it is virtually impossible for it not to have happened, because it already did happen so vividly in your mind.

In most cases, the actual result will match your visualization. But even at those times when it deviates a bit, you have at least further implanted in your mind the visualization of the correct shot, which may benefit you the next time that shot is attempted.

I'm reminded of Jack Nicklaus' reflection after he missed a putt that he had virtually guaranteed his Ryder Cup partner he was going to make. He said, "I made that putt—it just didn't go in." In other words, he did everything in a fashion that should have led to a successful outcome. He lined it up correctly, stroked it properly and even saw it coming off the clubface squarely and rolling end over end down the line true to the hole. The only missing ingredient was when he finally looked to see the result, to his justifiable surprise, the ball was not in the cup. In his mind, his visualization was so strong that he had already made the putt. In this case, however, the ball just didn't cooperate.

If you visualize perfect shots all the time, particularly during that split second after contact with the ball, you will always play a beautiful round of golf in your mind, no matter what the actual results might be. Indeed, successful results are the ultimate goal. But on the difficult road to objective success, wouldn't it be better to entertain positive visualizations in your head than to constantly observe nothing but painful reality with your eyes? Furthermore, the greater relaxation, motivation, perseverance and enjoyment that comes from regularly visualizing successful shots may ultimately lead to better results in reality, as our neuromuscular pathways become more familiar with what success feels and looks like.

Lesson #20

PLAY SLOW-MOTION GOLF FOR BETTER RESULTS

EVEN WITH THE RECENT emphasis on speeding things up on the course, when it comes to swinging the club, golf remains a slow-motion game. Sam Snead, despite his moniker "The Slammer," said he swung at 85 percent of his strength. Curiously, the modern-day slammer, Tiger Woods, has cited the same percentage as the level he gears down to in order to control his game.

Steve Thomas, a long-driving champion of a few years past, once was asked to swing as hard as he could with his driver so that his clubhead speed could be measured. The speed was mechanically recorded at 102 mph. Following that initial vicious swipe, Thomas took his normal swing. The speed surprisingly measured 167 mph. His normal, smooth, rhythmic swing produced a clubhead speed 65 mph greater than when he tried to swing as hard and as fast as he could.

Still more evidence supporting slowing things down comes from a study reported by sport psychologists Robert Weinberg and Daniel Gould in which a group of runners was initially asked to run all out—that is, give 110 percent. A few days later, the same runners were asked to run at a 95 percent effort level. Contrary to what one might have expected, the runners actually ran faster at 95 percent than they did at 110 percent.

> *When you swing as hard and as fast as you can, all your muscle groups are contracting at the same time, resulting in some working against others and interfering with the speed you are trying to produce.*

Byron Nelson said that when he was playing his best, he felt like he was simply dropping the club on the ball. Gravity was the only force that was propelling the club. Isn't that what Fred Couples seems to do with his guillotine-like swing? The clubhead drops from out of nowhere in a free fall, producing a powerful effect on a par with that deadly blade of the French Revolution. Curiously, like golf, the guillotine had its origins in Scotland where an early version was developed during the late Middle Ages.

Jack Nicklaus indicated that when the heat was on in a tournament, he concentrated on one thing—a slow backswing. Yet he hit some of his most powerful drives down the stretch with the tournament on the line.

Perhaps the epitome of the slow-motion swing is "The Big Easy," Ernie Els. What a marvel is the power that's produced by that big, slow-motion arc. It's also interesting to note that Tom Watson's remedy for producing a little more power when he needed it was a bigger swing, rather than a harder, faster swing.

From a teacher's perspective, the legendary Ernest Jones taught his students to swing the clubhead rather than hit the ball. The focus was on the rhythmic, swinging action of that weighted object attached to the end of the club's shaft. Swing the clubhead smoothly and simply let the ball get in the way. Again, this sounds like a rather slow, sweeping action.

Why Is Slow-motion Play More Effective?

By now you might be starting to feel quite relaxed as you envision all the lazy, smooth, slow-motion swings described above. Indeed, relaxation is likely to be a beneficial side effect of slowing things down. The importance of relaxation in sport is well-documented. Recently, Olympic swimmer Christina Teuscher stated that relaxation is one of her primary keys for getting into the zone where her "body knows what it needs to do." If slowing things down leads to relaxation, then it may be a way of getting your body to cooperate with your mind.

Weinberg and Gould have said that most sport activities are performed better when various muscle groups alternate contracting and relaxing. When you go all out—swing as hard you can—all muscle groups are contracting at the same time, resulting in some working against others and interfering with the speed you are trying to produce. Optimal mechanics involve certain muscles flexing while others are relaxing in an alternating fashion. Slowing down or easing off may help to facilitate this process.

Yet another reason why slow-motion play is more effective is because it's likely to produce better contact with the ball. When you are swinging at blinding speed, you may be just that—blinded to making pure contact between the clubface and the ball. For every degree off-center on the clubface that the ball is struck, a certain amount of distance is lost. When you slow things down, your balance is better, as well as your timing and control, all of which increases the likelihood of making solid contact between the clubhead and the ball.

> *When you slow things down, your balance, timing and control are better, which helps increase the likelihood of making solid ball contact.*

One last consideration regarding the value of slow-motion golf is that it allows the club to function as it was designed. The club is meant to do a lot of work for you, as should be evident from the price that is charged for clubs these days. The space-age materials in clubheads and shafts are intended to work together to propel the ball up in the air for considerable distances, assuming the club is swung properly. If you swing too hard, you may override the technical design of the club. That is, the club won't be able to do the job it was designed to do because you won't let it.

An analogy for this might be that of a sailboat. If the boat is moving along powerfully with a full sail and suddenly the auxiliary motor on the back of the boat is turned on thrusting the boat forward, the sail will lose its fullness and power. That is, the motor will have overridden the sail. The same applies to golf. If you try to motor the ball out there with nothing but your body, you will override all the technical power in the club. The golf club is designed to sail the ball quite well on its own, as long as it is swung in a slow, smooth, controlled fashion.

Why Is Slow-motion Play So Difficult?

One reason for our reticence toward swinging slower is that we have a hard time believing that slowing things down will truly produce more speed and power. "I'm already not hitting the ball very far; if I swing any slower, it won't go anywhere," is likely to be what's running through our minds.

An even more dominant reason why slow-motion play is so difficult is because we are so highly motivated on the golf course. While being motivated, in general, is a desirable state, it can create a problem because the higher the motivation, the faster we tend to do things. A person in a high motivational state is likely to walk faster, breathe faster, talk faster and swing a golf club faster. Remember Nicklaus saying that when he was under pressure, he made a concerted effort to slow down his backswing. Presumably, he was aware that the high motivation produced by tournament pressure had the potential to speed up his swing. By focusing on swinging slower, he brought his swing speed back into its normal range where it would be most productive.

How to Achieve Slow-motion Play

1. Remember that you are in a highly motivated state on the golf course and will have a tendency to speed things up. This realization alone is a starting point for getting yourself to focus on slowing things down.

2. Consider that this tendency will only become greater with the mounting pressure of shooting a good score or winning a match. So be extra vigilant under these extremely motivated conditions.

3. When the heat is really on, as in going down the 18th fairway with the tournament on the line, walk slower, breathe slower and slowly take in all your surroundings. If you slow down the things that are definitely

under your control, it might help you to relax and slow down other things, like your swing, that are about to get out of control.

4. Visualize your swing as if it were a slow-motion instant replay. Now, if you are going to be in the movies, you want to look as good as possible and make every move smooth and rhythmic, lest the slightest flaw be revealed in the slow-motion replay.

> *To help slow down your swing, imagine yourself encased in a large container of molasses.*

I can remember one of the best drives I ever hit was when a sports reporter was taking a picture of me. I knew that the only thing on the picture would be the point of impact, and I did not want to be falling off balance with my head looking straight up in the air. So, I concentrated on slowing things down, keeping my eyes glued on the ball and not even considering the outcome of the shot—since that wouldn't show up in the picture. To my surprise, when I got down the fairway I found that the ball had drawn perfectly into the dogleg, traveled about 280 yards and was resting precisely in the middle of the fairway.

5. It might also be reassuring to consider that as hard as you try to ease off and slow down, you will still be swinging hard and fast enough. The truth of the matter is, you just can't slow it down too much. All your efforts at slowing things down will only bring them into manageable proportions.

Consider further that the emphasis here is on easing off a bit, not stopping the action. The runners referred to in the earlier study cut back only 5 percent, not 50 percent, and certainly not 100 percent. You're not going to accomplish anything if you don't swing. The only suggestion here is to slow down just a bit, and the image of swinging in slow motion is likely to help you accomplish that.

A good image to leave you with is that of the golfer who, with club in hand, imagined being encased in a large container of molasses. It doesn't take much of a stretch of the imagination to appreciate how slowly the swing would move through that thick, gooey substance. But, oh, what a syrupy swing and sweet result it would be!

Lesson #21

THE MOST IMPORTANT MILLISECOND IN GOLF

DESPITE CLAIMS THAT YOU should not worry so much about keeping your head down, and despite the fact that keeping your head down may not be the most accurate terminology for the behavior it is trying to encourage, this age-old golf instruction is still the best advice for 99 percent of the golfing public. No single factor cures more mistakes in the golf swing than that of keeping your head in the proper position throughout the shot.

It is true, however, that misinterpretations, misconceptions and improper implementations of this idea do exist. So let's explore what keeping your head down means and how to get yourself to effectively do it.

What Keeping Your Head Down Does *Not* Mean

Keeping your head down does not mean to press your chin down against your chest. To do so would restrict the swing considerably. In fact, keeping your chin up and looking down your nose at the ball is the better approach. With your chin up, your spine is aligned straighter and your shoulders can rotate more freely under your. chin. Just because your chin is up doesn't prevent you from keeping your eyes focused downward toward the ball.

Also, keeping your head down does not mean keeping it down forever. Once the ball is gone and the shoulders are completing their turn, the right shoulder will naturally bring the head up to a position facing the target. The critical factor is that the head be kept oriented toward the ball at impact. Once impact has been witnessed, then the head is free to make its natural turn to the upright, position. The alternative—pulling the head up too soon—tends to distort the plane of the swing. This interferes with crisp contact between the clubhead and the ball and throws the body off balance during the follow-through.

Lastly, keeping your head down does not mean to keep it frozen in position. The entire body should always feel relaxed and fluid. Some slight lateral movement of the head may even occur, during some players' swings. What is ill-advised, however, is a vertical movement of the head, particularly on the backswing. To do so robs the swing of power and makes it harder to reliably get the clubhead precisely back to the ball. Actually, any movement, lateral or vertical, increases variability and makes it more challenging to reassemble everything back into its original position for clean contact between the clubhead and ball.

What Keeping Your Head Down *Does* Mean

Basically, keeping your head down means to keep your body steady next to the ball while your eyes intently watch for something as the clubhead passes through the hitting area.

While this mandate mentions only the head, the process actually has as much to do with the spine and the sternum as it does with the head. That is, the central core of the body (spine, sternum and head) must stay in a steady and consistent orientation to the ball so that the shoulders, arms and clubhead can rotate around that central core and back to the ball with the least amount of variability.

As far as what you should watch for as the clubhead passes through the hitting area, a number of choices are available in this regard. Keeping your eye on the ball is just one of those possibilities, and not a very good one at that. We will also explore others. The main point here is that in watching intently for the action in the hitting area, you are encouraging the steady position of your body next to the ball, which is the most important thing for clean, square and powerful contact.

The Psychology of Keeping Your Head Down

What has been discussed to this point is basically the semantics and physics involved in the recommendation to keep your head down. Now comes the psychology of it all, which involves coming up with the proper images for maintaining a steady position next to the ball and determining the most beneficial thing for you to focus on as the clubhead passes through the hitting area.

> *Thinking of your head as being at the center of a wheel, with your arms and the club shaft forming a long spoke out to the clubhead, is a useful image of steadiness during the swing.*

Keep in mind that a steady posture is not only fluid and flexible, but also solid and stable. It might be compared to a tree trunk or a flag pole. Both of these give and bend a bit so they don't snap in the wind, but neither changes its basic position in the process.

One useful image of steadiness during the swing might be to think of your head as being at the center of a wheel. Your arms and the club shaft form a long spoke out to the clubhead, which is analogous to a tire in contact with the ground. Now, if the center of the wheel (head) moves in the process of making a swing, the spoke (arms and club shaft) will pull the tire (clubhead) from its position at ground level. In the case of the tire, the result will be a powerless spinning of the wheel above the ground. In the case of the clubhead, the result will be off-center contact between the clubhead and ball, if not the absence of contact altogether.

Another helpful image might be to think of a rod on an angle implanted down your neck and spine so that your upper body coils and uncoils around the rod as you swing the golf club. With your body wrapped around this rod, you are helpless to do anything other than turn. Indeed, moving off the rod would do considerable damage to your body, at least figuratively. Your only option is to coil and uncoil around this angled rod down the central core of your body.

The game of tetherball, in which a vertical pole has a rope attached to the top of it and a ball attached to the other end of the rope, provides an additional image of steadiness. The object of the game is to smack the ball at the end of the rope so the rope wraps around the pole. When applied to golf, your body is the pole, the rope is your arms and club shaft, and the ball at the end of the rope is analogous to the clubhead. The beauty of this image, in addition to the steadiness of the pole (your body), is the fully extended rope (arms and club shaft) whipping around this stable base.

One last image of steadiness next to the ball is that of the hammer thrower in the Olympics. In contrast to the hammer in your toolbox, the hammer in track and field is a lead ball at the end of a chain that you swing around your body before giving it flight. Once again, you have a steady central core (your body) around which a weighted extension spins (the lead ball at the end of a chain) creating a powerful centrifugal force. If the central core is not steady and solid, the centrifugal force of the extended weight is greatly weakened. The same is true for the golf swing. If the central core of your body is not kept firmly in position, the centrifugal force of the arms and club shaft will be greatly weakened and make the impact between the clubhead and the ball much less powerful.

As the clubhead passes through the hitting area, it will do you little good to tell yourself not to look up. This is a negative thought. It tells you nothing regarding what to do to not look up, and at best it involves a two-step process of not looking up and then trying to do something else to keep your head down. Even the directive to "keep your head down" is not very useful. Following that instruction is as difficult as trying to relax simply by telling yourself to relax. Telling yourself to do something that is very difficult does nothing to actually make it happen. Similarly, the directive to keep your eye on the ball doesn't solve the problem and may even create another problem. Consider that if you truly keep your eye on the ball, then you must move your head to follow the ball as it moves forward, thereby lifting your head up sooner than is optimal for a crisp shot.

The better solution for getting yourself to keep your head down is to require some action on your part that, as a by-product, creates the phenomenon of keeping your head down as the ball moves forward toward its intended target. You need something useful to do rather than something not to do or some ineffectual self-directive. Following are a few things you might focus on that should result in your head staying in position as the clubhead passes through the hitting area.

Something Under the Ball—There is always something under the ball—a tee, blades of grass or a divot you are creating with your swing. Focus on seeing what is under the ball before you look to see where the ball itself has gone.

Absence of the Ball—Say to yourself, "The ball is gone," before looking to check its flight. If you can witness the absence of the ball created by the clubhead having just propelled it forward, then you will have kept your head down the required amount.

Clubhead Moving Low Along the Ground—Feel and see the clubhead moving low along the ground in front of the spot from where the ball has just vacated. Doing so will create a good forward move and arm extension toward the target, while at the same time giving you something to focus on in the hitting area other than the ball.

Exhale Forcefully at the Ball—Just before making your backswing, take a deep, relaxing breath and exhale 90 percent of it. Then, at the moment of impact between the clubhead and the ball, forcefully exhale the remaining 10 percent in the direction of the ball. This will create intensity and focus along with a moment of abandon that will consume all the time that is necessary for keeping your head in the proper position for crisp contact between the clubhead and ball.

Visualize the Desired Result—After the club strikes the ball, imagine the perfect ball flight before looking to check the reality of it all. With your head and eyes still oriented toward the ground, visualize that flight so vividly that you are surprised if it is not reality when you actually look to see the result. In the meantime, your head will be staying down the required amount of time.

See the Ball On the Clubface—Try to do the impossible of seeing the ball staying in contact with the clubface as long as possible. It's like imagining the clubface and the ball are made out of Velcro. Gary Player refers to this as staying with the shot or staying with the ball. Such a focus will again draw you low toward the target while at the same time keeping your head in position behind the ball just long enough to create crisp contact.

See Smoothness—Before looking up, ask yourself, "Did I see the club-head pass smoothly through the ball?" The time it takes you to ask your-self this question will be all that is necessary for keeping your head down sufficiently.

> No single factor cures more mistakes in the swing than that of keeping your head in the proper position throughout the shot.

See the Squareness/Feel the Firmness—This one is good for putts, par-ticularly short putts. Ask yourself, "Did I see square contact between the putter head and ball?" or "Did I feel the firmness of the stroke?" Then just listen for the putt to drop. By the time you answer "yes" to this question, the putt will be well on its way and you will have done your job of staying steady over the ball.

See the Success at the Target—Before you look up, if you can see the ball knocking down the flagstick, landing on the spot you picked for your chip shot or coiling smoothly into the center of the hole, you will have kept your head down long enough.

Indeed, a number of these suggestions are physically impossible to actually do (e.g., see the ball on the clubface, see the clubhead moving low along the ground). The questions and answers have to be processed in a split second in your mind, rather than enjoying the time normally required were you to recite them aloud. The important thing is that you are actively imagining and focusing on something as a means for enabling you to keep your head down. Try different images and points of focus and determine which ones work for you.

PART III

CONTROLLED
EMOTIONS

CONFIDENCE AND MENTAL TOUGHNESS

No shortage of different personalities exists on the PGA tour—or in any other gathering of golfers, for that matter. All kinds of golfers succeed, but some personality styles seem to lend themselves to success more so than others. Lesson #22 divides the personalities of PGA Tour players into four categories and reflects on "How Your Personality Can Affect Your Game."

The personality ingredient that every player craves the most is confidence. Who wouldn't like to be as confident as Tiger Woods appears to be? Lesson #23 suggests "Seven Ways to Build Confidence on the Course" and be more like Tiger.

Along with confidence comes mental toughness. Again, Tiger Woods has it, while most golfers do not! Mental toughness, like confidence, can be built. It's not easy or painless, it takes guts and determination, and you may be surprised to find that you no longer fit in with the typical run-of-the-mill golfer—anymore than Tiger does. But you can do it, if you really want to. Lesson #24 tells you how to "Sharpen Your Mental Toughness."

Lesson #22

HOW YOUR PERSONALITY CAN AFFECT YOUR GAME

D IFFERENT PERSONALITY STYLES ABOUND on the golf course. Some are beneficial to your performance, while others do more harm than good. Perhaps the most important thing is that your personality and game are compatible, as opposed to being at odds with each other and doing combat for 18 holes.

The following is a system for categorizing personality styles. It is adapted from the work of forensic psychologist Dr. William Foote, who used this approach in the process of jury selection. A favorable jury, like a favorable golf game, may ultimately revolve around the personalities involved.

Categorizing Personality Styles

At a very basic level, personalities might be divided into four categories based on two dimensions—the emotional dimension (high or low) and the thinking dimension (high or low). Combining the levels of these two dimensions results in four categories: high emotional/high thinking, high emotional/low thinking, low emotional/high thinking and low emotional/ low thinking.

The level of a golfer's thinking might be reflected in the way he talks about the game. Saying things that suggest strategy, playing the percentages, taking into account an opponent's situation, being realistic and calculating in making decisions all suggest a thinking player.

Golfers also say things that suggest emotionality. However, demeanor and actions provide a better reflection of emotion. For example, your facial expression, intense gestures and behavioral outbursts certainly betray your level of emotion over anything you might say about your feelings at the moment. Similarly, impulsive decisions that are lacking in strategy, calculation or realism might also be viewed as manifestations of high emotionality.

Now, without intending to slight anyone on the PGA Tour and recognizing that this is all conjecture based on limited information and observations, it might be interesting to speculate where a few well-known golfers might be categorized regarding personality style.

Personality Styles
of the Pros

High Thinking/High Emotional—How about Tiger Woods for starters? Based on quotes that often are very well thought out, and based on witnessing his intensity and occasional outbursts on the golf course, Tiger might be considered to be high in both thinking and emotionality.

Bobby Jones might have also fit into this category, particularly if the tales of his youthful temper tantrums are taken into account. along with the written and videotaped evidence of his detailed thinking about the game. In the more recent past, Gary Player was certainly a smart player who evidenced a certain intensity that might qualify him as high thinking/high emotional. A future candidate for this category, once we have more data to reflect on, might be Sergio Garcia.

High Emotional/Low Thinking—John Daly might fit this category. It's not too big of a stretch to view Big John as not always thinking too clearly on (or off) the golf course. By all accounts, his behavior seems a bit impulsive at times, as opposed to being strategically thought out. He also displays no shortage of emotion. If he is not outright verbalizing his feelings, he is wearing them on his sleeve for all the world to see.

Mark Calcavecchia and other high-strung players on tour could also be considered as high emotional/low thinking players. This isn't to suggest that these guys are lacking in intelligence. They just don't always apply their smarts when it comes to playing golf. Nor does it mean that they can't succeed on tour. Indeed, when they are on a roll, their lack of thinking might be beneficial in not disrupting their momentum. Certainly, Daly has had some great moments and even major victories. The bigger question regards sustaining a high level of success, which may be hard to do on emotion alone.

Looking back in time, you might find other quite successful golfers in this category, like Tommy Bolt and even Arnold Palmer. The latter certainly exuded emotionality with his swashbuckling, thrilling style on the way to some of golf's most memorable victories. Yet his equally famous collapses might be viewed as evidence of a lack of clear thinking, wise strategy and smart decision-making at times. You have to wonder how great all these players might have been with a little more thinking in their arsenal of skills.

High Thinking/Low Emotional—This type of player seems to be more common on the PGA Tour. Jack Nicklaus epitomizes this group—always thinking, calculating, strategizing and playing the percentages. While physically powerful in his day, Nicklaus' real power was his ability to cognitively dissect the opposition. He typically did it with hardly a change in expression, much less a burst of emotion.

The same might be said for Ben Hogan, who mentally and physically engineered his game in stoic fashion without much of a hint of emotion. This is not to say that these players weren't experiencing any emotion. They just didn't put it on display. They were very controlled.

Other players in this category might include Tom Watson, Phil Mickelson, Vijay Singh, Retief Goosen, Bernhard Langer and many others who emulate this seemingly successful way of negotiating the ebb and flow of the game of golf.

Low Emotional/Low Thinking—Players in the low emotional/low thinking group are an interesting lot. Fred Couples and Ernie Els might be placed in this category. Both of these easy-going guys seem to just play the game. Their demeanor suggests, "What's the big deal? Just hit the ball, glide down the fairway and hit it again." They are golfing machines.

For these low/low players, thinking is simply not an issue, and they don't see the need to get all emotional. Both are blessed with phenomenally beautiful swings, so much so that they can just put it on automatic and enjoy the walk in the park.

Sam Snead might have been included in this category. He certainly had the automatic, photogenic swing to qualify. So, with these examples in mind, which personality style is the best to emulate? How might you attempt to adjust your golf personality, if the one you currently take to the course isn't working for you?

The Best Personality Style

Successful golfers, even stars, are found in all four categories. This situation is probably due to a compatibility between these players' natural personalities and their style of play. They are not bucking their natural tendencies, but instead making those tendencies work to their benefit.

However, a closer look seems to suggest that those listed in the high-thinking categories (whatever their level of emotionality) seem to have had the more successful and balanced careers. The records of Nicklaus and Woods are unparalleled. Hogan, Jones, Player and perhaps Mickelson form an enviable second tier of strong thinkers who have enjoyed stellar careers.

The low-thinking folks, on the other hand, have had their moments and even good careers, but they are not quite in the same category as their higher-thinking colleagues. This seems to be particularly the case when you add in high emotionality and consider players like Daly who can hammer the ball and sometimes put it together, but has nothing sustained to show for the long haul. Even Palmer, as revered as he may be, was only on top of the competition for about four to six years, and much of that was strongly contested by the more cerebral Nicklaus and a more cognitive Player.

The low thinkers with low emotionality have also failed to put the whole package together. Who doesn't love Fred Couples? But has he lived up to expectations? Els also seems to be having a hard time closing the deal of late, particularly in the majors. It's hard to argue that Snead didn't have a stellar career, but the Slammer never won the U.S. Open, something every great player would be expected to accomplish at some point in his career.

These guys made their names because of the beauty of their swings, but apparently something was lacking when it came to the thoughtful management of themselves and their games.

So, if you were able to pick, you probably would want to be blessed with a personality style reflecting high thinking and low emotionality. Put yourself in with the Nicklauses, Hogans and Mickelsons of the world and you'd have to like your chances. Even Woods' success is probably more a result of his high level of thinking rather than his high level of emotionality. Indeed, his level of thinking may be so strong that he succeeds in spite of his high emotionality, rather than because of it.

In addition, Jones, who was another player high on both dimensions, had to retire at age 30, most likely because he'd had enough of the emotional strain of the game.

Cultivating a New
Golf Personality

If you want to develop a higher level of thinking on the golf course, a style that might lend itself to more enduring, long-term success, then you should consider the following suggestions.

1) Make a Game Plan—If your thinking goes up in smoke as soon as the course is in sight, then do your thinking at home before you leave for the course. At breakfast, or even the night before, plan your round for the day. Consider the percentage way to play each hole, which clubs to hit and where to place your shots. Come up with ways to ensure at least minimal survival on your particular jinx holes. Make a special plan for the unexpected and think about what you are going to do to contain the damage if you get in trouble. Anticipate everything you can, even down to how to handle the needling you know will emanate from one of your regular playing companions.

This game plan is your blueprint for thinking your way around the course. Write it down so you can refer to it when your old tendency not to think raises its ugly head, which you know is sure to happen. Old ways don't die easily.

2. Review Your Routine—Before you start playing, settle on what swing keys or imagery you are going to employ and don't let your emotions deter you from keeping those favorable thoughts in mind. Make execution of your routine the goal for the day. Judge the success of your round solely on how consistently you implement your routine, rather than on the emotionally laden matters of score and beating your opponents. Your routine is something you can also think about before you leave the house. Indeed, rehearsing your routine in your mind on the way to the course is a smart way to jump-start your round.

3. Talk Kindly and Wisely to Yourself—Positive self-talk can go a long way toward constructive thinking and emotional control. Analyze what you typically say to yourself when your low thinking/high emotional personality style is in control. Replace high-emotional self-talk (e.g., "You dumbo, you'll never figure out this game. Just get the round over with and chalk up another wasted four hours.") with more high-thinking self-talk (e.g., "This is where I kick in my game plan and pay more attention to my swing keys and routine. This might not be a round for the ages, but for the rest of it, I'm going to work on hitting as many well-thought-out shots as I can, whatever the score turns out to be.").

4. Consider Your Image—Do you want to be known as a hothead, a loose cannon, someone who self-destructs and is out of control? Instead, cultivate the image of a cool, calculating customer who will beat you one way or the other. At least your opponents will know that you are unlikely to beat yourself. Rather, you're a solid, in-control player who always hangs around until the end, just in case your opponents meet with some untimely disaster, perhaps losing their collective cools and self-destructing themselves. Even if you don't win on a given day, your strong thinking will earn the respect of your playing companions and serve notice that you are a force to be reckoned with anytime you tee it up.

Lesson #23

Seven Ways to Build Confidence on the Course

WATCHING TIGER WOODS PLAY golf is a clinic in confidence. Sure, he drives the ball a mile, hits surgical iron shots and gets up and down from the wildest of places. However, what really distinguishes him from his peers is the confidence he exudes in the process. He truly believes that he should win every time. Not just that he can win, but that he should win.

I'll take it a step further. He doesn't think anybody else deserves to win when he is on the golf course. You rarely hear any of this self-deprecating stuff like, "I was lucky to get out of there alive today," or "This or that other guy played great, and I'm just proud to have gotten the better of him today." Baloney! When Tiger debriefs a round, it's more along the lines of "I'm good, I've worked at it since I was barely able to walk, I deserve to win every time, so get out of my way because nothing is stopping me."

This attitude isn't meant to be arrogant, ungrateful or unsympathetic to those surrounding him. It's just a fact of life when you're Tiger Woods. You are supremely confident.

Now, the obvious questions: (1) How did he get this way? (2) Can he stay this way? (3) Is there any way possible that any of us could get this way?

How Did Tiger Woods Become So Confident?

I think you have to give a lot of credit to Earl Woods who capably applied key ingredients for building confidence from an early age. For example, from the very beginning he exposed the young Tiger to success experiences. I'm sure he challenged him, but he never asked him to do more than could be handled at each stage of development. In addition, I'm sure he was very reinforcing of his early attempts and that he talked to him like he was already a champion.

From these early beginnings, the elder Woods gradually upped the ante with new challenges, but never so much that the younger Woods would be doomed to failure. With each success, the evolving Tiger had more and more opportunities to associate himself with the feelings that go along with success, until eventually he did not have to directly experience new successes to feel successful. He, himself, became a signal for success. That's confidence.

But confidence did not happen quickly and magically. It happened gradually and methodically from repeated associations with success. Earl Woods patiently nurtured confidence over time in the developing Tiger.

Another astute move that Earl Woods made was to immunize the Tiger against threats to that confidence. Once the lad was good enough to succeed under normal circumstances, the elder Woods began throwing distractions his way so that Tiger could learn to succeed in the face of obstacles. Tiger learned to stay focused, to forge ahead, to come back from adversity, to win whatever the odds. Again Tiger witnessed himself succeeding time and again, and now even under undesirable conditions. Distractions, obstacles, insurmountable odds simply became additional cues for success. External circumstances were irrelevant. Tiger Woods came to embody success and confidence.

Lastly, from a young age Tiger seems to have developed a willingness to learn, even if the various teachers along the way happened to be mere mortals. He was proud, but not too proud to listen. Even now he is not afraid to change, to learn new things, to try anything that will make him a better performer. This openness to learning over time has resulted in him being optimally prepared for whatever he has to face, and there is nothing like total preparation for enhancing one's confidence.

Can the Tiger Remain Supremely Confident?

We all certainly hope so, and if anyone has a chance for sustained self-confidence, it's probably Tiger Woods. One thing on his side is youth.

It is characteristic of the young to feel invincible, timeless, even immortal. For example, if a young person has a healthy young body, does he or she worry about healthy behavior? Not particularly. Young people eat junk food, do not systematically exercise, stay up all hours of the night, drive fast and take risks that would give an older person pause. To be young is to be invincible, to have plenty of time to rectify things and, like Shakespeare's Caesar, to entertain feelings of never dying.

But then youth meets middle age, and for the first time in life there is the recognition of vulnerability. Suddenly what seemed a certainty now becomes a probability. What seemed timeless now begins to have limits. What felt like total control starts to be replaced with just hoping for the best.

Tom Watson in his youth confidently rammed putts into the hole with the speed of a freight train. But as he got older, he was confronted with the previously foreign realization that he might miss the hole. Indeed, stroking the ball that hard, he might miss it coming back. Once these thoughts of vulnerability set in, tentativeness starts to make inroads into confidence, and prudence becomes the better part of valor.

Tiger, too, will eventually reach middle age, which in a sport like golf is probably somewhere in the mid-30s. But with the early start he has on the record books, he could do a lot of damage before then. Furthermore, even if his confidence is eventually dampened a bit by realism, the calculating wisdom of age should emerge to become his ally and take him to still greater heights.

What Can You Do to Build Confidence?

1. *Associate Yourself with Success*—There is no shortcut to self-confidence. The key is to repeatedly pair yourself with success. After many pairings of yourself with success, just being yourself will signal feelings of

confidence even before new successes occur. The challenge, of course, is in creating the initial success experiences.

The first thing one can do in this regard is to eliminate situations that encourage failure. For example, it is difficult to succeed at any one sport if you are playing many other sports at the same time. The focus may have to be exclusively on golf if you want to truly succeed at golf. Other situations that may set one up for failure include playing with better players all the time, continuing to play when in a slump, attempting skills that haven't been mastered, giving opponents overly generous handicaps or playing when not feeling well or when distracted by outside concerns.

Once you have reduced the likelihood of failure, success will mainly come from that dreaded word "practice." Pay attention to where you are losing strokes in a round and be sure to practice the necessary skills to deal with these situations. Consider components of the game where you feel least confident, then learn fool-proof techniques for those situations that you can depend on and, therefore, feel confident about.

Engage in competitions that are appropriate for your stage of development. That is, give yourself a chance to do well. As your skill improves, sign up for gradually more demanding competitions, but be sure not to get ahead of yourself, thereby setting up potential failure experiences.

2. Simulation—Structure practice situations that simulate the actual performance situations where you lack confidence. For example, if short putts under pressure are your nemesis, use a practice drill that forces you to make 18 short putts in a row or you have to start over. I guarantee you will feel the same kind of pressure you do in a match when you get down to the 17th and 18th putts in your drill and want to go home. When you can make those last putts in this type of practice, the resulting confidence should transfer to the course.

3. Modeling—Pick a pro on tour or even a good amateur at your course who is about your same physical stature and who has a game similar to yours. Watch them play, watch them hit the shots in which you lack confidence. Get an image of their technique and try to imitate it. Most of all, entertain the realization that this guy built like me can do it, so I should be able to learn to perform this skill, too.

4. Think and Act Confidently—Talk to yourself with respect. You may not be supremely confident yet, but you can start talking to yourself like you are. You're certainly not going to become confident any faster by running yourself down. Act confident, too. Even when you are struggling and doubting yourself, smile, hold your head up high, persevere and look confident. You may just fool yourself and your opponents in the process.

> *There is no shortcut to self-confidence. The key is to repeatedly pair yourself with success.*

5. Relabel Emotions—No matter what level of confidence you reach, there will still be those times when you get that sinking feeling in your stomach and self doubts start to creep in.

No problem. While you used to label these emotions as a lack of confidence, now you can view them as cues for reaching back for a little extra. You're not doubting yourself, rather you're excited, primed, pumped and ready to show them what you can do. You are in your element. Thankfully, this isn't happening to someone else who hasn't cultivated the confidence that you have.

6. Physical Conditioning—If you are in good shape, you have all the more reason to feel confident in a physical event. At the very least, it's one less thing you have to worry about giving out on you. There's nothing worse than to be struggling mentally and to feel your body giving out at the same time.

7. Preparation—The ultimate security blanket is preparation. If you have not done everything you can to prepare, you may have no right to feel confident. On the other hand, if you have adequately prepared, you can say to yourself with absolute confidence that an opponent maybe better than me, but they can't be any better prepared. So, let's see whose preparation and confidence wins out on this given day.

To quote the British novelist, E. M. Forster, "The people I respect the most behave as if they were immortal." Ah, youth and confidence! It is a marvel to behold.

Lesson #24

SHARPEN YOUR MENTAL TOUGHNESS

A LERT! CODE BLUE! Dr. Heart! A dangerous virus is invading the game of golf. Many golfers are already infected, but few recognize the extent of their condition. Symptoms of the virus are hard to detect because they surface only when stress is put on the system, such as in the club championship.

The virus has a rather innocuous name—social rules. But don't be caught off guard by this innocent terminology. The virus is powerful, attacks the nervous system and, if left uncorrected, will undermine the very mental foundation of your game.

Symptoms include the inability to handle even the slightest amount of pressure that might be encountered, such as on the first tee. You may be rendered totally incapable of playing tournament golf at any level. Frustration tolerance is greatly weakened. If the virus is left untreated, you may find yourself completely oblivious to the difficulty of the game of golf. You may even think you are a scratch golfer when, in truth, your skill level dictates scores more in the 90s.

The virus spreads via other golfers, even friends who think they are being nice to you. Be on the lookout for carriers before they unwittingly do you in. Respond quickly to the earliest signs of the malady. If you are unfortunate enough to already be infected, don't panic. Immediate corrective action can produce dramatic positive results even at advanced stages of the disease. A complete cure is even possible.

The following are indicators of infection by the social-rules virus. Take them lightly and your golfing brain may turn to mush in a matter of months, accompanied by the demise of your ability to play anything resembling real golf.

Take Another One

Recently I was near the first tee at a resort course as a player was hitting a mulligan after his initial tee shot went awry. Observing the event was a young lad with a very British accent who looked aghast at the prospect of the gentleman disregarding his initial tee shot and hitting another ball. He leaned over and whispered to his father, "What's he doing?" His father disgustedly replied, "That's the way they play golf in America."

The "take another one" social rule tends to occur when golfers have neglected to warm up before a round. Sometimes it even extends to those who have warmed up but feel it's their right to hit two balls off the first tee. This practice is so prevalent it's now virtually an American tradition. Those recently introduced to the game think it's the way golf has always been played.

The result is that the golfer is bound to get one tee shot in play due to the relaxation factor of knowing he has two shots at it. A drive in play means the golfer is more than likely to have a reasonable score on the first hole.

But what happens when the club championship rolls around or some other serious match takes place where only one ball is allowed off the first tee. Now, facing unusual pressure, the golfer may find his single tee shot in unfamiliar territory, leading to a higher score on the first hole than has been typical. The shock may throw off the golfer's game for the next few holes, if not the entire round, since he is not used to proceeding to the second tee with anything other than a routine, acceptable, opening-hole score.

The Remedy—Warm up before your round and play one ball off the first tee every time you play. By doing this, you will get used to the first-tee jitters and to playing the ball from a variety of places along the first fairway. You don't want to send shockwaves through your mental game by being unprepared for the pressure of one ball off the first tee when circumstances demand as much. Learning to deal with adversity is part of the game, even when it occurs on the first hole.

Give Yourself a Shot

This social rule is applied when the golfer is stymied or experiences a bad lie. A playing companion, under the guise of doing you a favor, suggests that you move the ball to a more easily playable position and "give yourself a shot"—something the game of golf has not currently given you. A common variation of this practice is the root rule, which involves moving a ball from among roots so as not to hurt yourself or the club by swinging into the roots.

Certainly you are not expected to risk life and limb playing a shot, but that's no excuse to avoid taking your medicine when you hit a poor shot. All you have to do is chip off of the root just as you might off of hardpan or rocky terrain. You could also elect to follow the procedures dictated by *The Rules of Golf* for an unplayable lie.

Whichever course of action is chosen, the outcome is similar to that which a golfer incurs when he hits the ball into a hazard or lands behind a tree or other obstacle. Golf, unfortunately, involves negotiating obstacles, bad lies and hazards when less than perfect shots are struck.

The mental downside of "giving yourself a shot" under trying circumstances is that you don't learn to hit troublesome shots or to adjust to the difficulties of the game. Furthermore, being easy on yourself encourages a misperception of your scoring ability and skill as a golfer.

The Remedy—Refuse to allow yourself special breaks, even when friends insist. Such breaks are not really favors because you will pay the price sometime in the future when free drops are not allowed and you have to play the ball as it lies. Decline to be easy on yourself and you will be much better prepared when you are forced to play by the rules in their entirety. You will have been there before and experienced the interesting variety of unusual shots golf can throw at its players.

Pick It Up and Take a Double Bogey

This social rule applies when a single-digit handicapper is on the way to a triple bogey or more. The variation for the higher-handicap golfer who is encountering a disastrous hole is to pick it up and take a 7 or 8 or higher. In either case, the golfer doesn't have to finish out the hole. He just picks up the ball and pretends to have achieved a lower score.

This practice stems from the fact that the handicap system restricts the inclusion of single-hole scores beyond certain limits when posting an 18-hole score. Single-digit handicappers are restricted to including nothing more than a double bogey, while 10- to 19-handicappers are limited to no more than a 7. However, it should be noted that it is the posting of inordinately high scores that is restricted, not the counting of actual numbers of strokes on the way to a bona fide 18-hole score. To record a 6 or 7 on the scorecard when you actually were headed for an 8 or 9 is not only inaccurate, it also distorts a realistic perspective of your true scoring ability for 18 holes.

It is important to determine a true score on every hole. Consider all the painful double-digit scores the pros have recorded over the years on the par-3 12th hole at Augusta. Wouldn't they have liked to have simply picked up and taken a double bogey?

The Remedy—When a hole has gotten away from you, finish it out as expeditiously as possible and keep that big number as low as you can. Indeed, even a dreaded snowman is still better than a 9 or 10 in the final accounting. Post what the handicap system allows, but remember what you are really shooting so you are motivated to work on the prevention of disastrous holes in the future. Give yourself credit for not giving up and quitting on bad holes, and for keeping the score as low as possible.

You have to learn to handle trying situations because there are no "pick ups" in real golf. Furthermore, life still goes on after a difficult hole. Nothing is more rewarding than coming in with a respectable score, and maybe even a victory, when at an earlier stage all seemed lost. Exciting comebacks result from multiple past experiences with difficult situations that toughen you up for dealing with similar circumstances when they arise in the future.

That Makes My Putt Good

This social rule occurs when your partner makes a par to win a hole in better-ball competition, thereby rendering your 20-foot putt for par meaningless. A similar example might be when your opponent in match play is in for birdie, thereby making your long putt for par unnecessary. In either case, you pick up your ball and record a par as if you were playing medal play and had made the putt.

Now, it is understandable to pick up the ball for the sake of speeding up play in match play or better-ball competition. But as for recording a par all the time and turning in the score as if it were a complete medal-play round, that is questionable to say the least. What percentage of 20-footers or longer do you make in a round? If you pick up half of them and give yourself pars, I'll guarantee that your scores and handicap will go down precipitously over the course of a season.

A misperception of your scoring ability along with an unrealistic handicap does considerable damage to your mental game. Misrepresentation of how well you play puts undue pressure on you in handicapped competition, lets your partners down when they are depending on you being able to play to your handicap and destroys your self-confidence when you repeatedly see that you can't live up to an inflated view of your ability to play.

The Remedy—Establish an accurate perception of your scoring ability. Let your handicap fall where it may, based on medal-play rounds where you putt them all out. If you must turn in match-play rounds, be realistic about what you record as a score when you pick up your ball over the course of a round. Don't hurt yourself for future competition by unnecessarily improving your score just for bragging rights or handicap pride.

Inside the Leather

This social rule is so familiar that many new golfers would probably expect to find it in *The Rules of Golf*. If by the slimmest of chances you are unfamiliar with this practice, playing "inside the leather" refers to stretching your putter from hole to ball to see if the ball falls inside of the putter grip. If it does, you simply pick up the ball and count the stroke as if you had actually putted it and made it. What a stroke saver this generous procedure is since you don't have to make any knee-knocking, 2-foot, breaking, downhill putts during a round. Wouldn't Scott Hoch have liked this rule a few years ago during the Masters when he missed one such putt and saw his hopes for victory dashed right there "inside the leather?" I think it is safe to say that this social rule is worth as much as two to three strokes off a golfer's handicap.

The Remedy—There is no substitute for putting them all out. Not only does this practice harden your mental game for short pressure putts when the heat is on, but it also is good practice for longer putts as you firmly stroke the short ones into the back center of the hole. Putt them all out every time you play and you will be better prepared for any serious competition that comes your way.

Not long ago I met a fellow who was in a very advanced stage of the social-rules virus, having started playing golf only five years earlier. In an effort to administer an initial antidote, I persuaded him to play a round of real golf where we teed it up on each hole, didn't touch it again until we picked it up out of the cup and paid off for the lowest score at the end of 18 holes. We played strictly by the rules, which I had to teach him along the way. We had an enjoyable round, and this is what he had to say when it was over: "Gee, that was fun. I never played that game before! We'll have to try that again sometime." I could only imagine what he and his friends had been playing for the last five years.

Play the whole game. Don't cheat yourself and ruin your mental game by circumventing the rules and avoiding the difficulties of golf. Mental toughness, genuine lower scoring and honest handicaps come to those who avail themselves to the rigors of the game, struggle through its adversity, never give up and count all their strokes. Such game individuals can hold their collective heads up high and relish their membership in the honorable fraternity of true golfers.

PRESSURE
AND CHOKING

Pressure is inevitable in golf and you have to learn to deal with it. Otherwise, you are doomed to choke when the heat is on. Lesson #25 offers "Six Ways to Prevent Choking."

While golf is typically an exercise in individual effort and accomplishment, certain situations involve the less common demand of playing with a partner. Examples of such formats include *better-ball* and *alternate-shot*, as in the Ryder Cup, and *captain's choice* and *scrambles*, as in corporate outings and charity fundraisers. Lesson #26 discusses these formats and offers assistance in "Handling the Pressure of Partner Golf."

And, then, there's the issue of "Making the Big Putt" (Lesson #27). Every golfer will face this knee-knocking situation a number of times over a golf season, if not more frequently for those playing regular competitive rounds. It is, therefore, imperative to learn how to handle the pressure of *the big putt* without choking.

All in all, "Golf's a Struggle—So Why Not Enjoy It?" (Lesson #28). Gain insight into how great players have viewed the game, kept their heads about them and even enjoyed the struggle. Further strengthen your mental toughness and your ability to handle the never-ending struggle that is golf.

Lesson #25

SIX WAYS TO
PREVENT CHOKING

HANK AARON ONCE SAID that it took him 17 years to get 3,000 hits in baseball, but it only took one afternoon on the golf course. What went wrong for Hank? Was it lack of skill, poor preparation, low motivation, a challenging golf course or maybe Hank choked?

The Loss of Physical and
Psychological Control

Choking doesn't require much of an introduction since most of us have probably experienced it firsthand. Simply stated, choking involves the loss of physical and/or psychological control of your behavior due to pressure. The result is that your performance quickly deteriorates.

Loss of physical control might involve your legs getting weak, hands shaking, stomach getting queasy and coordination abandoning you. Loss of psychological control refers to your mind racing, difficulty with concentration, poor decision making and confusion:

Effort Tasks vs. Skill Tasks

An interesting distinction regarding choking has been offered by Dr. Roy Baumeister. He suggests that pressure helps you on effort tasks but hurts you on skill tasks. That is, pressure makes you try harder, which lends to help with effort tasks such as riding a bicycle, rowing a boat, lifting weights or knocking an opposing lineman back about 5 yards.

However, trying harder does not necessarily help with skill tasks such as golf that depend on a routine running off automatically. Indeed, sometimes when you try harder at something that is suppose to occur automatically, you mess it up. Skill tasks benefit from relaxing and not paying any particular attention to the automatic movements that are occurring. Choking tends to occur when, under intense pressure, athletes start paying conscious attention to otherwise automatic aspects of their performance.

Correct vs. Incorrect Tendencies

Another interesting distinction regarding choking is that it is more likely to jump up and grab you when you are playing poorly than when you are playing well. Poor play is likely to occur for beginners, those who have not been practicing and playing regularly, players trying complex techniques or experimental shots, or those who are simply in the early stages of their round and not yet into the rhythm of the game. These mistake-prone players are good candidates for choking because their errors are likely to be exaggerated under the motivation of competitive pressure.

In contrast, competent play is likely to come from veteran players, those who have been practicing and playing regularly, players using simple techniques and standard shots, and players who are warmed up and in the later stages of their round. These players who are displaying sound skills are not only less likely to choke, but may even benefit from some pressure and take their games to higher levels.

In considering the above distinction, the issue isn't so much whether pressure is good or bad, but rather when to apply it: Pour it on when you are playing well, and avoid it like the plague when your game is heading south.

How to Prevent Choking

Based on the distinctions made above, the following guidelines are offered for doing your best to prevent choking.

1. Minimize pressure in situations requiring more skill than effort. While all of golf is basically a skill sport benefiting from smooth, relaxed action, some aspects of the game can tolerate a little more effort than others. For example, when you are driving the ball, you can exert a little more effort than when the situation calls for a delicate cut shot with a lob wedge over a bunker. So, if you are under the gun and need to pick up some strokes, take your risks and let the pressure fall on the power shots, as opposed to leaving yourself with a delicate challenge to the short game where choking is more likely to occur.

> *The issue isn't so much whether pressure is good or bad, but rather when to apply it.*

2. Develop a routine. A pre-shot routine that is rigorously adhered to gets practiced thousands of times and becomes automatic. Develop a routine that is simple and deliberate so that when pressure mounts you can turn to that routine and depend on it to be so solid and tight that negative thoughts don't have time or room to slip in. Once you have developed an effective routine, overlearn it so that it becomes super-automatic and in effect freezes choking out of your game.

3. Create circumstances that encourage playing well as opposed to setting you up for failure. Practice and play regularly, warm up before you play, develop simple techniques that can hold up under pressure, and avoid experimental shots when the heat is on. Of course, maintain your health, get a good night's sleep before you play, and avoid drinking excessive amounts of destabilizing beverages the night before a pressure-packed round. In short, anything that contributes to playing better makes you more immune to choking.

4. Distract yourself under pressure so that you stay on automatic. Remember that choking occurs when you start paying too much attention to what is usually automatic. Therefore, if you distract yourself from thinking about how to swing, your automatic routine has a better chance of continuing undisturbed. Distraction may consist of talking with fellow players, appreciating the surroundings, strategically planning the placement of your shots on the hole before you or making up your Christmas list. It doesn't really matter. You just don't want to be attending too much to your pre-shot routine and the mechanics of the swing until you actually have to take action.

Lee Trevino seemed inclined toward the distraction approach when he said that he couldn't concentrate for four hours straight. He had to break it up by interacting with the crowd and his playing companions. He said, "All I need is five seconds to tap my foot and hit the ball. But that's a very serious five seconds." Note the simple, deliberate routine and the delay in focusing on that routine until it was absolutely necessary.

5. Insulate yourself and become absorbed in your routine. Suppose you are not a Trevino, but rather a Ben Hogan, who avoided distraction at all costs. Then, an alternative to distraction might be entering into a cocoon, insulating yourself in a trance-like state and becoming totally absorbed in your routine. The story is told about Hogan refusing to sign an autograph for a lady on his way to the practice tee because he was "already playing his round."

Any seeming contradiction between the cocoon approach and the distraction approach might be resolved by suggesting that Hogan became one with his routine. His whole round was a routine: If this conjecture is accurate, then there was never any variation in the amount of attention Hogan paid to his routine. He was always 100 percent focused and never paid any more or any less attention to the automatic aspect of his swing.

6. Practice under pressure so you get used to it. If choking occurs under intense pressure, then it is less likely to occur as the impact of pressure is reduced. One way to reduce it is to get used to it. If you dive into a cold swimming pool, it is quite a shock; but after you are in there awhile, it feels all right. It's the same with pressure. Swim in it for a while, and it won't be such a shock.

Thoughts and
Words to Live By

Remember, pressure makes diamonds, as well as causing lesser things to crumble. It also is the source of strength for the Roman Arch—as the stones above press down on the stones comprising the arch below, the latter become more firmly cemented together, making the structure stronger than it would have been had the pressure not been exerted from above.

If you want to take a more lighthearted view of pressure and choking, you might consider the response of downhill skier Alberto Tomba when asked how he handled pressure. The eccentric Italian replied, "I don't care if I win or lose—it won't affect the party tonight!"

On the other side of the coin, when Tomba was asked what he says to himself after a great downhill run, he responded in his finest Italian accent: "I say, 'Congratulations, Alberto!'"

With such a simple, positive and effective attitude of competition, I seriously doubt that Tomba ever considered choking.

HANDLING THE
PRESSURE OF
PARTNER GOLF

GOLF IS HARD ENOUGH when you play by yourself, but add a partner and the task becomes exponentially more difficult. Playing individually involves simply hitting the ball, finding it and hitting it again, ultimately seeing how many strokes you end up with. But add a partner, or even worse a team, and you have to contend with new formats, special strategies, various personalities and a new kind of pressure—not letting your partner or team down. The following offers some suggestions for handling the peculiar trials and tribulations of playing partner/team golf.

Best Ball—Grammatically correct golfers prefer to call this "better ball" when the team involves two players. "Best ball" is apropos when three or four players are involved. Whichever the case, the team score for each hole is the single lowest score by any player on the team for that hole.

Psychologically, the best advice with this format is to play each hole like you're the only player on the team. Play your game and let the chips fall where they may. If you are a conservative par shooter, don't suddenly start going wild for birdies. Do that and you'll more than likely end up with a card full of bogeys or worse. Steady pars will win or save many a hole.

Alternate Shot—This format used to be popular in couples golf under the name of "scotch foursome." It virtually disappeared until experiencing a renaissance with recent Ryder Cup matches. The alternate-shot format involves each player on a two-person team taking turns hitting one ball until that ball is holed out. The score on each hole is the total number of shots taken by both players over the course of the hole.

The psychological challenge here is to give it your best effort on each of your attempts, while at the same time considering the condition in which you are going to leave your partner after each of your attempts. It's a delicate balance between offensive and defensive golf. You can't let it all hang out anymore than you can in best ball, but at the same time, playing overly defensive won't win anything either. The important thing in alternate shot is for the two partners to understand that each is going to give it his best at all times. Neither player should expect to be left with any easy shots. Of utmost importance is to never give your partner the feeling that he has let you down. The aftereffects of such disappointment could last for many more holes than the one where the difficulty occurred.

Sam Snead reportedly preempted the pressure by saying to his partner on the first tee, "I just want you to know that I'm going to be playing as hard as I can out there today, even though it may not always look like it. I'm also going to apologize to you right now for all the mistakes I'm going to make. And this is the last time I'm apologizing." Well stated by a master. Does anybody really think any golfer tries to miss a shot? Absolutely not! And as for the continuous banter of "Sorry partner, I let you down" or "I'm a heavy load today," that gets even older than the mistakes you are making. So play as hard as you can, expect your partner to do the same and quit apologizing.

Captain's Choice (Scramble Format)—A team of usually four players all hit their drives, then the best drive is selected and all the players hit a second shot from that position. The best second shot is selected, and all four members of the team hit a third shot from that position, and so on until the team ball is holed out. The result is one team score for each hole based on the best shot hit from each point on the hole.

Of all the team formats, captain's choice offers the greatest ill-advised encouragement for taking wild and crazy chances. It is a popular format, however, especially for company or charity outings where the caliber of players in the field varies greatly.

A special psychological consideration with captain's choice is the order of play among team members. For example, the lead-off spot is usually considered the least pressurized position, since the lead player has three other players to back him up. Typically, the weakest player is granted the first position and is expected to just try to get the ball in play. The second spot is good for a straight but not particularly long hitter. Assuming this player can get a ball in the fairway a reasonable distance from the green, then the last two spots can be reserved for longer hitters who can take the foolish chances cutting doglegs or worse.

If you are a decent golfer, playing out of the third position may be the most fun because often one of the first two players will have already put a ball in play allowing you to swing a little more freely. Furthermore, you still have another player hitting behind you, which eases the pressure a bit.

The fourth position should be occupied by a seasoned competitor with a bit of ice water in his veins, somebody who doesn't mind taking responsibility for the team when the chips are down. Other team members should always be supportive of their anchor man, not only when he is saving their derrieres, but even more importantly when he does not come up with the miracle shot. Remember, none of the first three chaps made the shot, so what have they got to complain about when the last guy misses?

In general, for all of the above formats, play your own game. Don't be influenced by your fellow team members' style of play, general ability or performance level on that given day. If you play your steady game, just like in individual medal play, you'll make your contributions to the team effort.

In fact, I'd take it a step further. Don't depend on your partners at all! Approach the match as if it depends solely on your individual medal-play performance. Expect absolutely no help from your partners. From this mind-set nothing shocks, disappoints, frustrates or angers you. In fact, any wondrous shots that your partners contribute will be doubly uplifting because you weren't expecting any help from them at all.

Even more importantly, not depending on your partners puts you in a frame of mind to play your own solid, steady game of golf—the one that usually leads to the greatest success no matter what the competitive format might be.

While taking on full responsibility for the team effort may sound pressurized, it actually immunizes you from the pressure. If you are expecting your partners to save you all the time, you will not only be distracted from full focus on your own play, but the pressure will be overwhelming when you are called upon to produce after your partners falter. But if every shot depends on you, one situation isn't any different from another.

Once you've mastered the above general orientations to partner golf, specific challenges still remain. For example, should you offer advice to your partner? The rules allow for it, but, practically speaking, is advice-giving a help or a hindrance? This is where every golfer has to be a bit of a sport psychologist. You have to read your partner and know how he reacts to advice. If your partner is a rugged individualist who gets confused or defensive when suggestions are made, leave him alone. If, on the other hand, the guy is quick to make adjustments and open to a team approach, go ahead and make a suggestion and see how it goes. Your best judgment regarding whether or not to give advice is likely to come from the reaction you get to your first suggestion.

Should you measure your shot based on your partner's play? Once again, only if it helps. In general, it would seem wise to take advantage of any information from any source before your shot. But if watching your partner distracts you from playing your own game, don't do it. Putting provides a good example. Each player has a feel for a putt based on his own stroke. If your partner tends to ram his putts, taking a break out of them, you as a gentler putter are going to learn nothing about the line from watching the outcome of his putt. You're better off going it alone under these circumstances.

What if teams are assigned and you get a partner you don't like? Well, if you are playing your own game and not allowing yourself to be influenced by others, being paired with an undesirable personality should not make that much difference. This is certainly a time when you are not likely to be giving or receiving advice. Should the gentleman insist on giving you unwanted advice, assertively tell him that you are most likely to contribute to the team success by playing your own game as best you can, and if you need any help you'll let him know. Interestingly, solid play on your part may enhance the relationship faster than anything you might do socially or psychologically.

A tactic that helps me when I get in tense situations with particular golfers or with uncomfortably high gambling stakes is to avoid knowing the details of the format being played. I might say something like, "Sure, we can play anything you like. Just let me know how much I owe you when we get through." Of course, I'm really planning on them paying me when the round is over. But this strategy enables me to focus on my own game and not get distracted by all the point-counting gymnastics.

If things don't go favorably during a team competition or during any competition for that matter, look for something to achieve over the remaining holes. For example, "Can I settle down in the face of adversity and play steady the rest of the way? Perhaps I can make one birdie on the way in." Keep trying. You never know what might happen. At least, "I'm going to make my opponents win this 'already won' match. How about if I treat the remaining holes like the first holes of my next round?"

The one thing you can always do under trying circumstances is demonstrate that you are a struggler, someone who keeps his cool and hangs in there even under the worst conditions, conditions that have to be endured by all who want to call themselves true golfers.

Lesson #27

MAKING THE
BIG PUTT

W HILE PUTTING PRESENTS MANY different challenges, one special challenge is making the big putt. Sinking a putt with the match on the line has brought even the best players in the world to their knees on many heralded occasions. Let's consider how to view the big putt in a mentally constructive fashion, how to practice for such occasions and ultimately how to handle this important stroke in the heat of competition.

Keep the Big Putt
in Perspective

Don't make one putt any bigger than another. Since it's difficult to convince yourself that a truly important putt is not actually that important; the way to make one putt no bigger than any other is to make them all big. Each putt is important, no way around it. Treat all putts throughout the round like they are just as big as those to win the match. After all, whether the 4-footers are on the first, sixth or 18th green, they all contribute equally to the final score, so treat them all the same. Then when you get to the one that happens to be on the 18th, it won't be such a surprise to you. You've been facing big pressure putts all day long.

Each putt is practice for later putts. While you don't want to diminish the importance of any putt, you can still view each successive putt as valuable practice for even more important putts that lie ahead.

Say to yourself, "This putt on the fourth green is good practice for the one I might face on the 18th." Then when you face the big putt on the 18th, think of it as merely practice for yet bigger ones at other times in your career. That is, a putt just like the present one may be for the club championship someday.

If indeed you do eventually face that club-championship putt, that one might be viewed as practice for the even bigger one you could eventually face for the state amateur title, and so on. Bigger putts always lie ahead, so don't get too excited about the present one. It is simply practice for even bigger ones in your future.

Big putts are great opportunities. It is hard to manufacture pressurized opportunities, so relish them when they come your way. Enjoy them as tests of your developing skills and emotional control. Keep working at them and take it easy on yourself if you don't always succeed. Remember, each big putt is just one more opportunity to get comfortable with big putts in general. The more you take advantage of these opportunities, the better you will get in big-putt situations.

Practice Pressure
Putts Regularly

While manufacturing pressured putts is not easy, golfers must make the effort to simulate pressure in practice. The best pressure practice is to force yourself to make a set number of putts in a row with the requirement that you start the count over if you miss a putt before the set number is complete. For example, make 18 3-footers in a row, starting over if you miss one along the way. Believe me, when you get to Nos. 17 and 18 in the count, realizing that you can't go home unless you make the last two putts, your knees will get a little weak and your palms will sweat just like they do over the big putts on the 17th and 18th greens.

The same pressurized exercise could be extended to nine 6-foot putts, four 10-foot putts or two 20-foot putts. A semblance of big-putt pressure will exist in each occasion toward the end of the string of putts.

Another way to practice big putts is to play serious competition involving important putts on a regular basis. When you play serious competition, particularly medal play where the final score is all that counts, you get used to the importance of each and every putt. No single putt is a shock to the system because you are bearing down on all of them.

Ways to generate serious medal play might be a challenge ladder among your friends, playing one-day tournaments sponsored by the state golf association or playing all the local tournaments you can find that provide the opportunity to count your individual score.

However, simulated pressure cannot substitute for actual tournament golf in which you experience truly big putts with no artificiality involved. Don't expect to go out once a year in the club championship and be comfortable and successful with big putts. Proficiency with big putts requires getting tournament tough, mentally tough and big-putt tough by playing serious golf throughout the year.

Always putt everything out, no matter if you are playing serious or social golf. If you allow yourself to get careless by slapping away short putts or accepting generous gimmes, you have no one to blame but yourself when important short putts seem like a foreign experience. If you practice carelessness, you learn carelessness.

On the flip side, if you practice carefulness and precision, you learn carefulness and precision. Jack Nicklaus was renowned for never hitting a careless shot. That is why he rarely, if ever, played golf with his family during his prime. Golf was serious business for him. Each and every shot counted under any and all circumstances.

Handling the Heat
of the Situation

Finally, here you are—the 18th green, the match is on the line and the big putt lies before you. How do you handle the immediate pressure of the situation?

Develop a routine. Good putters have a consistent routine that is used every time they putt. It's the same routine they used on the practice green, on every putt early in the round and now once again on the 18th green.

Stay with your routine. Don't change it by spending more time lining up the big putt, by standing over the ball longer or by making changes in your stroke. Your regular routine provides the best chance of maintaining your composure. In some ways it is simply the routine that is executing the putt. You are merely the medium through which this routine operates.

Focus on the task rather than the outcome. When you get over the big putt, think about what you have to do rather than what the result might be. Worrying about what might happen simply distracts you from the task at hand. The proper mechanics will give you the best chance of a favorable result.

Keep it simple. The bigger the putt and the more worried you are, the greater the need to keep your key thoughts as simple as possible. Focus only on one thing—the one thing you are most likely to neglect under pressure. For example, if you tend to get tentative on big putts, think only about firmness in making the stroke. If you tend to pull up on important putts, focus on keeping the putter head moving low toward the hole. If you tend to move your head when the heat is on, then concentrate on nothing but perfect stillness over the ball.

Another simple thought for all occasions is squareness. See the square contact between the face of the putter-head and the ball.

Whatever you are concentrating on during the putt, ask yourself if you actually achieved it before looking to see the result. So often you can think you are doing things correctly, when in actuality the execution is otherwise. If you are trying to hit the ball firmly, ask yourself, "Was that firm?" before looking to see the result. If you are intent on stillness over the ball, ask yourself, "Is the ball gone and my head still in the same position?" before checking to determine the result. Better yet, don't visually check for the result at all—just listen for the clunk of the ball in the hole.

Be content with your effort. If you did what you were trying to do, take the result in stride. If the ball goes in the hole, such was to be expected since the putt was well-executed. If the putt happens to miss despite your having done exactly what you were trying to do, that's the rub of the green. You did everything you could to produce a favorable result.

Remember Nicklaus' response after his Ryder Cup partner chastised him for missing a putt he might have been expected to make. Nicklaus said, "I made that putt. It just didn't go in." In other words, he stroked the putt just the way he wanted to. Nine out of 10 times it would have gone in. This just happened to be the one unexplainable time that the putt didn't fall. The message is if you execute properly, consider yourself a success no matter what the result.

Maintain a consistent emotional state. If the execution of the putt is done properly, your emotional reaction should be no different whether the putt goes in the hole or not. That is, assuming you did exactly what you were trying to do, no one should be able to tell whether you made or missed a given putt based on your demeanor as you walk off the green.

How you handle and react to the task of putting on the first green may set the stage for your putting success or failure on successive greens during the round. That doesn't mean you have to necessarily make the putt on the first green. You just have to approach the task in a disciplined fashion that serves as a model for disciplined putting throughout the round.

Remember that putting is as much attitude as it is mechanics. You start cultivating that attitude on the first hole (or even the practice green) so that it is available to you throughout the round and especially for that big putt on the 18th green.

GOLF'S A STRUGGLE

So Why Not Enjoy It?

POPULAR PSYCHOLOGY WRITER DR. Wayne Dyer once said that neurotics aren't crazy, they're just wrong. They want the world to be some way other than it is. According to Dyer, the world is just the way it's supposed to be, and we are the ones who have to adapt.

I wonder what Dr. Dyer might have said about golfers who want golf to be some way other than it is. I'm talking about those who seem to want the game to be easy. Perhaps he would have said that they are simply wrong. Golf is a struggle, and that's just the way it's supposed to be. Golfers have to adapt.

Instead of merely adapting, why not find ways to enjoy the struggle, take pride in the mental toughness required to cope with it and view adversity as an opportunity to show off your ability rather than to complain and cave in.

Jack Nicklaus is a classic example of someone who enjoyed the struggle. Reflecting on the reaction of some players to the difficulty that defines the U.S. Open, Nicklaus commented: "I used to love listening to them gripe. 'The rough is too high.' Check him off. 'The greens are too fast.'

Check him off. You just check guys off as they complain, because they complain themselves right out of the championship."

A playing partner of Nicklaus related another telling incident. Nicklaus had the lead on the 18th. He hit a perfect drive and found it in a divot in the middle of the fairway. A long iron was required to reach the green that was guarded on two sides by water. Now, many a modern-day player would point to his bad luck, stomp around with steam coming out of his ears and gesture so as to exclaim the unfairness of the situation. But not Nicklaus. In contrast, the Bear didn't even pay homage to the lie. He simply calculated his yardage, calmly stepped up and smacked a 2-iron to the middle of the green for the win.

When questioned later regarding his ho-hum reaction to the bad lie, Nicklaus responded in a manner that suggested what's the big deal, what could I do about it, this is just golf and I can handle it. In other words, I'm Jack Nicklaus, and the struggle isn't too much for me.

Tiger Woods appreciates the struggle. Consider these comments from Woods during the 2002 U.S. Open at Bethpage, a layout that played extremely difficult even by U.S. Open standards: "I tried to stay as patient as I possibly could today. I hung in there and made some good par saves to keep the round going. I think a good par save is always better than a birdie. All you can do is hit good putts, at least try."

On trouble situations, Woods suggested: "When you put yourself in a place where it doesn't look like you're going to make par, grind it out so you don't make double. Go ahead and make your bogey, and let's get out of here. Try and bury those par putts. Those par putts are key. You're going to have to make them to stay in the tournament."

Most people think of Woods as a tiger who easily prowls the course for birdies. Apparently that's not so. Tiger is a struggler who appreciates the difficulty of the game, keeps his head during tough times and never gives up.

Of particular interest is his attitude toward par-saving putts. He says he actually enjoys them more than birdies. This is quite in contrast to many amateurs who, once they make a miscue on a hole, give up the struggle and just accept the inevitable bogey. Indeed, even Woods has said that bogey is sometimes the best you can hope for on a hole. But on many other occasions, if you hang in there and scratch and claw, you may find yourself in position to make a very satisfying par-saving putt.

Despite these powerful examples, today's golfers do not seem to want to participate in the struggle that is golf. They would rather play short courses that require no more than 7-irons into greens. They insist on two balls off the first tee, improving their lies in the fairway, moving the ball off of roots and giving themselves 3-foot putts. They expect to play par golf without systematic daily practice. When par golf doesn't materialize, they prefer to hide their individual scores in better-ball competitions, captain's choice formats or Stableford point systems, rather than post those scores in their entirety as an accurate reflection of their level of play.

In effect, many golfers seek to avoid the threat of pain, disappointment and embarrassment that has been integral to the game from the very beginning. In doing so, they also miss out on the joy and exhilaration that accompany true improvement and accomplishment in a difficult game.

So what is the answer to this deplorable malady that might be called easyitis? What psychological vaccination might be administered to bolster golfers' immunity to the pain and suffering of golf, making them more willing to venture into the struggle that is presently being avoided?

Mental toughness is the vaccination. It can help you tolerate the struggle, even relish it as another thing to conquer in golf. Mental toughness is one more domain in which you can better your opponent, outlast him and stand tall in a game that brings lesser players to their knees. Mental toughness is the epitome of golfing maturity. You cannot consider yourself a complete golfer until mental toughness is part of your arsenal of skills.

What is mental toughness? Admittedly, mental toughness is not easy to define. As alluded to previously, it is generally reflected in how you handle adversity.

In his early days as head football coach at the University of South Carolina, Lou Holtz said his team was not strong enough to overcome adversity on the field. In other words, his team was not mentally tough enough. Holtz went on to say that this comes only with practice.

Amateur golfer Brandi Jackson, in her senior year on the Furman University golf team, turned around what was an otherwise unheralded career to earn her first collegiate victory, become runner-up at the U.S. Women's Amateur Championship, qualify for the LPGA's Futures Tour and be named Carolinas Golf Association Women's Player of the Year. How did she make such a big improvement in her performance in such a short period of time? She said the big change was in her mental attitude.

"Before, when I would get off to a bad start, I would want to quit," she said. "Now I have learned to shake it off, because you never know what might happen."

Her new mentally tough attitude was one of calm persistence in the face of adversity, using her head in realizing that good breaks may lie ahead as long as she didn't self-destruct before giving them a chance to happen.

Mental toughness also involves emotional control. After he won his third green jacket at The Masters, extending his perfect record to 7-0 when he had at least a share of the lead going into the final round of a major, Woods had this to say: "I've done it before. I know what it takes to win here. I know how to handle my emotions. I was able to outlast the other guys."

All of this might be summed up to define mental toughness as emotional control in the face of adversity. But how do you learn this important skill? As already mentioned, you have to practice mental toughness in order to learn it. Holtz came right out and said that mental toughness is something that comes only with practice. Woods was more subtle when he simply said, "I've done it before." That is, he'd practiced mental toughness before, experienced it many times and now was ready to handle it when the situation called for it.

No easy way exists for practicing mental toughness. The only venue is regular exposure to adversity, which usually comes in the form of competitive matches and tournaments. Does that mean you have to immediately thrust yourself into the highest levels of competition? Of course not. Begin by setting up individual matches against just one other person, but make those matches mean something so that you feel the pressure and have the opportunity to face the adversity that will make you tough.

The adversity might come in the form of bad breaks during the round, a tough ruling, not being totally on your game that given day, bad weather, a nagging injury or a tough or lucky opponent. Against this backdrop, you practice mental toughness by not complaining, staying calm and persistently plowing ahead despite the difficulty and frustration you are facing. Your efforts at mental toughness may not always lead to victory, particularly at first, but that toughness will be building gradually over time and enhancing your chances for future success.

To help ease the burden a bit, think of each difficult situation as merely practice for still tougher situations in the future. At the moment, you may have a pressure putt in an individual match. No big deal! Consider it a great practice opportunity for a really big putt you may have in the club championship. When you get to that championship putt, consider it as tremendous practice for the one you may eventually have for the city championship. Be thankful for these special practice opportunities. They don't come along very often, and you have to take advantage of them in order to practice mental toughness.

Similarly, when you are in trouble on a hole, view it as an opportunity to practice recovering. When you are down in a match, it's an opportunity for a comeback. The mentally tough golfer is the one who seeks out opportunity in situations where others wallow in disaster.

In the absence of matches and tournaments, simulate pressure and adversity in practice by creating situations where you must succeed or there are undesirable consequences. For example, make 18 short putts in a row or, as a consequence, keep repeating the process until you do. Those 17th and 18th putts can be real knee-knockers.

Before you end your practice session, successfully execute three difficult trouble shots in a row from the rough or in the trees. This exercise could keep you on the range for a while if you haven't yet developed mental toughness.

If you really want to apply the pressure and test your mental toughness, take one ball to the first tee (i.e., no reloading allowed) and make an agreement with yourself that if you don't drive it in the fairway, there will be no stopping at the 19th hole after practice that day.

Just as in the learning of mental toughness, no shortcuts exist for maintaining it. You have to keep putting yourself on the line in order to stay sharp. Ben Hogan said that he was afraid to miss one day of golf for fear that he would forget how to play the game. It's not quite that bad with mental toughness, but I would recommend exposing yourself to adversity with at least one serious match per week. Otherwise, you will certainly lose your edge. When you move to the tournament level, play monthly to keep your competitive legs about you. Every two or three weeks would provide even greater assurance of consistent mental toughness.

Mental toughness is further enhanced by learning all the psychological skills available so that your mental game, in general, stays ahead of the competition. Learn relaxation skills, learn to concentrate better, improve your visualization and work on your emotional control. All these skills will help you build your confidence and be at your service when adversity comes calling.

Mental toughness is also well served by a good knowledge of the rules of golf. Play by the rules at all times, make them a routine part of your play and you will reduce the likelihood that a rule infraction will sneak up on you and create unexpected adversity.

Moreover, playing by the rules, even during practice rounds, provides yet another way to face up to adversity. That is, no matter how careful you are, the rules of golf are always ready to jump up and grab you. They'll do it during practice as well as during formal play. So turn the rules into an ally, an ever-available competitor that's always there to challenge you in your quest for mental toughness.

PART IV

EFFECTIVE
ACTION

PRACTICE

According to coach Lou Holtz, he "never met a player that didn't want to play; they just don't want to practice." Ironically, Tiger Woods once said that he liked to practice more than he liked to play—and it's worth noting that he's done pretty well with that set of priorities.

Lesson # 29 explores how to "Make the Most Out of Limited Practice Time," including designing practice sessions so they are efficient, effective and enjoyable. The key to getting oneself to practice is to make it fun, as is prescribed in this lesson.

One way to make practice more enjoyable and effective is to get beyond the driving range, take your practice to the course. Lesson #30 offers some on-course practice drills that revolve around "Hitting Great Shots Under Pressure." Excitement is generated, as well as a great learning experience.

A subtlety of practice is the difficulty of generalizing what one *practices* to the *playing* situation. The problem is the dissimilarities between practice and play. For example, the driving range is different from the course; the practice swing is different from the real swing. Lesson #31 teaches you to "Rise Above the Situation—Make Similarity Your Friend," so the transition between different situations is more seamless.

MAKE THE MOST OUT OF LIMITED PRACTICE TIME

Golf writer Doug Ferguson once described a practice session of a young Annika Sorenstam. Annika was cold, wet and tired of hitting balls in the rain when she called her father and asked him to take her home. Tom Sorenstam couldn't help but notice the other teenagers still practicing.

"He didn't say anything when he picked me up," Annika said. "But when we drove away, he said, 'I just want you to know that there are no shortcuts to success.' I knew what he meant. To get better, you have to practice. Just by saying that, it hurt me that I went home."

That lesson transformed Sorenstam, whose success comes more from determination and will than raw talent.

Vijay Singh's dedication to practice is also legendary. Indeed, not many have reached the PGA or LPGA tours without years of commitment to systematic practice. In fact, psychological research tells us that it takes 10 years of full-time practice, ideally starting at a young age, to reach the status of an elite performer.

So where does that leave the amateur player who doesn't have the time or dedication of a professional golfer when it comes to practice?

Where does it leave the average golfer who wants to play the game in his free time rather than spend hours and hours practicing? Unfortunately, the answer remains that practice is still necessary. It's just that busy people have to learn to practice all the more efficiently and effectively (i.e., get the most out of their limited practice time), as well as make it enjoyable (have fun so they are more likely to want to practice).

Efficient, Effective and Enjoyable Practice

Lessons are important for a number of reasons. First of all, you are shown the correct technique so that you practice and learn the correct technique. If you spend time practicing faulty mechanics, you will do nothing but learn mistakes. Subsequently, your work is doubled because you will have to unlearn mistakes before establishing proper technique. Doubling your work is not efficient use of time. Efficient and effective practice dictates practicing and learning correct technique right from the beginning.

In contrast to golf schools, lessons permit ample time to work on what you have learned in between sessions. Once you feel like you have incorporated the new learning into your game, you can return to your teaching professional on your own schedule for a check-up or to pursue further improvements. Lessons without practice in between are a waste of time and money. Golf schools lasting even several days may not allow enough intervening practice time, not to mention the difficulty of getting back with the same instructor for remedial work in the months ahead.

Lessons from the same teaching professional give the pro a chance to get to know you and your game. Find a pro you are comfortable working with, see him or her regularly and put in ample practice between lessons. This is the most economical way to learn, and you will also get more for your money in terms of efficiency and effectiveness.

Once you understand what you have been shown during your lessons, the next consideration is to practice the new techniques precisely and carefully. If you were to inadvertently practice carelessly, then carelessness would be learned instead of carefulness. The storage area for practice in the brain records only what you do, not what you intended to do.

But how could anyone practice carelessly? Consider a few examples, such as players joking around the chipping green while presumably getting in some last-minute practice for the day's round, players hitting balls on the range in rapid fire without any particular focus on a target or the distances the shots are traveling, or players leaving the little markers in the hole on the putting green while practicing short putts.

> *Efficient and effective practice dictates practicing and learning correct technique right from the beginning.*

How careless these actions are in relation to the carefulness demanded on the course when the joking stops and matters turn dead serious. What happens to careless golfers when, on the first tee, only one ball must be accurately hit the correct distance with no extra balls to drag over for rapid-fire backup attempts? Upon reaching the green, how do careless golfers react to nothing but a hole without the aid of the little pin they are used to seeing out of the corners of their eyes? There's no backstop this time, and again dead silence.

Make your practice as realistic as possible. Get off by yourself and concentrate. Focus on the elements that will be required of you in the round, like targets, distance and precision. Put some pressure on yourself to make short putts to holes without any markers in them. Take your time. Line up each shot and go through your pre-shot routine just like you do on the course. This is careful, efficient and effective practice.

The efficiency of your practice is contributed to by whether you have to go to extra trouble to make it happen. Keep a few clubs in the car so you can stop at the range or putting green on the way home from work, rather than going all the way home and having to motivate yourself to go out again and retrace your route back to the course.

Identify times you tend to waste, such as the hour between dropping the kids off and picking them up from swimming lessons, and make that a regular practice period.

Yet another convenient practice opportunity might involve the clubs in the trunk again, this time being applied to any available patch of grass where you can work on your chipping when you have an unexpected wait for someone at the doctor's office or the mall.

Other than these little convenient practice opportunities, resist dissecting the game too much. The reality is that golf rarely involves hitting two shots of the same kind in a row. Playing golf is complex, and efficient and effective practice mandates practicing golf in all its complexity.

If circumstances allow, practice on the course so as to provide the best opportunity for generating the complex variety of shots that playing the game demands. Take shots over until you get them right. Keep score of how many extra attempts it takes you to shoot a perfect round.

A reasonable simulation of on-course practice can be achieved on the driving range if you use your imagination. For example, work through the holes on the course in your mind. Hit the drive on each hole until you hit it correctly, then move to the club that would be required for the second shot and repeat the process. Be sure to give yourself some variation in lies. Drop a few balls in the rough off to the side of the practice tee. Hit a few shots from downhill lies off the front of the tee. Try a couple out of divots. You might even make trips to the chipping and putting greens when the times for those shots arrive during your imaginary round.

Don't shy away from practicing in the wind and rain if you are going to have to play under those circumstances. Remember, you learn what you practice. If you don't practice in the wind and rain, those elements are sure to throw you when you face them unprepared.

Make Practice Fun

Nothing is more frustrating than rushing around and having little to show for time ill spent. When you rush, mistakes occur, you don't have time to correct them and you go home discouraged at your lack of progress.

Allow enough time for adequate practice so that true learning can occur. If you only have 45 minutes, better to have three holes of quality practice than to rush through nine just to have a nine-hole score. So be patient and don't expect overnight success. Savor the journey as you watch your game improve gradually over regular, unrushed practice sessions.

You should also try to create pressure for yourself. Technique does not occur separately from pressure during a round, so why should they be separated during practice? Indeed, you have to work on technique, so do it in the context of simulated pressure.

The pressure of competition makes play fun and can also make practice fun. When it comes to practice, you have an ever-present opponent—yourself. Every stroke becomes important as you try to better your previous performance on the practice range or putting green. By creating practice scores and keeping records and striking averages of those scores, you are always under a little pressure.

Pressure can also be simulated by establishing criteria you have to meet. Commit to certain consequences if you don't meet the criteria, such as not going home until you make 18 short putts in a row. Reward yourself if you meet the criteria sooner than later. For example, indulge yourself with a visit to the 19th hole if you meet your criteria on the first or second try.

Another source of pressure is having others observe your performance. During practice on the range, ask another golfer to watch you hit a few balls as you call your shots. Match shots with other golfers on the range, perhaps with a few coins at stake.

All of this will help to simulate the ingredients of a round of golf. When you include them in your practice routine, your practice will approximate the demands and enjoyment of an actual round of golf.

In addition to being efficient and effective, practicing on the course adds enjoyment to your practice routine. Walking between shots, getting off by yourself and the variations in the scenery and terrain can all add peace and tranquillity to your practice. If you carry just a few clubs in your hands, you can even jog from point to point on the course to add the efficiency of getting your daily exercise in while you are working on your game.

Of course, courtesy for other players and care for the course are paramount if this type of practice is going to be tolerated. So, go out of your way to avoid other players and do extra repair work on the course, even beyond any marks of usage that you create.

Another helpful bit of advice is to stop practicing while you are still enjoying it. If a reader puts down a book at the most exciting part, he is much more likely to eagerly return to it. The same is true for a golfer when it comes to practice. Stop practicing while you are still enjoying it and excited about your progress, and you will be much more likely to eagerly return for your next practice session.

Once you have figured out something during your practice session, repeat it enough times to build confidence in it but don't run it in the ground to the point where you lose what you have gained due to distraction and boredom with the process.

Finish your session by making some notes regarding what you are doing well, tuck them away for the start of your next practice session and head home with a feeling of success that will entice you back for yet another effective, efficient and enjoyable practice session.

Lesson #30

Hitting Great Shots Under Pressure

IF I COULD JUST hit the ball as far as Tiger, I'd break par, too." "If I could consistently drive inside 150 yards for my approach shot, greens in regulation would be no problem."

"If I could hit as many greens in regulation as the players on tour do, I'd make a lot of birdies, too."

"If I could just put my ball in the middle of every green, I'd shoot lights out every time."

So go the assumptions about how easy the game would be if only certain stipulations were met. However, the following mental practice drills will test these assumptions on the golf course. They will challenge what you think and feel about the game. They also will either validate your assumptions about your alleged abilities or force you to face reality as to what you have to learn and practice to play better golf.

Drill 1: Tee Shots/Scores

Place a ball in the prime location in each fairway where you think Tiger would be after his tee shot. For the par 3s, put the ball on the green, since that's probably where Tiger would be.

Now, see if you can break par like Tiger given these ideal tee-shot placements for all 18 holes. Whatever the results, it should be clear that Tiger doesn't break par simply by hitting long tee shots. He finishes off holes with great approach shots and a deft short game.

With tee shots out of the equation, the results of your play will tell you how much you need to practice approach shots and your short game. As with all drills, keep records and see if you can improve over time. Don't be surprised if you start out over par. Just look for improvement as you keep trying to shoot Tiger scores.

Drill 2: 150-yard Drill

Starting from the 150-yard marker on each hole, see how many greens in regulation you can accumulate for the 18 holes. Remember, getting the ball anywhere on the putting surface is considered a green in regulation. You don't have to putt and you don't have to be close to the hole—just get it on the green.

Here again, tee shots are not a factor. Therefore, if you do indeed hit more greens than you normally do, it will tell you that you have to drive your ball in the middle of the fairway a reasonable distance from the green on a more frequent basis.

On the other hand, if you don't hit any more greens than usual, consider that you may be target-bound—not swinging freely when the target gets within range. To remedy this, try to swing through the green, as if you were going to hit the ball over the back. With the proper club in your hand, the ball should simply drop out of the sky onto the green, instead of continuing over the back.

To avoid using the same club all the time with this drill, vary your approach shots from between 130 and 170 yards, averaging 150 yards over the entire 18 holes. Allow yourself the same range of yardage on the par 3s, no matter where the actual tee markers might be.

Drill 3: In the Short Grass

While distance is king for most golfers, accuracy can also go a long way toward better scoring. Take a test drive out on the course regarding your accuracy off the tee. On each of the par-4 and par-5 holes, tee up one ball and see if you can hit the fairway. No approach shots are required on any hole. Just smooth it out there and simply hit the fairway with no particular concern about distance or playing the rest of any hole.

Despite this limited objective, more of a challenge exists here than might be expected. If you experience difficulty, back off from the driver and use the 3-wood or a hybrid. Indeed, find out just how far down the clubs you have to go in order to hit every fairway. You might have to back off all the way to a 7- or 8-iron in order to hit absolutely every fairway over 18 holes. If that is the case, at least you will have identified a major area in need of instruction and practice.

Also, consider the shape of your shots. For example, if you are a right-handed player and more comfortable hitting a fade, play that shot on as many holes as possible that allow for a left-to-right ball trajectory. Just start the ball down the left side of the fairway and use the generous landing area of the entire fairway to the right of the initial line of flight. Remember, again, with this drill all you have to do is get the ball in the fairway. You don't have to hit the second shot to the green.

Drill 4: Up and Down

This on-course drill can be done in endless ways with a variety of clubs. The basic format calls for hitting pitches and chips from various locations around the green. The objective is to see how many shots you can get within 5, 10 and 15 feet of the pin.

Use three balls at each green, pitching or chipping each ball from a different location. Take only one shot from each location, mimicking the pressure of playing conditions where only one shot is allowed from each point on the course. In other words, there are no mulligans, not even in practice.

For scorekeeping purposes, 3 points are allotted for each shot inside 5 feet, 2 points for each shot in the 5- to 10-foot range, and 1 point for each shot from 10 to 15 feet. Of course, a more accomplished golfer could reduce the range of feet to make this drill more challenging.

With this drill, be sure to repair any and all ballmarks to perfection, lest you incur the wrath of the maintenance staff, the pro and your fellow golfers. The best time to do any of these on-course drills is during slow periods of play—early or late in the day, during the off-season, when the weather is less than perfect, etc. At these times, you will be less conspicuous and limit the risk of inconveniencing anyone.

With all the above considerations, think about all the shots you might practice in getting the ball up and down—chip and runs, short and long pitches, lobs over bunkers, sand shots, little putt-chips with a 3-wood or hybrid, chips to long and short pin placements, bump-and-run shots from varying distances, etc. There are endless ways to do this drill.

As always, keep records of your performance and note the improvement. Once you find yourself easily racking up points using the 5-, 10- and 15-foot parameters, tighten up the requirements by demanding 3-, 6- and 9-foot precision in order to obtain your points. Get good at this drill and your scores will drop precipitously.

Drill 5: Middle of the Green

So, you think you could shoot lights out if you were just able to get your ball to the dead center of every green in regulation. Well, that should be easy enough to test.

Take one ball and your putter, put the ball in the geometric center of each green and consider that you have hit each green in regulation to that point on the putting surface. Then, putt to each pin wherever it might be for that day. If you are playing on average-sized greens, your longest putts should be in the 35- to 40-foot range. Sometimes, you'll get lucky and find the pin set near the middle of the green, leaving you with a short putt no more than 5 feet from the cup.

See what you can shoot under these circumstances with your ball on every green, right in the dead center. But don't be surprised if you have just as many three-putts as one-putts when you first use this drill. It's not as easy as it sounds. With practice, however, you should be breaking par fairly regularly with this drill.

Keep in mind that if the green is odd shaped, the front of the green is the farthest point forward, and the back of the green is the farthest point back. These points don't have to line up with each other north to south. The same goes from side to side—farthest point left and right. They don't have to line up east to west.

Try walking up to the front of the green and looking at it from left to right. Position yourself in the center between the two sides. Then, walk toward the back until you are in the center of the green, front to back. Drop the ball at that point and you should be in the center of the green. It will be surprising at times where you find yourself on the green. But rest assured you have systematically determined the center of the green.

Drill 6: Do or Die
on Short Putts

Putt all you want on the practice putting green, but you will never fully simulate the feeling and challenges of actual scoring putts until you get out on the course. To test your on-course, par-shooting putting skills, take one ball out to each of the 18 greens and putt nothing but one 5-footer. Each putt is for par, and there are no second chances.

Vary your ball placement on each hole so that you experience just as many downhill and uphill 5-footers as sidehill putts from right and left. Remember, hit only one putt on each green so you mimic actual playing conditions. Make it or miss it, take the long walk to the next green before putting again. You'll feel the pressure in this drill because you would rather make the long walk to the next green reflecting on the putt you just made, rather than the one you just missed.

If statistics are correct, you'll do well to make half of these critters. But who knows, maybe you'll do better. It would certainly take a lot of pressure off the rest of your game if you knew you could make the 5-footers, be it for birdie, bogey or par.

Incidentally, if 5 feet is too much at first, try it from 3 feet. You'll be doing well to make 18 three-footers in a row with just one attempt on each hole.

Drill 7: Be a Tiger
from the Forward Tees

Once you have it all together, test out your entire game from the forward tees. While this should be fun, watch your course management because of being unfamiliar with the layout from the shorter yardages. In addition, the short game and putting are always a challenge, no matter what tees you play from.

This drill will indicate, once again, how much distance is a factor in your game. If the only thing holding you back from stellar play is not hitting the ball far enough, then playing the forward tees should elevate you to professional status. After all, you'll be right out there with Tiger on your drives. But if you find that your scores don't change much despite playing from the forward tees, look to your iron play, short game and putting for solutions to your scoring difficulties.

Many variations of these drills could be designed and other entirely different drills could be constructed. For example, how about going out with a friend and matching shots from near impossible situations on the course. While you may never have that particular shot again, I bet you will learn a lot about creative ways to play unusual shots.

Or try doing what Gary Player used to do—hit two balls from each point on the course, then play the worse one. This drill will challenge your shotmaking and scoring ability, as well as your frustration tolerance. You'll also have to force yourself to concentrate for two shots in a row, since you don't want either of them to be poor shots.

Practice on the course and develop an appreciation for just how difficult golf is. Then, maybe, you will allow yourself to be more patient with the game and also with yourself.

RISE ABOVE THE SITUATION

Make Similarity Your Friend

A SHOT ON THE course can feel entirely different from one on the driving range. Similarly, a shot that can't reach the green can differ considerably from a shot within striking distance of the putting surface.

The practice swing and the real shot can also provide quite a contrast. That is, the smooth tempo of a practice swing can totally desert a golfer when he steps up to the ball and actually has to produce. Casual rounds and pressurized competition differ, too, as typically routine shots turn into something much more difficult when a match is on the line.

All of the above are examples of situations affecting performance. From the driving range to the course, shots far from the green versus close to the green, a practice swing versus the real thing, and casual rounds versus pressurized competition—all represent contrasts between different situations that can greatly affect the physical and mental game.

The general solution for dealing with such situational shifts is to engineer dissimilar situations so they become as similar as possible, which is sometimes easy and sometimes difficult. Let's explore how this general solution might be applied to each of these scenarios.

Moving from the Driving Range to the Course

The problem of dissimilarity begins with the fact that limited targets present themselves on the driving range as compared to the course. Flagsticks in an open field or mounds representing greens can hardly compete with the variety of pin placements encountered on the finely manicured greens of an actual course.

Another dissimilarity between the driving range and the golf course is that golfers on the range don't pay as much attention to the direction shots are traveling as they do on the course. Range balls tend to be aimed in a general direction with the focus more on feel and ball flight than on how accurate the shot might be.

Just like a high-wire walker who focuses only on the wire no matter how high it's set, you should not change your routine when you come under pressure.

Distances are also difficult to determine on the driving range. Golfers cannot typically walk onto the range, step off shots and gain familiarity with the distances various clubs produce. Even yardage markers are of questionable value considering how frequently teeing areas are repositioned on the driving range. Furthermore, range balls are of inconsistent quality and may bear little resemblance to the performance of new balls put in play on the first tee.

Obstacles or unusual lies are also absent on the driving range. When is the last time you tried to hit a low shot under a tree limb on the driving range, or a high cut shot around a tree to a tight pin? Any downhill or sidehill lies lately? What about hitting shots out of divots? Most golfers give themselves only perfect lies for shots on the driving range.

Still another thing missing on the driving range is score. It doesn't matter how many shots you mess up because a whole bucket of balls is waiting to back up miscues. Mistakes are reversible on the range, which is not the case on the course.

Lastly, spectators are absent on the driving range, or at least they are more concerned with their own activities than they are with yours. However, when you move to the first tee, the situation changes considerably.

Suddenly, a terrifying silence settles over the environment. All eyes are fixed on you preparing to hit your first drive. Just imagine if all the golfers on the driving range suddenly stopped, became silent and watched you hit your next warm-up shot. It would become quite a different and unnerving situation.

The Remedy—To facilitate the transition from the driving range to the course, make the situation on the range similar to that on the course. If targets aren't provided, generate them by aiming at trees in the distance, bare spots on the ground or irregularities in the terrain. Obstacles and unusual lies can also be created by positioning yourself at the end of the range where the tree line can mimic a similar threat on the course or an irregular surface can be found for practicing downhill or sidehill lies.

You can even make up some games and keep score regarding your practice shots so even your driving-range shots count for something. Ask others to watch you hit a few shots. Put additional pressure on yourself by telling the observers where you are aiming or what you are trying to do with the shot.

Unfortunately, calculating distances will have to be done on the course with high-quality balls and shots stepped off to determine the distance each club produces. Once these measurements are established, they shouldn't change unless you face different environmental conditions, get new equipment or make a drastic swing modification.

Transitioning from Distant Shots to Close-in Shots

Distant shots far from the green call for a general focus at a wide fairway. Close-in shots within striking distance of the putting surface require a more specific focus at a precise pin placement on a small section of the green.

The more general the demands of the situation, the more likely you are to relax and swing freely. After all, it's not going to matter that much if the ball is slightly off line or a little bit short or long of the intended landing area. However, when you get within striking distance of the green and the target gets more specific, two unfavorable tendencies are likely to creep in—steering the ball to the target and looking up to see the result. Both the target and the result are more critical now than they were with a wide fairway. The fluid swinging motion that allowed you to make a free and relaxed pass at the ball is now harder to reproduce.

The Remedy—You have two options to make the distant and close-in situations more similar: 1) Pick precise targets on all shots, including tee shots to wide fairways, so steering the ball shouldn't be an issue for one type of shot any more than any other. 2) Focus through the green as if the green weren't there and approach shots were simply progressing down a continuation of the fairway. With this strategy, steering should be eliminated as you swing freely through the green.

Regarding the tendency to look up to see the result, consider what you are likely to observe if you do so—a ball pulled left, sliced right, skulled over the green or hit fat and short. None of these scenarios is hardly worth seeing. Better to keep your head focused on the contact between the clubhead and the ball and let the result take care of itself.

Shifting from a Practice Swing to the Real Shot

The practice swing is dissimilar to the real shot because there is no ball to hit on the practice swing and no result to worry about. When you are swinging at nothing but air, it's hard to miss. With no ball in flight, little temptation exists to look up and see an outcome. Consequently, a still head and a stable axis for the swing result in a graceful, free-flowing rotation of the body and a beautiful practice swing.

Now step up to the ball. That's right, you actually have to hit the ball this time and a result will follow. At this point you have a tremendous temptation to see the outcome. The free-swinging gracefulness and stable axis of the practice swing escape you as you jump out of the swing to get an early glimpse of the dreaded result.

The Remedy—To reduce the dissimilarity between the practice swing and the actual shot, Harvey Penick suggested picking an object on the ground (e.g., a leaf, weed or acorn) to use as an imaginary ball during the practice swing. Use your typical routine over the object and make contact with it, as you will do shortly with the ball.

Build results into the practice swing by imagining the flight of a ball as you stay down and follow through. Visualize a long, straight ball flight just like the one you intend to see in reality momentarily. This procedure mimics precisely what you are to do on the real shot—stay down and visualize the perfect shot before you look to verify the imagined result.

The above suggestions will help make the practice swing more similar to the actual shot. However, if you want to attack the dissimilarity issue by making the actual shot more like a practice swing, try the following: 1) align your stance with the target before the practice swing, 2) make your practice swing close to the ball, 3) then quickly step up to the ball and repeat the practice swing, allowing the ball to simply get in the way. The ball will be struck before you realize it is there.

One last possibility is to skip the practice swing altogether. If you never do anything but hit real shots, then dissimilarity will be a mute point when you execute a real shot. Shot after shot—will be the same, as you simply do what you always do—hit real shots.

Executing Under Casual Situations
vs. Pressurized Circumstances

The dissimilarity between casual play and pressurized competition is fairly obvious to most players. The latter involves sweaty palms, dry throat, pounding heart, hyperventilation, etc. Bobby Jones made the point very well when he said, "There's golf, and then there's tournament golf."

When the shift is made from casual to pressurized situations, results become more important, hypersensitivity to distractions can occur and your pre-shot routine might change.

The Remedy—It is almost impossible to fool yourself into thinking a pressurized situation is casual and doesn't mean anything. Indeed, the best hope for creating similarity between the two situations is by making the casual situation more pressurized.

For starters, never allow yourself the luxury of a casual shot. In his prime, Jack Nicklaus rarely, if ever, played casual golf, not even with family. He avoided hitting anything other than a serious golf shot.

Always make results an issue, even when practicing or playing a friendly round. In addition to 18-hole scores, keep records or charts of such things as fairways hit, greens in regulation, ups and downs and putts. When you know a score is going to be recorded, each shot is important.

Another helpful tactic is to practice amidst distractions. Creating distractions provides a chance to get used to them. Earl Woods was renowned for throwing things around the young Tiger while he was practicing so the future star could get used to the chaos of large galleries. If galleries aren't a distraction for you, maybe it's something like blades of grass, leaf particles or pine needles flicking up behind your ball as you begin the backswing. If so, create these distractions by putting pieces of natural debris behind practice balls and hitting the balls until you get immune to all those little distractions.

You also will need to develop a precise routine and use it all the time, whether in casual rounds or serious matches. Make the routine so automatic that you never hit a shot (practice, casual or pressurized) without it. Always include the same steps along with the same sequence and timing.

A related suggestion would be to employ the same procedure for lining up putts during casual play as you would under pressure. When you come under pressure, don't change the routine by taking more or less time than you normally would in the casual situation.

In the book *Be the Ball,* Ken Venturi relates a story about Ben Hogan and his admiration for Karl Wallenda, the great high-wire walker. Hogan said that when Wallenda was asked if he got more nervous the higher the wire was set, the "Great Wallenda" replied, "Why should I? The wire never changes." Hogan took that as his model for pressure shots in golf. This could hold true for you, too, if you do the same thing on every shot— casual or pressurized.

PLAYING THE GAME

It's time to play. But, first there's "Getting Ready—The Proper Way to Warm Up" (Lesson #32). Now, this does not mean to simply slap a few balls around the range. Rather, you are about to engage in a disciplined process that will lead smoothly and effectively into the round.

Before heading for the first tee, consider "How to Play the Mental Game for 18 Holes" (Lesson #33). This lesson lays out a detailed example of what happens psychologically over the course of an 18-hole round. It will give you an idea of what you have to plan for.

Any game plan must have a strong course management component. You have to strategically navigate the course and make percentage decisions with a balance of patience and courage. Pace yourself, manage your time, control your emotions and learn "Eight Secrets for Better Course Management" (Lesson #34).

To more effectively "Gain Control of Your Game—Learn to place the ball (Lesson #35). As in a game of chess, always be thinking a number of steps ahead.

Despite all our best efforts, sometimes things don't go as planned and we find ourselves in the throes of a bad round. Damage control is suddenly called for and we have to implement what we know about "Staying with a Bad Round" (Lesson #36). You have to figure out "How to Get Your Head Back in the Game" (Lesson #37).

Ultimately, every golfer wants one thing, and it's not just a low score. I'm not going to tell you "What Every Player Wants" (Lesson #38). You'll have to remain in suspense until you read this lesson on playing the game.

Lesson #32

GETTING READY

The Proper Way to Warm Up

W ARMING UP BEFORE A round is one of those "you can pay me now or pay me later" kind of things. That is, if you don't spend at least a few minutes before your round warming up at the practice area, then you can expect to spend the first nine holes warming up out on the course.

Think about it. In nine holes, you hit approximately 18 full shots, which amounts to about a half-bag of balls at the range. Add another half-dozen or so pitch and chip shots and about 18 putts, and all you have in nine holes is what might be considered a minimal warm-up if the same number and variety of shots had been executed at the practice area. So, let's consider the better alternative—warming up before the round rather than during the round. Indeed, let's design the ideal warm-up, the kind a low handicapper might employ on the day of the club championship.

Begin Warming Up
the Night Before

You can start by putting together a game plan you can sleep on. What swing keys will you employ? Which clubs will you use for tee shots? What is the best placement for certain shots at given points on the course? How will you play difficult holes so they don't turn into disasters? What will be your "go to" shot under pressure? How about your overall attitude toward the round—conservative, aggressive or play the percentages? What's a reasonable outcome to expect from the day?

Write down your responses to these questions and then go peacefully to sleep knowing the plan is in place and only requires your review in the morning.

On the Way to the Course

Before leaving the house, take a look at your reminder notes so you can rehearse your swing keys and strategies as you drive to the course. Get your mind loosened up on the way so you will have one less demand on your time when you get to the course.

Planning Your Time
at the Course

Plan on getting to the course 90 minutes before your tee time, allowing plenty of time for getting your equipment together and yucking it up with your friends before your official warm-up begins in earnest. This little extra time will also give you a chance to acclimate to the situation.

The Warm-up Sequence

With 75 minutes or so remaining, warm up in the following sequence.

1. Putting—Test the speed of the greens on some expansive, flat area of the practice putting green. Then, locate a hole with a relatively level surface around it and knock in a few short putts. Be sure to take the little pin out of the hole and line up each putt. A careful warm-up is the only thing that will adequately prepare you for the carefulness that will soon be required during the round. Follow the short putts with a variety of long-putt/short-putt combinations, the kind that you will repeatedly face during the round.

In both cases, putt to some criterion (e.g., four short putts in a row, four combinations without a three-putt, etc.), in order to acclimate yourself to a bit of pressure. The time spent at the putting green should amount to 15 to 20 minutes.

2. *Short Game*—Proceed to the pitching/chipping green. Hit a few chip shots with your favorite club, gauging how far the ball is rolling after it flies a certain distance. Now make a series of chips, again to a criterion so you are not just slapping balls around without getting mentally focused. Repeat this procedure with pitch shots and sand shots, allowing again at least 15 to 20 minutes.

If you don't spend at least a few minutes before your round warming up, then you can expect to spend the first nine holes warming up out on the course.

3. *Full Shots*—Finally, it's off to the range with 30 to 50 balls. Remember, this is only a warm-up, not a wear-yourself-out practice session. Nor is it a contest to determine who can hit the most balls in the shortest period of time. Instead, you want to concentrate on each shot right from the beginning, being deliberate with alignment and using your usual pre-shot routine, just like you will be doing shortly out on the course.

Begin with several practice swings, perhaps with a weighted club, so you don't waste any balls loosening up. Then, start by swinging the short iron that you have the most confidence in. Follow that with the best mid-iron, then your favorite hybrid or fairway metal. Repeat the process with other short-iron/mid-iron/fairway-club combinations until you work through all the clubs.

Hit each club until one solid shot is obtained. If a solid shot with a club comes on the first swing, move onto the next club. Work the driver in as merely another club in the sequence, rather than as some special weapon. The "big dog" shouldn't get any favored treatment, just the same effort and tempo as your pitching wedge. For a low handicapper, this should be accomplished with 25 to 30 balls in another 15 to 20 minutes.

Now, with the last 10 to 20 balls, "play a few holes" (on the range), simulating actual holes out on the course. For example, if the tee shot on the first hole has trees down the right side of the fairway, set yourself up at the end of the range that actually has trees down the right side. Once you hit an acceptable drive (i.e., take it over until you get it right), pick a realistic target for the second shot on the imagined hole and hit that shot until you're comfortable. Repeat this process for two or three imaginary holes.

With the remaining balls, keep playing imaginary holes but now play your mistakes. That is, instead of taking the shots over until you get them right, figure out where a less-than-perfect shot might have ended up and then hit the follow-up shot that would be required. Don't hesitate to simulate a downhill lie in the rough, if necessary, by looking for a similar patch of grass on the edge of the practice tee that might afford you such a lie.

> *Invest a little time warming up before the round, and you may soon find yourself accruing big dividends beginning at the first tee.*

Conclude the full-shot warm-up by hitting one last tee shot that reflects the demands of the first hole. To more fully simulate the dreaded first-tee phenomenon with everyone watching, ask someone on the range to observe your last shot. Even if you don't hit it perfectly, you've got the feared bad shot out of your system, and your actual first tee shot will be a second chance to get it right. At the very least, you will have been observed, so it will not be such a shock to be watched by others as you begin your real round.

4. Retrace Your Steps—On leaving the range, stop back by the chipping/pitching green and hit one or two chips, pitches and sand shots in order to re-familiarize yourself with the feel of those shots. Don't worry about criteria this time. Just focus on the feel.

Lastly, throw down a ball on the practice putting green at a distance that might be required for your first putt on the first hole. Make a very serious effort to two-putt it—stepping off the distance, lining it up judiciously and taking all the time you will be taking on the first green. If you have time throw down a few more representative putts and repeat the procedure before you head to the first tee.

Brief Warm-up

Sometimes circumstances don't lend themselves to the ideal, complete warm-up described previously. You might be running late, your tee time might have been moved up or it may be a casual round. In these particular cases, consider the following options.

1. Selected Clubs—Select four clubs that present the greatest challenge for you—perhaps the lob wedge, the 5-iron, the 17-degree hybrid and the driver. Hit a few pitch shots with the lob wedge and full shots with all four clubs in the time available. Don't rush the shots. Better to hit a few quality shots than a whole bag of rapid misfires.

An even quicker alternative might be to select your two best clubs, perhaps the 3-wood and the 8-iron. A few shots with these old reliable friends may give your pre-round confidence a shot in the arm.

If you're really rushed, make a choice between your toughest club and your easiest club. The rationale for the former might be that if you can get your toughest club working, you ought to be able to hit anything. The rationale for the latter might be that since you only have a few swings to work with, you want to generate some positive images, rather than running the risk of introducing something negative right before you start your round.

2. Selected Shots—If you are limited to one shot in warming up, try the pitch shot. In addition to providing a manageable task that allows you a few solid contacts with the ball, the main advantage of the pitch shot is that its tempo is a good model for swinging every club in the bag.

Begin by hitting a few short pitches. Then, maintaining the same tempo, extend the swing a bit to hit longer pitch shots. Gradually, in the same tempo, square up your stance and hit what might be called full pitch shots—a swing that can be used for all full shots, from the wedge to the driver.

As you make your way to the first tee, keep saying to yourself that every shot is just a pitch shot. You'll be amazed at how effortlessly you'll play and how well the ball will respond to such a simple and rhythmic technique.

You might also try a few sand shots. The softness of the sand is nice when you are starting out a little stiff, and the resistance against the clubhead might serve to loosen you up a little faster than otherwise. The sand is also a good venue for easing into the relaxed tempo of the swing.

Treat your warm-up as an actual part of your golf game. If you were making an investment in the stock market, wouldn't you do a little research before plopping down your hard-earned money? A round of golf is also a sizable investment of time and effort. Therefore, doesn't it seem appropriate to prepare for this important event also?

Get ahead of the game. Don't waste nine holes reconstructing your swing keys from last time. Invest a little time warming up before the round, and you may soon find yourself accruing big dividends beginning at the first tee.

How to Play
the Mental Game
for 18 Holes

GOLFERS FREQUENTLY ASK, "JUST what is the mental game?" Curiously, when they observe themselves playing a round of golf, all they seem to grasp is the concrete physical things they are doing, even though mental events are always occurring simultaneously.

I recently had the occasion to play a serious match in which the mental game was very obvious to me. Indeed, without my awareness and manipulation of the mental game, the outcome of the match might have been quite different. Walk with me, if you will, through that match and see for yourself where the mental game entered in.

The Setting
The match involved the first round of a match-play competition. I was paired with a solid golfer of about my same age and physical ability. I was concerned because he was a more powerful player than me and was an intense competitor. I wasn't sure what gamesmanship might occur, but I knew I would have to stay focused for 18 holes if I was going to have a chance.

Game Plan

In the service of staying focused, I planned to talk as little as possible. I would respond minimally to whatever he offered in a cordial fashion, but I would initiate very little communication, if anything, and not participate in any type of needling.

Since he was exercising the option to ride in a cart while I opted to walk, I made up my mind from the outset that I would not let him rush me. In fact, while not intending to do so, I realized that my walking might slow his pace a bit and if anything throw him off his usual rhythm.

The Match

Hole #1—I won the toss, and my first tee shot was tentative and to the right, while he split the middle with a long one. From a bare lie I faded a 2-iron around some trees to the front fringe about 25 feet from the hole. He put his second shot on the green about 30 feet away. After he left his first putt short by about 7 feet on the slower than normal greens, the first notable mental action kicked in for me. First of all, I was relieved to have gotten this close to the hole from where I had left my drive. Now I have a chance to capitalize after his poor first putt. So, I'm thinking, "Just get it close and get your par." Unfortunately, I leave it 8 feet short and miss my putt. He makes his, and I'm 1 down with a grade of D for the mental game.

Hole #2—As I head for the tee on the par-3 second hole, I tell myself that tentative play isn't going to pay off. I have to go for it. So, after we both hit our tee shots on the green and he again leads off with a putt that falls well short, I make a critical mental move to go for the birdie, despite the fact that he may miss his short putt. I make the 18-footer for bird and experience a tremendous lift. The match is now all square.

Hole #3—I stroke a drive down the middle on this No. 1 handicap hole, while he hits his power hook into the lake. Still not quite loose, I dribble one up the fairway and in three shots end up on the back fringe, where my opponent also ends up in four shots. After he two-putts for a double bogey, I lag one down about 3 feet from the hole. Enter again the mental game.

This is the first important 3-footer of the day for me. It could set the tone for the match. I have to take my time, focus and make it. I do, and I'm now one up after three holes.

Holes #4 and #5—After routine pars for a halve on the fourth hole, I split the middle with a drive on the par-5 fifth hole. My opponent blocks it right in the roots of a dry creek bed. I'm thinking he's dead, but he makes a miraculous recovery and ends up in birdie range after his third shot.

Meanwhile, I'm hacking it around and end up hitting my fourth shot about 12 feet from the pin. After he just misses his birdie putt and makes par, I say to myself: "First, it looked like I had him in the bag on this hole. Now, it looks like he's got me. If I can knock in this par putt from 12 feet, it will take the wind out of his sails because he is thinking he has really stolen one here." So, I bear down, don't even look up to see the result and knock it in the cup for a halve. On to the sixth tee, still one up.

Hole #6—On six he knocks his drive in the trees again, while once again I'm in the garden spot with a perfect angle to the pin. But once again, he recovers, this time hitting the pin on one bounce for a gimme birdie to even the match.

Hole #7—By now, we are getting in our stride. We both hit the par-3 seventh in regulation, but he is 50 feet away and three-putts, while I win the hole with an easy two-putt from about 15 feet.

Holes #8 and #9—The last two holes on the front nine were somewhat uneventful, except for the minor fact that he won them both, finishing birdie-par to complete the front nine with yours truly down one for the match.

Between Nines

Now, between nines, is a critical time for the mental game. A must for me is to stay in the game and not be distracted. So, I go straight to the 10th tee and continue to stay focused on my swing thoughts and game plan, making occasional practice swings with the clubs I am likely to use on the next hole. In other words, I am already playing the 10th in my mind.

Back to the Match

Hole #10—Despite my best laid plans, I miss my drive, hit a weak chip and end up with a bogey on the easiest hole on the course. Fortunately, after his break between nines, my opponent blows one over the green and hands me a halve on the hole. So, I remain one down and feel relieved that I got away with one.

Hole 11—On the difficult par-4 11th, the wheels come off for me. Out of a fried-egg lie in the trap, I skull it over the green and make 7 from the woods. This quickly puts me two down for the match.

Hole #12—Now is where the mental game really begins. I had been thinking all along that if I could get to the 13th and 14th holes in good shape, I'd be in the driver's seat because there are big lakes down the left side on both holes, and he can't always control his hook. But now I'm two down after 11. I've lost three out of the last four holes, and if I lose the 12th, I'll be three down going into the 13th and 14th, which will take considerable pressure off his drives. I've got to win the 12th, so I make up my mind that I am going to quit watching him altogether, play my own game and see if I can scrape out a par on this long par 3. I succeed, but it takes a downhill 15-footer for par to accomplish the feat.

Hole #13—So, low and behold, here I am on the 13th tee only one down instead of the envisioned three. However, the script once again goes awry when I bail out to the right away from the lake but into the rough, while my opponent splits the middle. What the heck happened to his power hook into the lake? After I smothered one from a sidehill lie out of heavy rough into the same lake that wraps around in front of the green, I end up with a double-bogey. He manages only a bogey, but that was still good enough to take back his two-hole advantage.

Hole #14—Now I am two down with five holes to go, but I'm thinking, "He has won two out of four holes on the back nine, and he hasn't had so much as a par. Indeed, I've only made one par back here, but that was good enough for a win. If I can just start making pars, I think I can still win this thing. So. I recommit myself to not watching him play, and I say to myself, "Just stay down and hit the fairway, put it on the green in regulation and get your par. Bobby Jones said that they'll all crack if you just keep throwing pars at them. Let's try it. If he can do better, then the match is his."

I also abandoned all swing thoughts about this time, since they already had abandoned me several holes earlier. From this point on, I was just going to visualize a favorable result down the center of the fairway, on the green and into the hole. I also was going to intensely entertain this image before I ever looked to see the result on any shot.

Well, my opponent cooperated, and this time he bailed out into the trees away from the lake. I did find the fairway on both my first and second shots on the par 5 and ended up with a routine par for the win.

Hole #15—Now just one down going into the 15th. I again found the perfect angle down the right side of the fairway, while he once again shied away from the trouble to the left with a drive into the trees on the right. Of course, I didn't know that until we got there because, remember, I truly was not watching his shots. After he chipped back into the fairway, I carved a 4-iron to a pin tucked behind a trap from where I sank a treacherous downhill 22-footer for birdie to even the match.

Holes #16 and #17—Nice pars by both of us at the par-3 16th sent us to the 17th tee all even. From there each of us put our drives in play. He hit the green in two, while I totally missed my second shot and left it up against the cart path with a bunker between me and a tight pin placement. Now, I could have justified a drop from the cart path, but I had a lie that was sitting up and a little uphill, and I needed to get the shot up if I was going to have any chance of stopping it within 25 feet of the hole. So, I played the lie, hit a full cut shot and got it within the 25-foot objective.

But I was lying 3 to his 2, and his first putt ended up within 3 feet to make things worse. I had to make this putt, but I left it 6 inches short. I'm now preparing myself to go down the 18th one down, when he misses his 3-footer, the only short putt we missed between us all day. Quite a lift at a critical juncture in the match.

Hole #18—So, here we are on the 18th tee all even. And I am very lucky to be so, although I have done pretty much what I planned to do starting back on the 14th hole. We both hit our drives in perfect position. Once again I lay my second shot on the par 5 up the middle. My opponent blocks his right, but again I don't know the exact result because I'm still refraining from watching him. I put my wedge on the green, and when I get up there I find that he has recovered beautifully again. His birdie putt from 25 feet hangs on the lip, and he has to settle for par. Now the match is mine if I can make a downhill 10-footer for bird. I lip it out, and we go to extra holes.

Hole #19—Well, to make an already long story a little bit shorter, my opponent chops up the first extra hole, while I continue to stay with my closing game plan and par the hole for the victory. On the mental side, during the playoff I did draw on the memory of past successes in sudden-death, where I'm fortunate to have an almost perfect record.

Debriefing

The round ended graciously as it started with the reward of knowing that we played an intense, hard-fought match. There was not one rule infraction, no undue gamesmanship—only pure golf. I've always had three objectives when I play a match: 1) play well, 2) have a good match and 3) win. On this day, I gave myself a B on the first, with A's on the second and third.

Regarding the mental game, I was quite proud of myself for having a good game plan and being disciplined enough to stay with it. I also was adaptive enough to make changes when necessary and to endure until the end. The one thing that stood out the most was that despite a less than perfect physical game on this given day, the mental game carried me through. And, therefore, I offer this as an example of just what the mental game is in a round of golf.

EIGHT SECRETS FOR BETTER COURSE MANAGEMENT

C OURSE MANAGEMENT INCLUDES JUST about everything you do on the golf course other than swinging the club. For example, the mental game contributes enormously to how you manage a round. Understanding the rules allows you to take advantage of all your options when critical decisions are to be made. Time management protects you from the distraction of rushing to catch up.

Course management even involves style and demeanor. The manner in which you play the game and the aura conveyed while navigating the course communicate volumes to others and can, in turn, affect your play. Ultimately, all of the above converges into a game plan, which is a blueprint for course management.

Devise a Game Plan

Elite athletes report that they consistently prepare and adhere to disciplined game plans. Those game plans involve an ideal strategy for proceeding from the beginning to the end of the contest, and also include contingency plans for obstacles that might arise under less than ideal conditions.

Evidence of such detailed planning came in the 2001 Women's U.S. Open where post-round interviews revealed how the leaders had a game plan, stuck to it and climbed to the top of the leaderboard.

In contrast, problems with the game plan appear to have occurred earlier in the year at San Diego when Frank Lickliter declined to play safe after his opponent, Phil Mickelson, drove his ball into trouble on the third playoff hole. One might have assumed that Lickliter would have had a component in his game plan that suggested playing conservatively when his opponent shot himself out of a hole. Such a strategy might have saved him from driving his own ball into trouble and the eventual loss of the tournament. Of course, Lickliter's snafu was nothing compared to that of Jean Van de Velde on the 72nd hole of the 1999 British Open.

Devising a detailed game plan takes a lot of work and thus is not the daily fare of the amateur player. The typical recreational athlete just wants to get out there and play. But without thorough consideration of strategy, a golfer is likely to fall victim to poor decisions in the heat of the action.

Make Strategic Decisions

The best strategic decisions are based on knowledge, which in the case of golf refers to knowledge about yourself, your equipment and the golf course.

Yourself—Most people are aware of their strengths, but good course management also requires an acceptance of personal limitations. Ask a golfer how far he hits a drive and the common response is 250-plus yards. That's a long ways! Just think, if you hit every drive 250 yards, you regularly would be hitting a 7- or 8-iron into 400-yard par 4s. A more realistic assessment of driving distance on a flat, soft fairway with no wind, even for a lower handicapper, is about 230 yards in the air with a few additional yards of roll—and that's still a nice drive!

The point here regarding course management is that if you know and accept your typical driving distance, you can swing within yourself and hit more typically good drives. The macho alternative of swinging from your heels and knocking the ball all over the place lends itself to very poorly managed rounds.

Equipment—Even more important in making strategic decisions is knowledge of the distances that all your other clubs hit the ball in the air. This mandate extends from the 3-wood all the way to the shortest of pitch shots. This knowledge alone allows you to select the right club and commit to the shot without the tentativeness that follows from uncertainty about club selection.

I'm sure you've stood at the edge of a lake wondering whether a 3-wood was enough club, only to over-swing and dunk it in the water. That result may not have happened if the calculation had been made that the carry over the water was 190 yards, and you knew that your typical 3-wood shot flew 210 yards in the air.

Or how about looking at a sand wedge into a green and thinking that it is too much club, with the result that you decelerate and hit the shot fat. This wouldn't have happened if you had known the carry was 70 yards, the precise distance you hit a full sand wedge.

Golf Course—Wise decisions also are based on intimate knowledge of the environment, which is why players have a much easier time managing their home course. Yet skilled players still manage to survive on unfamiliar venues because they take advantage of all the information available to them.

The best source of course knowledge is gained from playing practice rounds. When practice rounds aren't possible, knowledge might still be accrued from walking portions of the course, studying the scorecard or reflecting on a yardage book in sketching out a game plan.

Consider comparing unfamiliar holes at the new course to familiar holes at your home course in terms of yardage, shape and design. Then, apply how you play the old familiar holes to the new ones you are about to face. Another tactic is to pay close attention to yardage markers and to be objective in trusting those yardages when choosing clubs. Most importantly, play conservatively for the middle of the fairways and greens, avoiding temptations to cut doglegs and go for pins until you are a little more familiar with the course.

Play Percentage Golf

Choose to play shots that offer the highest percentage for success. For example, if you are facing a tight driving hole, consider hitting the tee shot with a fairway wood or long iron, giving up a little distance to increase the chances of keeping the ball in play. The pros on tour gear down in this fashion more often than viewers realize. In the 2001 U.S. Open, it was estimated that Tiger Woods' game plan might call for hitting the driver only four times per round.

Consider playing for the side of the fairway that affords the easiest approach to the green. If a bunker guards the right side of the green and the flagstick is behind the bunker, select a club that will enhance your chances of approaching the green from the left side of the fairway, thereby providing a friendly opening to the well-guarded flagstick.

If you are better at hitting full 9-irons than half-wedges into greens, consider laying up on par 5s to a distance that accommodates your full 9-iron shot. A full 9-iron to 20 feet from the pin is a lot better than a chunked half-wedge to a bunker in front of the green.

When in trouble, take your medicine and ensure escape. Don't try to bite off too much at the risk of leaving yourself in the same trouble or

Measuring Course Management

If you are going to get serious about course management, it will be necessary to monitor your progress in this department.

For the sake of an example, a scratch golfer who skillfully manages a round would expect to be on each green in regulation, followed by two putts on each green. If a green were missed in regulation, then the expectation would bet to chip close and one-putt. Of course, the scratch golfer does not accomplish such a feat every time he plays, and one of the reasons is poor course management leading to extra shots beyond those described above.

A simple way for the scratch golfer to measure these extra shots would be to award a point for each green in regulation, as well as a point for each one-putt green. Subtract the total of these points from the number of strokes over par, and the difference would be the extra strokes wasted during the round—a rough measure of course management. The above formula could accommodate less-skilled golfers by simply adjusting the criteria for the measures mentioned.

Of course, extra strokes might also come from bad luck, difficult conditions or being out of practice on basic skills. But if the extra strokes are coming from drives out of the fairway because of improper club selection, unfavorable angles on approach shots resulting from an overly aggressive strategy, or three-putt greens caused by poorly placed long putts, then you can bet the culprit is course management.

worse. Get out of the situation and try to make up the stroke with a solid pitch shot or a well-stroked putt, as opposed to trying some high-risk shot from among the thistles, tree trunks or overhanging branches.

Balance Patience
with Courage

Course management involves an interesting mix of patience and courage. Patience epitomizes the front nine where matches are seldom won but frequently lost. The player who goes for broke right off the first tee may indeed be broke by the ninth green, while the player who patiently goes for the safe side of the fairway and middle of the green is likely to be ahead or well within striking distance when the turn is made.

Once you are on the back nine with the holes running out, courage might be necessary in taking some risks required for victory. As the maxim goes at Augusta, "The Masters doesn't begin until the back nine on Sunday," which has been the theater for many courageous heroics over the years.

Ultimately, whether with patience or courage, skilled course management comes down to placing the ball around the course as in a chess game. At first, the placement is patient and conservative. But as the game wears on, courage must be called upon to move in for the kill or to take some chances just to stay alive. However, the overall strategy is best considered beforehand when you can think clearly about your options, instead of trying to figure them out with the contest on the line.

Pace Yourself

Course management can be thrown into chaos if you try to concentrate on too much at one time, as in trying to play the entire 18 holes on the first tee box. Pace yourself. Begin by planning exclusively for the first tee shot. Once you are past that, have a plan ready for the first three holes, then the next three holes and so on for the entire round.

There may also be special plans for troublesome holes that should be adhered to no matter whether you have played poorly or fabulously up to that point. It is often tempting to cast the best-laid plans to the wind under extreme duress or irrational exuberance. Anyone who follows the stock market will recognize this pitfall and know that the same caveat applies to golf.

The main point is to let the game plan unfold over the course of the round, stick with it and don't try to execute something that can't be done until you get there. Pace yourself, and the game will prove to be more manageable than you think.

Understand the Rules

Course management requires knowing your options. In this regard, the rules can be as much a friend as a foe. For example, knowing where to drop the ball from an unplayable lie might save several shots. I was playing with someone recently who faced an unplayable lie and took the option of returning to the spot from which the original ball was last played, a choice that left him with the same obstacle in his way that resulted in the unplayable lie in the first place. Had he considered the rule more thoroughly, he might have taken the option of keeping the spot of the unplayable lie between him and the hole and dropping back as far as he wanted on that line, thereby allowing him an open shot to the hole that avoided the initial obstacle.

Manage Your Time

Course management and time management complement each other beautifully. Course management contributes to time management in that having a game plan prepared beforehand saves time when it comes to making last-minute decisions. Conversely, time management contributes to course management in that being ready to play eliminates rushing, which can only be a distraction when it comes to good course management.

Consider the following tips regarding time management as you prepare to play:

• Whether walking or riding, get to your ball as soon as possible. It is only at the site of the next shot that you will be able to check the lie, the wind and the distance; clear loose impediments; consider your options on how to hit the shot; and ultimately select the proper club, align yourself and be ready to play. In other words, you can't fully manage the situation until you get there.

• The same thinking applies to putting. While your playing companions are preparing and executing their putts, assess the distance and line of your putt, remove loose impediments and repair ballmarks as much as possible without distracting other players, and take a few practice strokes so you are ready to spring into action when your turn arrives.

• Don't let carts or scorekeeping slow you down. Park your cart where it allows for a quick exit from the green and mark the scores down at the next tee while others are preparing their tee shots. Also, after you play a shot from the fairway, jump in the cart with your club. You can clean it and place it in your bag while your partner is engaged in his equipment duties at the site of his next shot. Efficiency is far better than rushing when it comes to course management.

• Take responsibility for your own game rather than everyone else's. Find your own ball before helping others look for theirs. Attend to your own performance rather than giving lessons to others. Get ready to initiate your pre-shot routine rather than watching and commenting on the complete flight and outcome of the shot that immediately precedes yours.

These suggestions are not made simply with regard to etiquette. They are made in the service of course management. The more time you create for yourself on the course through efficiency, the more time you have to deliberately manage your round and avoid careless mistakes. If you put yourself in situations where you have to rush, course management will definitely suffer.

Control Your Emotions

Lastly, how you handle yourself when playing is an aspect of course management that should not be overlooked. Your style might be dignified and reserved like Ben Hogan and Bernhard Langer, swashbuckling and daring like Arnold Palmer and Greg Norman, playful like Lee Trevino and Chi Chi Rodriguez, intense and fiery like Tiger Woods, or polite and gentlemanly like Phil Mickelson. Which particular demeanor you possess is not as important as the fact that you are in control of yourself.

Many a great player, from Bobby Jones to Tiger Woods, has had to battle his temper, but none became great players until they conquered that demon. When emotions take over and your demeanor starts to distract you, self-control is lost and course management is the victim.

GAIN CONTROL
OF YOUR GAME

Learn to Place the Ball

GOLF IS NOT A game of distance. It is not even a game of accuracy. Golf is a game of placement. It's like chess—thinking moves ahead, finding the best spot to locate the ball so you can reach your objective while encountering the least resistance.

Consider the following: The long hitter can actually hit it too far at times, with the ball ending up through the dogleg or too close to the green for a comfortable full swing on the approach shot. That's assuming, in the first place, that the ball stays in play. The straight shooter, on the other hand, might be so hung up on straightness that he doesn't swing freely enough to get adequate distance. The straight hitter also might be accurate, but to the wrong spot. Distance and accuracy are worthless unless the ball ends up in a wisely chosen place that contributes to the overall game plan.

Thinking in terms of placement changes the whole game. Golf should be played in a more controlled fashion with a smooth, repeating swing. Golfers should play within themselves and play smart. There should be a feeling of knowing where the ball is going at all times.

Placing the ball takes pressure off the swing because the ball is fed to a certain spot, as opposed to being banged somewhere. It's a kinder, gentler manner of play applying to drives as much as to chips and putts. Thinking in terms of placement puts golfers more in control of their games.

Golf's Simple Formula

Golf actually has a very simple formula: 1) Drive the ball somewhere in the fairway; 2) Stroke the approach shot somewhere on the green; 3) Ease the first putt somewhere in the vicinity of the hole; 4) Firm the short putt in the hole.

> *Golfers should play within themselves and play smart. There should be a feeling of knowing where the ball is going at all times.*

Unfortunately, golfers tend to do things other than what is dictated by this simple framework. Distance and accuracy are obsessions, as discussed above. In addition, golfer's minds are on automatic: When they are on the tee, out comes the driver every time. If it's an approach shot, automatically go for the pin. For a pitch shot, loft it in there. And for the 30-foot putt, ram it at the hole at all costs.

Automatic is great for a repeating swing, but it's no way to handle the strategy side of the game. Golf offers many choices, and all the alternatives should be considered in playing golf as a game of placement.

Endless Choices

The Tee Shot—The driver is, of course, one of your options. But other possibilities include the fairway woods and the long irons. The key consideration is the location from which you want to hit the next shot (i.e., which side of the fairway, how far from the green). Another consideration is the percentage way to get to that spot (i.e., which club feels most comfortable and what shape of shot is the hole begging for). The answers to these questions dictate the placement of the tee shot on the hole.

The Approach Shot—The approach to the green affords, perhaps, the greatest number of choices. The first consideration involves the risk/reward ratio for going directly at the pin vs. the middle of the green. Next, if the shot happens to be struck less than perfectly, which side of the green is more friendly for a follow-up pitch or chip shot? Is it possible that laying up in front of the green for an easy chip might be the percentage way to play, considering the hazards around the green? Which level of the green will leave the easiest approach putt? What kind of shot (club and shape) feels most comfortable? The answers to these questions produce the placement decision for this particular shot.

Pitch or Chip Shot—Once again, alternatives present themselves. Should this shot be run up or flown in? Which club feels most comfortable for producing the shot? Where do you want the ball to land on the green before its smooth roll to the hole? If the ball doesn't go in, where is the best place for it to come to rest?

The Long-approach Putt—The key issue here is giving the ball a chance to go in the hole, while at the same time ensuring the success of any second attempt. The choices have narrowed down to the putt's speed and break. When there is indecision in this regard, playing more break (with less speed) is likely to result in a more favorable outcome than vice versa.

Of course, a successful outcome should always be visualized, but it's still prudent to consider the position from which one would like to attempt a short second putt, if such a putt becomes necessary. That position will probably be a place on the green that produces a flat or slightly uphill putt. It's also worth remembering that a putt that rolls slightly past the hole not only has had a chance to go in, but also provides information on the line of the return putt.

The bottom line is to choose a type of putt that feels comfortable in meeting a combination of the above placement demands. Anything less will result in an unconfident, tentative stroke that is unlikely to meet with success.

The Short Putt—Most of the time a short putt will benefit from a firm stroke into the back of the hole. However, if the putt is ticklish and will gravely punish the player if the firm effort is missed (e.g., a fast, downhill, breaking 3-footer), there is nothing wrong with allowing for a little break and letting the ball fall in whatever side of the cup it ultimately finds. Still, there must be an element of firmness and conviction to whatever line has been decided upon.

Note that most of the above choices relate to placing the ball in certain strategic areas on the way to its ultimate destination—the hole. This is placement golf, a way of playing that gives you more control over your game.

Developing a
Placement Game

1. Build a Strong, Repeating Swing—Such a swing probably will be simple and compact with minimal moving parts. The more complex the swing, the more that can go wrong on the way to placing the shot. Simplicity, on the other hand, will be more likely to hold up under pressure, repeat itself over the long haul and allow for controlled placement of the ball.

2. Learn Distances—Precisely calculate how far a smoothly struck ball will travel for every club and shot in the bag. This is tedious, dedicated work, but it is the price of being able to play placement golf. You can't reliably get the ball to specific places on the course if you don't know the precise distances that the various clubs produce. This knowledge comes from physically going out and stepping off distances. Of course, these distances will be more consistent when generated by a solid, repeating swing.

3. Refine Shot Alignment—Alignment is important not only for the obvious aiming of the shot in the desired direction, but also for enabling you to make a confident swing through the ball. That is, misalignment seems to result in the body instinctively trying to correct the misalignment by distorting the swing, which makes control of the shot even more difficult. In short, proper alignment encourages a proper swing toward the place where you are trying to strike the ball.

4. Practice Considering Choices—Making proper placement choices does not occur automatically. It comes from practice, which initially should be done solo on an uncrowded course where adequate time can be taken pondering the alternatives each shot presents. Consider writing down the alternatives and your ultimate decisions and reviewing each situation after the round to see if any patterns emerge as to which ones worked and which ones didn't. With practice, considering all the choices will soon become quick and routine.

5) Play Percentage Golf—Pick safe, reasonable landing areas based on consideration of all the choices. Swing within yourself using a club and shape of shot that feels comfortable to you in the given situation. Calmly accept the result and repeat the procedure from the next ball position without overreacting to whatever happened on the previous shot. Become a decision-making, shotmaking machine, methodically placing the ball at strategic locations around the course en route to your ultimate goal—the lowest score possible on that given day.

Lesson #36

STAYING WITH
A BAD ROUND

G OLF CAN SEEM FAIRLY routine when cruising along in the comfort zone. For example, a 15-handicapper is in his element when he's on a run of straight bogeys. But give him a day when he starts off with three pars, and he begins to feel the old lump in the throat. *This could be the day*, he thinks, and all of a sudden the cruise is over. For the next 15 holes he has a new psychological challenge: Is he mentally tough enough to keep a good round going?

At the other end of the comfort zone is the day when the 15-handicapper starts off with three straight double bogeys. Now the cruise seems more like a ship about to sink before it gets out of the harbor. Instead of the lump in his throat, he experiences anger and frustration. While a rough start may not seem as exciting as one that opens with three pars, it also presents a mental challenge that may be equally important to the golfer in the long-range development of a sound mental game.

First of all, it's unfortunate but true that golfers are more likely to encounter bad starts than good starts. Players often rush out to the course insufficiently warmed up for the round, leading to less than fluid shots on the early holes. At other times they may be playing with a new group about which they feel a little nervous, requiring a few holes to calm down. Whatever the circumstances, most days it takes a golfer a little while to settle into the round and get into the flow of his or her usual game.

Major golf tournaments like the U.S. and British Opens afford us the rare opportunity to see the pros struggle with this phenomenon. With these tournaments on television, we not only get a chance to see the players playing well and finishing strong, but we also get to suffer with them through the early hole jitters that often lead to poor shots and three-putts on the opening holes. But the pros have learned to rise above these rough starts, to stay with the round, hang in there, steady themselves and finish with a respectable score. This ability is what makes them successful pros and what can make you a better amateur.

The Temptations to
Bail Out of a Bad Round

The biggest problem with being caught up in a bad round is that golf is no fun. You find yourself looking at four hours of drudgery on a day that was supposed to be enjoyable. This state of affairs can lead to one of three escape mechanisms:

1. The quickest way out is to quit after nine holes or even sooner by just walking off the course. This is problematic if you have a match going with other golfers, and even more problematic for your own personal development because you have deprived yourself of an opportunity to deal with the adversity that the game so often presents.

2. Another way to end the pain is to give up and quit trying. You play out the round with a look of disgust on your face or mess around and act silly in an attempt to communicate to others that you really don't care. "How I play is no big thing," you try to convey. The problem is that nobody believes you. You don't even believe yourself.

3. The more subtle way to bail out of a bad round, particularly if you aren't embroiled in a formal match, is to quit keeping score and start hitting practice balls. Certainly, practice is to be encouraged. However, on this given day you had set out to practice shooting a score, and you abandoned that objective. Swinging the golf club and generating a score are somewhat distinct skills, and both have to be practiced at appropriate times. Staying with a bad round is one of the best opportunities for practicing the scoring side of the game.

How to Stay with a Bad Round

Since the biggest problem with a bad round is that golf has ceased to be fun, it stands to reason that the solution lies in how to make the round fun again. To be more specific, how can you inject meaning, challenge and interest back into the round? Consider the following:

1. Get your swing back on track. While producing low numbers for the scorecard is proving difficult at the moment, you can at least start making a few good passes at the ball. See if you can just hit one pure shot. Can you hit one shot the way it's supposed to be hit, no matter what the result? Forget the outcome for a moment, concentrate on your swing keys and just try to hit some good shots. If nothing else, you will be practicing something constructive for the next round.

2. Find some goal to shoot for during the remainder of the round. See if you can make one par before you worry about the rest of the holes. Or can you make a birdie on one of the remaining holes? Could this possibly be your day for a hole-in-one? There are still a number of par -3s left. Sometimes holes-in-one occur in the midst of the worst of rounds. Wouldn't you hate to miss your day by giving up? Consider what a famous baseball pitcher once suggested to his professional golfing partner when the latter got down during a bad round in a pro-am: "Pretend this next hole is the first hole of tomorrow's round." How about the next six holes being the first six of your next round?

3. Keep the score, at least, respectable. You may be off to a bad start, but three double bogeys is only three strokes higher than the three bogeys you usually start off with. Therefore, if you get back on track right now with bogeys and a few pars, you will only shoot three strokes higher by the end of the day than you would have shot anyway. So, your usual 85 becomes an 88. Big deal! A score in the 80s is respectable. What you want to avoid is the alternative of just letting the round get totally out of hand and turning a very achievable 80s score into an unacceptable score over the century mark.

4. See if you can win even when playing poorly. Pro golfers win tournaments even when they are not at the top of their games. They just know how to win, how to score or how to keep it together enough to get the job done even when they have to scratch and claw to do it. Ben Hogan, Arnold Palmer and Jack Nicklaus did not become legends by giving up when the

game became a struggle. They just found another way to survive and win on that given day.

When Lee Trevino had back surgery near the end of 1994 and couldn't hit a 4-iron any farther than he usually hit an 8-iron, he relished the opportunity to go out and beat his fellow competitors with his short game. In other words, he turned the struggle into a challenge and actually found a way to enjoy it. In validation of his positive attitude, he came back and won two tournaments when he returned to the tour in 1995.

Lesson #37

HOW TO GET
YOUR HEAD BACK
IN THE GAME

WHEN REFLECTING ON ALL the things that can go wrong in a round of golf, Walter Hagen said he was fortunate to realize early in his career that he was not a machine. He would hit many a shot like those of a beginner, but he couldn't let that bother him if he intended to persist and win matches and championships.

Golf is certainly not a game of perfection. Rather, it is a game of managing imperfection. Ben Hogan said he hit only a couple of perfect shots in any given round, and yet those rounds still led to scores around par. That would mean even his par rounds were made up of a bunch of imperfect shots. Good thing Hogan, like Hagen before him, didn't let imperfection bother him.

Make an Unplayable Lie
Your Friend

As an example of the kind of thinking that can get you through imperfection during a round, consider the following medal-play competition I had with a friend. The fact that it was medal play is important because with medal play (versus match play), if you let a bad break get to you, multiple strokes can be lost on one hole, as opposed to just losing the hole.

As events unfolded, we were all even after nine holes, having had a tight front side where neither of us could break away for a lead. On the par-4 10th hole, my drive found some shrubbery about halfway down the fairway. With the ball unplayable and no favorable place to drop, my best option was to crawl into the shrubs and bump the ball out backward and back into play. Meanwhile, my opponent had split the fairway with his drive. He was threatening to pick up maybe two strokes on the hole, which called for some quick adaptive thinking to keep myself in the hole and the match.

Naturally, my initial thoughts were of potentially losing two shots. However, I considered that if I could hit my third shot somewhere in the proximity of the hole, he'd experience extra pressure to hit his close to pick up two shots on the hole. If I could actually stick my ball close enough to knock in the putt and all he managed was a routine par, that would kill him since he would walk away with nothing, instead of the previously anticipated two-shot lead that looked very likely when my ball was unplayable in the shrubbery.

As it turned out, I did hit my ball to about 10 feet. He followed with a shot to about 12 feet, missed his birdie try and then watched my 10-footer drop for par. He gained nothing on the hole, felt helpless to get a lead and eventually faded as I went on to win the competition.

In looking back, we both had to agree that the 10th hole was the turning point in the match. Curiously, I was actually better off having had the misfortune of an unplayable lie. If I had made a routine par like my opponent did, no momentum swing would have occurred. But with my unexpected recovery from the unplayable lie, he was deflated, I was invigorated, and the match was virtually mine after that.

Other Situations Requiring Adaptive Thinking

Adaptive thinking calls for finding hidden value in less than desirable circumstances, rather than just wallowing in misfortune and imperfection. Following is a list of difficult situations, each with a suggestion of how to think yourself through them constructively.

A Difficult, Unfamiliar Course—"A round of golf is always a challenge,

but this one is really going to be an adventure. The course is not only difficult, but I am also unfamiliar with it. I remember that Arnold Palmer shot
86 the first time he played St. Andrews. If Arnie can struggle like that, I
know I have to be reasonable about my present expectations. Indeed, it
will be quite an accomplishment if I can shoot 10 shots over my handicap—five for the extra difficulty of the course and five more for the unfamiliarity. To improve my chances for success, I'll avoid unnecessary risks
and just keep the ball in play."

Even the pros miss 50 percent of their 5-footers.

Your Scores and Handicap Aren't as Low as You'd Like—"Indeed, I
would like my scores to be lower, but good reasons exist for why they are
not. First, I'm not a pro. I don't practice and play every day, and I live for
more than just golf. Secondly, I play by the rules and count all my strokes.
If I took two drives off the first tee and gave myself 3-foot putts, I'd have
lower scores, too. Lastly, golf is difficult. Legitimate low scores are hard to
come by. According to the late Harvey Penick, the average score in golf
would be more than 100 if everybody played by the rules and actually
counted all their strokes. So, all in all, I ought to be quite happy that I
score as well as I do. On the brighter side, with a little more practice and
commitment to improvement, I bet I can lower my handicap to a more
respectable level."

A Tight Driving Hole—"This is a hole where brains will win out over
brawn most every time. Just put the ball in play, even if it requires hitting
a 5-iron off the tee. Get the second shot up around the green and take your
chances with an up and down to get the par. Let the others air it out with
the driver and flirt with disaster off the tee. I'll take a sure bogey (and
maybe a scrambling par) and move onto the next friendlier hole with my
round still intact."

A Shot in Trouble on the First Hole—"So, I made a bad decision and
got myself in trouble early in the round. This could be the start of just
another lousy score, or it could be an opportunity for a great comeback
that might have never happened if I hadn't duck-hooked that first drive. If
I can just get the ball back into play and somehow make bogey, I'll still
have plenty of holes left to shoot a good score. Considerable pride will also

be experienced in that I didn't give up early in the round. Just think, if every player in history who was down in a contest had given up, none of the great comebacks we love to remember would have happened. This may be the chance for my great comeback. I'd sure hate to give up and miss the occasion."

A Treacherous Chip Shot You Want to Get Close—"I'd like to get this close, but a chip to gimme distance is only one way to get up and down. Pars are also made with 10-foot putts. The one thing I want to be sure of is getting the ball safely up on the green, rather than be chipping again, as could easily be the case if I don't get the shot up there. In short, I have two ways to make par, and I'll have a sure bogey on the card if the par attempts fail. A careless double bogey, however, is not an option."

Not Hitting Enough Greens in Regulation—"Hitting greens is a noble goal, but the fact remains that even the statistical leaders on the PGA Tour still miss five to six greens per round. Yet they manage to shoot scores of par or better, which suggests that a whole lot of scrambling is going on out there. Golf is anything but routine (i.e., a drive in the fairway, an approach on the green and two putts for par). Instead, golf involves getting the ball in the hole in various ways from a variety of situations in which you find yourself. So, quit worrying about the greens in regulation. Hit the ball, go find it and hit it again. There is no required way to par a hole or shoot an even-par round. Just get the ball into each hole as soon as possible and see where the score ends up."

Missing Short Putts—"These 5-footers are driving me crazy! But then I'm told the pros make only 50 percent of their 5-footers. It sure doesn't seem like it on TV, but that's because all they show are the leaders, the guys who are playing exceptionally well that week. If the whole field was televised, including those missing the cut, we'd see a lot more missed 5-footers. What's hard to realize is that short putts are difficult, just like everything else in the game. Without a commitment to practicing them, I may have to accept missing as many or more than I make."

Playing a Hustler Who Is an Expert at Applying the Needle—"Oh, great! I'm playing Nick the Needle. Well, I'm just going to play my own game, not his. I can't compete with his mouth or personality, but I can compete with him through my play. One strategy I'll try is staying away from him. If that doesn't work, then I'll try to ignore what he says. Perhaps I'll even agree with him or compliment him. That should be disconcerting, since he's not accustomed to receiving that kind of reaction. The bottom line is that I am a gentleman, and I'm not going to change, particularly for someone whose own character is suspect."

You're in the Semifinals of the Club Championship—"Can you believe it? I'm down to the final four of the club championship. The question is do I belong here. Well, I've worked hard, played well and nobody handed me those first three matches. Furthermore, I even have one advantage—nobody expects me to beat my opponent and move onto the finals. The pressure is really on my opponent, who is expected to win easily. So, I'm just going to use the strategy that got me this far. I'll stay with my game plan and let the chips fall where they may."

The thinking in the situations described above is similar to that of Tom Kite in the days when he was the PGA Tour's leading money winner and leader in scoring average, yet saddled with the moniker "best to have never won a major." Kite reportedly said, "I hope to win majors, but it's not life and death. I have a good life. Christy (his wife) is pregnant, and she's feeling fine. Everything is going very well for me. If the majors come, they come. If they don't, things still are going very well for me." Of course, that major did come in the 1992 U.S. Open.

Lesson #38

What Every Player Wants

W HAT DOES EVERY GOLFER want—distance, direction, low score? No. What every golfer really wants is control—the feeling that he or she is going to make clean contact with the ball and be able to predict the general outcome of the shot.

Consider the following example. You are about to hit a tee shot on a par-3 hole. A hole-in-one is not likely to be the realistic expectation, nor is sticking the shot for a "gimme" birdie. Happiness would be merely teeing it up with the confidence that you can reliably make crisp, square contact with the ball and get it somewhere on the green for a reasonable run at birdie or an easy par.

In contrast, no worse feeling exists than to stand over the ball and have no idea where the shot may go. It's almost better to be assured of a slice or a duck hook, because then you can at least play for that malady or do something to correct it. Having no idea what's going to happen leaves you in an uncomfortable state of confusion that detracts considerably from the fun of the game.

The desire for control actually extends beyond the swing to include your emotions on the course as well. Living in constant fear that you are going to blow your stack makes you tense out of concern for ruining your day at any unforeseen moment. The golf course becomes a dreaded place, rather than a place to relax and have fun.

Rest assured that the ever-present issue of control reaches beyond golf to life, in general. We all want, need and deserve control of our lives for as long as possible. Therefore, to the extent-that golf mirrors life, the desire for control on the golf course should not be very surprising at all.

So let's explore control regarding the golf swing and our emotions on the course, along with a brief reflection on the role of control in life.

Putts

The smallest of swings—the putting stroke—would seem to offer the best opportunity for control. Yet we are all aware of the twitches that can occur during this little stroke, particularly the real little strokes very near the hole.

To enhance control while putting, keep swing keys and images as simple as possible. For example, a simple image for an abbreviated, accelerating stroke might be that of shuffleboard; with a short backstroke and shoving the ball toward the hole. A player using a longer stroke might envision the pendulum of a grandfather clock—back and through. The point is that control benefits from avoiding complicated thoughts and images.

Another perspective on simplicity in putting is to concentrate only on distance for long putts and direction for short putts. Keep the focus simple and where it belongs. It's much easier to control distance or direction if that is all you are thinking about.

Chip and Pitch Shots

As the swing gets longer with chip and pitch shots, control issues shift from the fine-tuning of the stroke to making crisp contact with the ball. To gain control over chunking or blading shots, develop a simple technique that offers the assurance of getting the clubhead back squarely to the ball.

Have you noticed how Vijay Singh puts the ball way back in his stance so that the club is coming down sharply on the ball? If the lie is tight, he may even address the shot with the ball situated on the target line but behind his right foot. Using this approach, Singh is almost assured of striking the ball first on his forward stroke.

Another approach that should provide better control is to set the angles of your arms and wrists before the shot, and maintain those angles throughout the stroke. Once the structure is set, all you do is rock your shoulders to bring the clubface down on the ball. Once again, simplification is occurring by setting the structure beforehand and then having to think of only one thing (rocking your shoulders) during the actual shot.

Full Shots

With full shots, the control issue moves beyond making good contact to moving the ball a reasonable distance in the general direction of the hole. This aspect of control heightens the involvement of the mental game.

For example, it may help to remember that any club, including the driver, is meant to hit the ball only a certain finite distance. Think of hitting each shot to a specific reasonable landing area, and you might be more likely to make a controlled swing. To "grip it and rip it" is likely to lead to control problems for the average golfer.

Control on full shots benefits from placing the ball around the course, as in a chess game. Constantly ask yourself where you want to be hitting the next shot from, which will indicate to you where you want to place the current shot.

A related control question would be which club and which shot trajectory will give you the greatest likelihood of accomplishing a particular placement of the ball. Get multiple factors working in your favor, and more confidence will be generated toward making a controlled swing.

One last thing to consider on full shots is that anything that reduces variability in the swing (i.e., the number of moving parts) will serve to increase control. The compact swings of Arnold Palmer and Doug Sanders may have looked funny, but there wasn't much that could go wrong with them. Extraneous movement was virtually eliminated.

Arnie once said that he didn't understand what was so difficult about the golf swing. "All you do is take the club back as slow as you can and bring it through as fast as you can."

He might have added that if you can do that with an abbreviated arc, you will have a reasonably simple and efficient swing.

It is worth noting that, in all of this instruction, the overriding principle is simplicity. Keep things as simple as possible and you will likely experience greater control.

The Emotions

Controlling your emotions is quite a different animal from controlling the swing, and there is nothing simple about this creature. It comes down to two things—considering what you are communicating to others when you let your emotions all hang out and learning how to talk to yourself in a way that calms you down.

> *In all of this instruction, the overriding principle is simplicity. Keep things as simple as possible and you will likely experience greater control.*

When your temper gets out of control while playing golf, the first thing you communicate to others is that you are beat—the game is beating you, the course is beating you, your opponent is beating you and you are most certainly beating yourself as you get more tense and distracted with each successive temper tantrum. It might help to remember what it looked like during childhood when a kid started crying in a fight. That kid was beat, even if he hadn't totally given up yet. Well, that's what it looks like on the golf course when anger takes over—a crybaby losing a fight.

Temper tantrums are also an attempt to say to others, "I'm a more talented player than is currently being demonstrated. The problem is that I can't actually demonstrate it, so I'll settle for trying to convince you by throwing a fit."

Of course, the truly skilled player will suck it up in the face of adversity and say to himself, "If everyone thinks this poor play is the real me, let them stick around for a few more shots and allow my clubs to do the talking. They'll see the true skill that my current play does not accurately represent."

Of course, handling your emotions reflects your level of maturity, something we all value to a high degree. People have long memories for immature behavior. An ill-timed emotional outburst on the golf course may later come back to haunt you in some far-removed social or business setting that has nothing to do with golf.

So what do you do to calm yourself down in the heat of the action? Consider the following examples of coping self-talk that may help you when you are about to lose your cool.

- "Good thing it was me who missed that little putt and not some-one of lesser skill. I can come back from it, while a lesser player couldn't keep it together."

- "I bet they think they've got me after that poor drive. Won't it take the wind out of their sails when I knock the heck out of this 3-wood and hit the green in regulation anyway."

- "I'm a mature individual, bigger than any game. My image is more important to me than winning on this given day. I'll have plenty of days to win, but I won't have many days where I can resurrect my image if I throw it away now."

- "Sometimes it is more impressive to face adversity, not give up and keep on playing with a professional demeanor than it is even to win. This may be an opportunity to serve as a model for others. They all know I'm high strung. So if I can keep it together, won't they be surprised, not to mention having to believe that they can do it, too?"

Another key tool for moving on after misfortune is to focus imme-diately on what you have to do on the next shot or hole. That is, if intense emotions can distract you from what you have to do (as is widely assumed), then it seems reasonable that focusing on what you have to do should be equally capable of distracting you from intense emotions.

Consider a basketball player missing a lay-up, getting mad and then immediately fouling someone going back down the court. If the player had focused on his precise defensive assignment right after the missed lay-up, then he might not have had time for the anger that led to the quick foul.

The same goes for golfers. A missed putt should be a cue for imme-diate focus on the game plan for the next hole. Fill your mind with thoughts of the next task at hand and anger won't have space to intrude.

Golf and the Game of Life

As with golf, life is all about control, too. We start out as infants, totally dependent on others and with little control over anything. It doesn't take long, however, before we are trying to exert control over our environment by crying and screaming for attention. The battle to extend our control becomes quite tumultuous during adolescence, even more serious during young adulthood and probably reaches its apex during the middle-aged years, when we expect to have the most control over our lives. Alas, the whole process of successful aging depends on maintaining as much control as we can over our lives for as long as possible.

As with golf, the key to staying in control for as long as possible is to keep matters simple. The more complicated we allow our lives to become, the harder it is to maintain control.

GAME IMPROVEMENT

With each new season, hope springs eternal: Surely this will be the year when my game really improves. "Preparing for the New Season," (Lesson #39) may be your best hope for getting off to a quick start.

Once you get rolling, consider "Seven Things You Can Do to Improve Your Scores and Lower Your Handicap" (Lesson #40). I personally took these steps over a five-month period and cut my handicap in half while doubling my winning percentage. You're going to want to take a look at this one!

In general, it's hard to make progress toward a goal if you don't know what the goal is. Lesson #41 explains "How to Reach Your Goals This Season" by setting reasonable and achievable, yet challenging goals that you will be motivated to pursue.

One thing to consider is more "Aggressive Play—When Going for the Pin Pays Off (Lesson #42), which may enable you to "Take Your Game to the Next Level" (Lesson #43). If you want to "Win Tournaments—Think Like a Champ" (Lesson #44).

Finally, just because the season is over doesn't mean there's any time to rest. "Stay Sharp in the Off-season" (Lesson #45), so you're ready for the next one, which is just around the corner. Get a head start on the new year and you won't have to begin again from square one.

Lesson #39

Preparing for the New Season

Seven Tips

THE GOLF SEASON IS rapidly approaching. Time to hit the ground running, shoot your career round and be on top of your game—all on the first day out of hibernation.

Wait a minute. Before putting all your stored-up potential back into action, pause a moment to formulate a plan for the new season—a plan that takes into account learning as well as motivation.

It should be emphasized that you need to consider both learning and motivation. For example, you can try to learn all you want from lessons, but unless you are truly motivated to become a better golfer and are willing to put in the necessary effort, your improvement will be limited.

On the other hand, you can be so motivated that you would trade half your life savings for a lower golf score, but unless you learn the proper technique, again you will see little improvement. So let's begin with a plan for learning and then take into consideration the motivational factors that will enhance your chances for perseverance and success in the new season.

Commit Yourself to
Getting Expert Advice

Some golfers never seem to improve. Usually in life when you do something repeatedly, you get better at it. But if you look back over the past 15 years, you'll probably remember quite a few golfers who had weird swings and couldn't break 100 back then, and today have the same weird swings and still can't break 100. Curiously, these same golfers will tell you that they play regularly, work at the game and heed the advice of others. They just happen to have a 36 handicap.

Now, if the truth were told, regular play for these non-improving golfers probably amounts to once a month. Working at the game refers to hanging around the driving range and hitting a few balls while yucking it up with their friends. The advice they get probably comes from fellow high-handicappers and results in substituting one swing flaw for another.

Therefore, the first thing to do to improve in the new season is to get expert advice. This will most likely come from a local club pro whom you are comfortable with and who fits your style of play. Identify that professional in your community and commit to an extended teaching relationship with him or her well into the new season.

Prepare for Lessons

Learning does not happen during lessons. Lessons provide a prescription as to what you have to learn. The learning itself takes place during hours of practice between lessons. The few attempts you try in the presence of the pro do not translate into permanent learning. Only your own repeated attempts between lessons will accomplish the permanent change you are seeking.

To take a lesson and not practice is like buying a product and not using it. In planning for spring training, be sure to allow ample time for practice sessions between lessons.

Practice takes time, and thus learning takes time. Be patient. Don't expect overnight miracles. Instead, look for gradual improvement over the span of the entire season by setting realistic seasonal goals, keeping records of your progress and looking for small gains. Furthermore, when one part of your game is lagging a bit (e.g., your ball striking), look for and appreciate the improvement you are making in other parts of the game (e.g., the short game).

Practice carefully so you learn the correct thing. You learn what you practice. It is as simple as that. However, you have to be careful not to inadvertently practice the wrong thing.

A classic example of practicing the wrong thing is practicing carelessly. That is, if you practice carelessly, you learn carelessness, when carefulness is what is actually required.

I'm always intrigued by golfers on the practice green who carelessly slap putts around while joking with their companions, hit several balls without reading the line on any of them and never bother to take the little pins out of the holes.

> *Commit to an extended teaching relationship with a local pro well into the new season.*

When the actual round starts and they get ready to hit their first meaningful putts, their brains receive a sudden jolt of reality—one ball, the pin out, no jokes from their playing companions and a putt to line up without the benefit of several previous putts to show them the line. Understandably, they panic. This is now a careful, measured situation, which is quite different from the careless, random activity they had been practicing in their pre-round warm-up.

This season carefully analyze the details of what you are trying to accomplish on the course, then make sure your practice regimen parallels the real situation as closely as possible. Don't waste time and delay your improvement by messing around during your valuable practice and warm-up sessions.

Build in Small but Complete Steps

The principle that you learn what you practice has far-reaching implications. For example, when you learn to type, the initial suggestion to type slowly and accurately sounds good, but only if you want to learn slow, accurate typing. If you want to achieve the ultimate goal of fast, accurate typing, there is no alternative but to type fast and accurately right from the beginning. This feat is quite readily accomplished by starting with small, easy steps (e.g., repeatedly striking "d" and "e" on the keyboard as fast as you can), and then adding increasingly difficult finger-letter combinations over time. The key is to do each little move correctly (as well as quickly and accurately) right from the beginning.

Jack Nicklaus understood this principle. When asked if, in teaching beginners, he would teach them to hit it hard first or hit it straight first, Nicklaus said he would teach them to hit it hard and straight. You can't separate the two aspects of a good golf shot—not even for beginners.

But how do you hit hard, straight golf shots right from the beginning? Just like with typing, it starts with small, manageable steps and gradually building the golf swing.

Ben Hogan's approach to teaching novices was to start them out on the putting green practicing short putts until that stroke was learned. Then he would shift them to gradually longer putts and chips. Later would come short pitches, short irons, and eventually longer clubs and shots in succession.

In this way, the golfer could build the swing in small steps, doing each component fully and completely right from the beginning.

It is well within anyone's capability to set a ball down 6 inches from the hole and hit it as hard and straight as will ever be necessary, squarely into the back of the cup. Indeed, anyone should be able to do this with absolute correctness from his first day of practice onward.

Whatever facet of the game you are practicing in the new season, break it down into its smallest components and then practice them in their complete form. Build a powerful full swing by starting with short pitch shots, attacking them with a strong and abbreviated stroke, and then gradually extend the stroke toward making a full swing.

Even the mental game can be built in small steps. You may not be ready for the full-blown pressure of tournament golf, but you can still create very real pressure for yourself on the practice green by saying you won't leave until you can make 18 short putts in a row. If you can indeed make 18 consecutive short putts, there's no reason to think you're ever due to miss a short putt anywhere in an 18-hole round. With this ability on the putting green, you're well on your way to matching your mental toughness against that of other golfers.

Distribute Your Practice

Cramming didn't work in school, and it doesn't work in golf either.

Learning occurs most efficiently when practice is distributed. If you have 10 hours to practice, the result will be better if you distribute those 10 hours over 10 days than if you mass them all into one day. In other words, a little practice every day is better than a lot in one day.

Similarly, playing once during the week and once on the weekend is more beneficial than playing 36 holes on Saturday. Also, spreading lessons over many weeks, with generous amounts of practice in between, is better than a series of five lessons crammed into a week-long vacation.

Make Practice Convenient and Fun

Keep your clubs handy. You never know when you might have a few minutes to practice. A few clubs in the car lend themselves nicely to a stop at the practice range if you happen to get away from work a little early. Or say your spouse wants to run into the shopping mall for a few minutes. This is another opportunity to seek out a little patch of grass and work on your chips and short pitches. The wait for the kids during swimming lessons might go a little more quickly if you spend it at a nearby practice area rather than twiddling your thumbs by the side of the pool. At the very least, a handy club always provides the opportunity to practice your grip, review your swing keys and visualize a few shots in between actual practice sessions and rounds.

Keep records of practice and play. Record keeping was mentioned earlier as an aid in maintaining patience. That is, by observing small, recorded gains in improvement, you bridge the long gap between your starting and ending points.

Similarly, record keeping can enhance motivation. It gives you something to shoot for each time you practice or play. Every shot becomes important, and you have a permanent, reliable golfing companion every time you want to practice or play—yourself.

Record keeping might benefit from the use of alternative scores. If your only measure of progress is 18-hole scores, it can be difficult to maintain your motivation. It doesn't matter how capable you are as a golfer. Eighteen-hole scores still vary all over the place. Many single-digit handicappers will predict only that their score for any given day will fall somewhere between 70 and 90. Too many variables affect such a global measure of performance as 18-hole scores.

In comparison to 18-hole scores, alternative scores (such as fairways hit, greens in regulation or number of putts) are much more under your control and should serve as a better reflection of consistency and improvement in your game.

In addition to such objective alternative measures as fairways, greens and putts, consider also a more subjective alternative score—shots hit the way you intended to hit them. That is, in the split second after contact between the club and the ball, assess whether you did what you were trying to do, regardless of the outcome of the shot. If you did, give yourself a point for your records.

Another game you can play is a match against the course. Par or birdie means you win the hole. Make bogey or above and the course wins. After each round, record how many holes you won against the course.

Also, stop practicing while you are still enjoying it. When you put a book down at the most exciting part, you are much more eager to pick it up again and read on. In fact, you can hardly wait to do so. The same is true with golf. Quit practicing while it is still fun and you won't be able to wait to get back to it. Burnout isn't good for you or your game.

Design Competition
to Reinforce Practice

Competition is an important source of motivation. Even the most casual golfer displays a distinct shift toward seriousness when pride or a few coins are on the line. While ego and money are important, the most important thing about competition is its compatibility with what you are trying to achieve. Any competition you design should be consistent with your ultimate goal—improving your score.

> *Record keeping can enhance motivation. It gives you something to shoot for each time you practice or play.*

Along this vein, medal-play competition (total stroke count) generates much greater focus on lower scoring than does match play (number of holes won). After all, the score is the defining factor in medal play.

A constructive wager for improving your scoring ability is for the loser to pay the winner a set amount for each stroke that separates the two at the end of 18 holes. This bet encourages both players to keep trying even if the match seems lost. Give up and each shot that is carelessly thrown away costs more money, whether the shot is on the first or the 18th hole, or whether the match is close or a runaway.

> *Learning occurs most efficiently when practice is distributed over several days and not crammed into a single day or weekend.*

Match-play competition does just the opposite in terms of sustained effort toward a low score. If you are out of a hole, you pick up your ball and, in effect, give up on the hole. In best-ball matches, if your partner makes a par, your 10-footer for par or bogey is now meaningless. So, again, you pick up and give up. All of these pick-ups result in an invalid, meaningless individual score. Bets involving carryovers, presses and greenies all tend to make match play fun, but they also make the competition so distracting that you have little energy left for concentrating on the bottom line—a low score.

Of course, match play is still a fine form (indeed, the original form) of competitive golf. Nonetheless, if the goal is to learn to shoot low scores, playing pure medal-play golf on a regular basis is the quickest and surest route to that objective.

Get It Right This Time

Consider the people you know who make the same investment mistakes over and over again, take other jobs with the same headaches as the ones they just left, get into new relationships that are no different than the ones that came before and play the same golf game they have been playing for the past 15 years. Perhaps it is part of the human condition that we seem to never learn. At the very least, it is difficult to learn new ways of doing things without expert analysis of our past mistakes and a commitment to a systematic plan for change.

SEVEN THINGS YOU CAN DO TO IMPROVE SCORES AND LOWER YOUR HANDICAP

I F YOU HAVE ALL the answers, why aren't you a better golfer? That's a question that sport psychologists frequently are asked. My standard response has been that being a good golfer is more than just knowing sport psychology. Other contributing factors include physical prowess, raw talent, mastering the technical mechanics of the game and finding time to practice and play in order to maintain your skills. Furthermore, just because a person knows psychology does not mean he or she is immune to mental difficulties anymore than a good business person is immune to financial reversals or a medical doctor is protected from disease.

Despite the validity of the above rationale, I decided to take on the challenge and see if I couldn't use a little psychology to improve my own game. Specifically, could I lower my handicap, improve my competitive (win-loss) record and ultimately feel more at ease with scorekeeping and the pressures of competition? What follows are the seven things I found that you can do to improve scores and lower your handicap.

Two preliminary cautions are in order. First, the following does not involve psychological gimmicks and tricks aimed at a quick fix. This is nuts and bolts psychology. Second, I do not separate the physical from the psychological. The two are hopelessly intertwined in golf. Therefore, you will notice as much physical as psychological in what follows.

The Program

Step 1: Get Proper Equipment and Know Your Yardages—When you are making a serious effort to improve, you do not want to be wondering if your tools are holding you back. This does not necessarily mean throwing out your arsenal of existing equipment. In my case, I just took my current set of clubs to a clubfitter and had them adjusted for my build and swing. When I returned, the clubs felt better, and I could depend on the distances produced by each club.

You have to know the yardage for each club, and this is accomplished only by hitting shots and stepping off distances. However, you get double duty out of this exercise because you also get practice making the solid, repeating swings that are necessary for producing consistent distances.

The psychological focus of Step 1 is that I no longer could blame my equipment for poor play or lack of improvement. Also, knowing the yardages for each club allowed me to make a confident swing, where previously I might have been tentative, wondering whether or not I had the correct club in my hands.

Step 2: Settle on a Few Productive Swing Keys—Before you can improve your scoring and competitive success, you have to commit yourself to a swing that is comfortable and productive for you. This might be as simple as reflecting on what has worked consistently for you over the years, or as complex as beginning a series of lessons to guide you in building your most productive swing. The swing doesn't have to be perfect, but at some point you have to stop experimenting and settle on the mechanics you are going to take on the road to improvement. Of course, the same analysis also must be done on your short game and putting.

The psychological focus of Step 2 is that you can stop wasting mental energy on tinkering with technique and start devoting all of your effort to honing the mental skills involved in scoring and winning.

Step 3: Channel Your Emotions—One of the biggest risks on the road to improvement is that you will get discouraged and throw in the towel if things don't come around fairly quickly. What I did to control my anger and frustration was to remind myself that this program wouldn't be easy, success wouldn't happen overnight and persistence was the key to gradual improvement. Record keeping also was useful for keeping me in touch with my gradual progress. But ultimately, I just had to tell myself that angry outbursts and giving up would only interfere with and delay my quest to become a better golfer.

The psychological focus of Step 3 is that knowing you are in control of your emotions further frees you to concentrate on the important work at hand.

> *Taking your clubs to a clubfitter for adjustments can help your clubs feel better and prevent you from blaming your equipment for poor play.*

Step 4: Commit to Some Daily Golf Activity—Ben Hogan once said he was afraid to take a day off for fear he would forget everything he was working on. There is actually quite a range of things one can do on any given day. On a busy day, you might do no more than review your swing thoughts or swing a club in the backyard. Practicing for 20 minutes on the putting green might suffice for another day. Of course, the more hours you spend in thorough practice sessions, playing rounds or engaging in competition will only lead to better results.

One of the little things I did was to make 18 short (2- to 4-foot) putts in a row before I would allow myself to go home. Another was to engage in mastery practice, a special regimen for on-course practice that I describe in my book, *The Complete Golfer: Physical Skill and Mental Toughness* (Allyn & Bacon, 1996).

Such an option may not be available to you, but whether it is or not, I encourage you to spend most of your practice time on the course. If you are limited to the range, at least pick targets, vary clubs and lies, and play imaginary holes in your mind. Simply pounding balls with the same club time after time is going to lead to limited improvement when you try to improve your scoring on the course.

The psychological focus of Step 4 is that successful completion of 18 short putts in a row made me confident that I could complete 18 holes without missing a short putt. It also took some pressure off my long game and chipping.

Mastery practice on the course enabled me to learn what I needed to do in the context where I ultimately had to perform. It also afforded much more realistic shots, situations and decision making than can ever happen on the range.

Step 5: Play Serious Golf—Playing seriously meant first and foremost having a scrupulously honest handicap that I could live with under the toughest of competitive conditions. This meant learning the rules of golf in all their subtleties and applying them to my scoring whenever I played, with no exceptions. If the rules would affect my score in competition, I wanted them to affect my score while I was establishing my handicap.

> *Channel your emotions to avoid angry outbursts after a poor shot, such as missing a short putt.*

Playing seriously also meant not messing around when I was playing. Each round was a serious attempt to shoot the lowest score I could on that given day. It's been said that Jack Nicklaus never hit a careless shot. Becoming an expert is serious business.

The psychological focus of Step 5 is that serious play reduced mental errors that led to higher scores, and it also kept me trying even when I was having a bad day. Having an honest handicap took pressure off me in competition, because I knew I could play to my handicap and didn't have to apologize to anyone for any bogus impressions of skill I didn't yet possess.

Step 6: Engage in Medal-play Competition—Since lower scores were the objective of this program, medal play was the competitive format of choice. Match play wouldn't do since it allows for inconsistency and higher scores in contrast to medal play, where a low score is the bottom line—the only line. The medal-play competition in this program was handicapped so as to assure an equally challenging match, whomever the opponent was.

It should be noted that medal-play matches can initially be a shock to the system, particularly if you have become accustomed to playing best-ball and scramble formats where the only identifiable score is a team score. When you play individually by the bona fide rules of golf, you'll have an honest starting point and your scores will generally improve from that point on.

Another consideration about medal play is that it requires delaying gratification—you have to wait 18 holes to win anything. This can take some adjustment if you are used to getting paid off after nine holes, as in a Nassau, or even sooner after each hole, as in a skins game. Indeed, the ultimate in immediate gratification is winning after one shot, as in closest-to-the-pin competitions, driving contests or when playing greenies, sandies, etc. With medal play, you have to learn to wait for the payoff and find value in the journey along the way.

Regarding that value, I find medal play to be a challenge right from the beginning. The early holes give you a chance to get off to a strong start, sending a message to your opponent that you are someone to be reckoned with. If, on the other hand, you get off to a shaky start, you have to exercise patience so as to keep yourself in position to make a move on the back nine or whenever your opponent falters. The back nine tests your courage and staying power. Can you come back? Can you hold a lead? Can you withstand the pressure of the final holes?

Medal-play competition by the strict rules of golf is the closest we come to experiencing what it's like on the PGA Tour. You know you are playing the real thing and experiencing something like what the best golfers in the world experience on a regular basis. Also, you are never closed out in medal play until the last putts are holed. Anything can happen, and often does, if you just hang in there.

The psychological focus of Step 6 is that I was amazed at how quickly I got used to the pressure, conquered my emotions and mastered the strategy involved in medal-play competition. Medal-play competition under the strict rules of golf is where the mental game of scoring is practiced, all of which probably led to my great improvement.

> *Make a serious effort to improve by committing to some type of daily golf activity, such as making 18 short putts.*

Step 7: Take Yourself to the Next Level by Playing Shorter Tees—Once my improvement reached a plateau, I took a radical step to jump-start my scores to an even lower level—I played the forward tees for awhile. My thinking was that playing from the shorter tees would tell me how much my limited driving distance was holding me back from further improvement vs. how much my approach and short games were the culprits. That is, if I could break through to a new scoring level when playing from the forward tees, then maybe driving distance was indeed creating a limit to my improvement. On the other hand, if I couldn't score any better from the forward tees than from the championship tees, then I knew I had some work to do on my approach shots and short game.

The other consideration was that if I could shoot some fantastic scores from the forward tees, I could establish a new scoring comfort zone that wouldn't be that hard to transfer back to the senior tees. If I could continue to score that well hitting 6-irons into greens from the senior tees, couldn't I shoot the same score with 4- and 5-irons from the regular men's tees that weren't that much farther back? And then what about taking it one step farther back to the championship tees? It's still the same course and the same game, and now I'm familiar with shooting these low scores. I've been there and experienced them.

The psychological focus of Step 7 is that starting at the forward tees and gradually moving back to the championship tees shapes your feeling of comfort in shooting previously "forbidden" scores. From the forward tees, unrealistically low scores are no longer forbidden. Indeed, they become expected, and you feel uncomfortable if you don't shoot them. This expectation gradually is extended back to the longer tees where such scores previously were never even considered. Playing the shorter tees instills in you a go-for-birdie mindset that is hard to forget even when you move back to the championship tees.

The Results

When I started this program, I was coming off a 7.1 handicap for March. From April to August, the program was implemented to include playing 47 medal-play matches. The results showed a gradual decline in handicap to 6.1 for April, 5.6 for May, 5.5 for June, 4.6 for July and finally 4.1 on August 11. During that same time period, my winning percentage (per every 10 matches) went from 44 percent for the first 10, to an unexplainable 100 percent for the second 10, back to a gradual improvement trend of 56 percent for the third 10, 67 percent for the fourth 10 and 86 percent for the last seven of the 47 matches. In other words, while the handicap was decreasing from 7.1 to 4.1 in less than four months, the competitive winning percentage was increasing from 44 percent to 86 percent over the same time period.

An interesting footnote is that, with the end of the program due to the beginning of a new academic year for this college professor, my handicap again rose slightly, but the competitive successes continued, with winning percentages staying in the 80 to 88 percent range for subsequent 10-round segments stretching into November.

> *Playing from the forward tees will instill a go-for-birdie mindset that you can maintain when you move back to the championship tees.*

Furthermore, the carryover effects of the program have led to subsequent handicaps as low as 3.5. Even more exciting is that the experiment with the forward tees resulted in an under-par performance when I moved back to the regular men's tees, followed shortly thereafter by a 1-over-par score from the championship tees.

Conclusion

So there you have it. A sport psychologist practiced what he preached and ultimately cut his handicap in half. He also doubled his competitive winning percentage and increased his comfort considerably with scorekeeping and the pressures of competition.

If there is a next step in this program of improvement, it would be immersion in official tournament golf, which would provide the opportunity to play with the best competition, as well as a chance to get acclimated to having scores publicly posted all the time. Indeed, I tried it in a recent Senior U.S. Open qualifier, shooting a 78, which was better than 60 percent of the field but still seven strokes off the pace. But the good news was that the competition was not a shock to the system. I was prepared for medal play, I knew how to handle the pressure and I kept on trying until I shot the lowest score I could.

HOW TO REACH
YOUR GOALS
THIS SEASON

I N GOLF, AND IN life, it is difficult to get where you want to go if you haven't focused yourself in the right direction and made a good plan for getting there. However, setting goals is more than simply establishing certain outcome criteria (scores, victories, etc.). It is a matter of skillfully determining realistic intermediate goals or steps along the way to what you want to achieve. It also involves strategies and rewards for making each of those steps, as well as flexibility in adjusting your plan as the situation demands.

According to sport psychologists, the difficulty in goal setting is not so much in getting people to identify their goals. Rather, it's in getting them to set the right kinds of goals and to stick to and achieve those goals.

All goals are not created equal. Some goals are virtually worthless because of their vagueness and unachievability, while others are of great value because of their clarity and reasonableness. Consider setting the following types of goals.

Performance Goals

Focus on what you intend to do, not what you would like the result to be. For example, rather than setting a goal of lowering your handicap (a result), set your sights on hitting one more green in regulation or having one less putt per round (performance factors). If you perform these tasks on average, the result of a lower handicap should follow.

It cannot be stressed enough that you should focus on the task at hand—the thing you have to do or perform. Results or outcomes, such as the score or beating an opponent, are not entirely under your control. But achieving some task and executing it properly are under your control. These are things you can do on the road to achieving favorable results.

Specific, Measurable Goals

You should stay away from vague, abstract objectives such as being a champion golfer or a better putter. Strive for concrete goals by being specific about how you will measure what you are trying to accomplish. For example, a measurement for being a better putter might be lowering your 10-round putting average from 32 to 30 putts per round.

To measure means to count something, to place a number on it, such as the number of putts, driving distance, number of greens in regulation, number of fairways hit and so on. It is hard to count something if it has not been identified concretely and specifically. So if you can count what you are trying to accomplish, you can be relatively assured that you have done the job of being specific.

Another way to encourage specificity and concreteness is to state your goal in a way that a 5-year-old could understand. If a 5-year-old can comprehend what you are talking about, then chances are the objective is clear and specific in your mind as well.

Challenging, Realistic Goals

You will be more motivated to pursue what you perceive as an achievable goal than you would be in pursuing some pie-in-the-sky goal that deep down you know is unrealistic. Realistic, achievable goals encourage persistence as you see successive goals being regularly met. This is not to suggest being easy on yourself. On the contrary, goals should present a challenge. It's just that the challenge should appear manageable with the skill and effort you are able to produce. A good adage is, "Make your goals high enough to inspire you but low enough to encourage you."

Short-term Goals

If you win the day, then the weeks, months and years will take care of themselves. Set short-term goals for each practice session and each game. By setting short-term goals, you experience the joy of daily achievement and don't have to wait for long-term accomplishments to feel like you are making progress. Conquer the short-term goals, and the long-term goals will take care of themselves.

Sticking to Your Goals

Whether you stick to your goal depends on how well you prepare for the journey. Consider a few challenging questions before you begin your quest toward higher achievement.

For example, have you ever achieved this goal before? If the answer is "yes," then you know you can do it. If the answer is "no," then perhaps you should re-assess how realistic your goal is and consider adjusting the degree of anticipated achievement to a more realistic level. Once the more realistic level is achieved, you can always set higher goals.

How was the goal achieved previously? What was your approach last time? Maybe previously proven resources and strategies could be drawn upon again, instead of reinventing the wheel. If something worked before, consider trying it again, perhaps with some modifications that will make the approach even better.

What is the most you might expect regarding this goal? What is the least you would accept? Again, this is a matter of being realistic. Most people think in terms of the most that can be expected, which actually means the most they would like to have, realistic or not. The more practical option is likely to be the goal that represents the least you would accept. Again, you can always crank it up a notch if you easily reach your initial objective.

What will happen if you reach your goal? Typically, nothing but good and happiness is expected from reaching a goal. Joy would certainly emanate from hitting more greens in regulation and draining a few long putts. Once the handicap starts decreasing, however, a certain downside to reaching your goal can also make the scene—expectations rise, pressure to consistently play better mounts and you may even start losing money to opponents you used to beat handily when you had a higher handicap.

You have to be prepared to cope with all the outcomes that go along with reaching a goal. Otherwise, you might sabotage your own efforts to achieve success. That is, if you feel threatened, you might not stick to your goal, thereby quietly saving yourself from the heightened expectations, pressure and financial loss that you see beginning to develop.

What will happen if you don't reach your goal? Contrastingly, if you don't reach your goal, it is no particular surprise that undesirable outcomes occur. For instance, you remain a less-accomplished golfer, you feel defeated and you suffer the boredom of being stuck indefinitely at the same level of achievement.

> *Make your goals high enough to inspire you but low enough to encourage you.*

But, curiously, some benefits also stem from not reaching your goal—no new expectations, no new pressures to perform at a higher level and continued ease in winning in your handicapped competitions. Again, if you are not prepared to move on from your comfort zone, you might find yourself unwittingly hanging onto your old ways.

What resources do you need before you begin? If equipment, facilities, money, etc., are needed to achieve your goal, line up these things before you begin. Otherwise, the lack thereof will emerge later as an excuse for not sticking to your goal.

Finally, what are the potential barriers that might keep you from achieving your goal? If six months after you begin your program you are asked how you are doing, what excuses will you come up with to explain not achieving your goal? Those anticipated excuses are likely barriers between you and your goal. Predict those excuses beforehand and pre-empt them before they derail you.

For example, if lack of time always gets you, make a schedule that ensures enough time to pursue your goal. If undependable social support typically lets you down, then ensure that your initial planning doesn't include other people having to be involved.

The same old excuses tend to resurface time and again. Therefore, an inventory of old excuses will help identify potential barriers and allow you to deal with them upfront so they don't interfere again.

Ultimately Achieving Your Goals

Once you have identified appropriate goals and considered the challenges related to sticking to those goals, the next thing is to make a strategic plan for goal attainment. As with goal identification, the plan should be clear and cover all the bases.

First, devise a strategy for achieving each short-term goal. Make a staircase of short-term goals, each step increasing in difficulty. Make the incline of the staircase gradual and uniform so you will be able to smoothly make the climb.

Now, devise a strategy for each step. For example, if the first step is to have one less three-putt green per round, the strategy might be to get long putts closer to the hole, rather than going all out to make them. If the goal is one more green in regulation, the strategy might be to aim for the middle of each green, whatever the location of the flag might be.

Next, set an appropriate reward for reaching each goal. When you reach your initial goal, have a previously identified reward ready to deliver. It might be as simple as the top-shelf beverage at the 19th hole that day. Or, for more demanding goals, the planned reward might be springing for a green fee at one of the top courses in your area.

It is always best to give the reward as soon as possible, so that it can easily be associated with what you have achieved. Then you can put that accomplishment behind you and concentrate on the next goal and the next reward.

It is also important to enlist significant others in support of your plan. While you don't want to depend on others in achieving your goals, significant people in your life may still encourage you, hold you accountable and perhaps even reliably join you on the journey. Obtain the support of these folks, as long as you can still move along toward your goal even if they fizzle out.

You might consider telling just one other person about your plans. Telling everybody would produce debilitating pressure, but one significant other in your life holding you accountable might provide an optimal measure of motivation for goal achievement.

Another key step is to make a timetable but remain flexible. Set a target date for each step in the staircase, but don't panic if you don't quite make the date. If the latter occurs, simply set a new date and continue on. Plateaus occur in any climb, so enjoy the progress you've made, maintain your plan and press on toward your new target date. Allow for the fact that you couldn't precisely predict beforehand the amount of time it would take to climb each step in your staircase.

Of course, you will need to determine when you will take the first step. It's true that you can't get much done by starting tomorrow. But it's also good to realize that you don't want to begin until you're absolutely ready. Remember, it's better to look ahead and prepare than to look back and regret.

So once you have made all the preparations for the journey, set a date for embarkation. Look forward to that date with great anticipation and excitement, for all your planning is about to come to fruition.

Finally, you must monitor your progress. Charting your progress via a table or graph can be a useful reward in itself and thereby encourage persistence. That is, a glance at your graph showing the line moving in a favorable direction can be reinforcing and get you to carry on, especially when you feel like you are making only minimal progress. The trend may be a bit more gradual than you had initially expected, but at least you will see that the plan is working, so encourage yourself to continue on.

How to Proceed if You Get Bogged Down

What if the line on the graph starts moving in the wrong direction? First of all, remember to look where you are in relation to where you started. You will likely find that you are in a better position than your starting point and that your program is having an impact.

Secondly, avoid the saint or sinner syndrome. That is, if you can't be a saint (e.g., always making progress, never diverting from your program, always being perfect in your behavior), that doesn't mean you have to go off the deep end and become a total sinner (e.g., stop your program, give up, resign yourself to failure).

Other alternatives exist between St. Peter and Beelzebub. While you might not succeed at being completely perfect, you still have many other options other than totally giving up. Take a break, control the damage, get some help but don't throw in the towel and assume you will never achieve your goals.

Lastly, do an inventory of your initial plan to make sure you did not make the common mistakes discussed previously, such as forgetting to set specific goals, failing to set performance goals, setting too many goals too soon, refusing to adjust your goals or neglecting to follow up or monitor your progress toward your goals.

If you find a flaw, make adjustments and set out on the journey again. Even if it takes multiple tries, stick with it and keep experimenting until you find the right formula that allows you to achieve at least some approximation of your objective. So, it's not the perfect result you initially envisioned. It may still be a better state of affairs than that which prevailed when you initially set out on the road to higher achievement.

AGGRESSIVE PLAY

Why Going for the Pin Pays Off

T HE PROS MAKE A lot of pars because rather than just hitting the ball on the green, they hit it close to the pin. I would say that if you or I regularly had two putts to make par from inside 20 feet, we'd make several pars also, not to mention some birdies.

On the flip side, when the pros find themselves with a 50-foot putt, a putt through the fringe or a wicked downhill chip from high grass around the green, they struggle like we do. Despite their exquisite skill, it is not easy for them when they don't put the ball neatly on the putting surface near the pin.

As an amateur at the Masters in 1995, Tiger Woods lamented that the three-putts that contributed to his third round 77 were not the fault of his putter. "I put myself in almost impossible positions to even two-putt," he said. Senior pro Jim Dent concurred that Woods ". . . never hit it consistently close to the hole. Everybody who gets on tour can do that." Obviously, Tiger has rectified this situation over the past few years.

It takes skill and practice to get the ball close to the pin on long approach shots. But, unfortunately, ability to execute is not the complete answer. Golfers also must introduce an aggressive mindset that encourages going for the pin.

Curiously, an aggressive style of play hasn't always been prevalent in golf. Consider Bobby Jones' maxim that ". . . if you keep shooting par at them, they all crack sooner or later." Such a conservative approach was reasonable in the days of match play and when even par actually could win a golf tournament.

But medal play and Arnold Palmer changed that. I remember hearing a story from Palmer's college days that had the King trotting down the fairway to his drive in the woods, hollering back to his companions that he couldn't wait to get to his ball so he could see how he might make birdie from there. With that attitude, it wouldn't take long before you would stop winning golf tournaments unless you made a bundle of birdies, which in turn required regularly hitting shots close to the pin.

So, how does a golfer develop a more aggressive style of play? Consider the following suggestions:

1. *Focus On the Target*—An accomplished tour player was overheard once in the following conversation with a local caddie as he prepared to play the first hole of an unfamiliar course: (Player) "Tell me where to hit this drive." (Caddie) "Just don't hit it left." (Player, flinching) "I said to tell me where to hit it, not where to hit it."

Thus, the most basic principle of aggressive golf is to focus on the target rather than on all the impending dangers surrounding the target.

2. *Knock the Ball in the Hole*—As soon as you get in range of the hole, try to knock it in. I wonder how many more holes-in-one might have been enjoyed over the years if every player who ever stepped onto a par 3 really had been trying to knock the ball in the hole. Indeed, all varieties of long shots occasionally find the hole. But those seemingly miraculous events must have a higher percentage of occurrence for those who are trying to knock it stiff as opposed to those who are praying to get it somewhere on the green. Frank Ford once said that the only thing he thought about concerning the ball was knocking down the pin. That mindset took him to seven South Carolina Amateur championships.

In a similar vein, Canadian greats Moe Norman and George Knudson were known to gamble on how many pins they could hit in a round. Norman described one particular round where he hit four pins and Knudson hit six.

Each time you stand over a shot within 200 yards of the green, consider it a chance for a memorable shot. You have at least 18 of those exhilarating attempts every round. Make it your goal to knock in at least one shot from the fairway (or tee) every round and recognize that the shot you currently are standing over may be the one. Go for it!

3. Think "Birdies"—Some golfers live in fear of the golf course. Each hole is a threat, and each round is something they try not to ruin. But for you, each hole is an opportunity. You're going low, and messing up is not a concern. Even in the unlikely event that you do mess up, who cares? You're an aggressive golfer, and you love it.

Go for birdies, and not just a few of them. You want to birdie every hole. Your goal each time you play is to shoot 18 under (or better). Two birdies in a row is nothing. You still need 16 more. Don't let up. If you miss a birdie opportunity, that's a shame. But how many can you make in the remaining holes? If you happen to bogey a hole, no big deal since your goal is to birdie the rest of them. The question you pose to yourself on every tee is, "What do I have to do to birdie this hole?"

> *Go for birdies, and not just a few of them.*
> *You want to birdie every hole.*

4. Hit the Shot the Way It's Supposed to Be Hit—Sometimes golfers actually make choices and adjustments in anticipation of bad shots. They may assess a shot and think that they are going to hit it fat and leave the ball short. So, what do they do? They take more club to allow for the fat shot. Then, to make things worse, they get over the ball and look at the target only to envision the ball slicing right of the green. So, they wiggle themselves around until they are aiming left of the target, and they prepare to yank the club farther left in order to compensate for their feeling of the ball going right. The end result is that they hit too much club while not aiming at the target and using a swing that creates the very monster of a shot that they feared.

This scenario exemplifies a very tentative style of play with the player holding back on the shot instead of confidently and aggressively hitting it the way it's supposed to be hit. Aggressive play mandates that you pick the appropriate club, aim it precisely at the target and hit through the shot with conviction. Don't back off, even if you aren't 100 percent sure of the decisions you've made. I venture to say that an imperfectly planned shot hit with conviction will end better more often than a perfectly planned shot hit tentatively.

5. Imagine Absolute Success—Getting the ball close to the pin is one thing, but you still have to negotiate the putt into the hole. At this critical juncture, it is important to entertain images of nothing but pure success. Employ all your senses in the process of preparing to execute the putt. Feel the fluid stroke and the ball rolling softly off the clubface. Visualize the ball rolling squarely into the hole. Hear the delightful sound of the ball dropping into the hole. As you stand over the putt, imagine all these sensory dimensions vividly again. Now, stroke the ball and one last time entertain these images before you look for the result. When you do look, be absolutely surprised if the vivid result you have envisioned hasn't actually happened.

In closing, let me relate a personal anecdote that goes a long way in supporting the above suggestions. I was once in a foursome that agreed late one evening to squeeze in six holes before dark, and for the fun of it to pay off on nothing but birdies. In other words, the only thing that was going to be rewarded this evening was aggressive play. After about an hour of golf and a combined 24 birdie opportunities for four golfers playing six holes, the final scorecard curiously reflected only two birdies. But what the scorecard didn't show was that 21 greens were hit in regulation, nine more birdie putts burned the hole and a combined even-par score was recorded by the four players for the 24 holes. Not bad for a foursome whose handicaps projected that they should have shot a combined 14 over par for the 24 holes.

So, even if you don't shoot 54 with your new aggressive mindset, you may at least beat your best-ever score by more than a few shots. Indeed, the first time I related the twilight story above, a gentleman called me soon after and said he tried the birdie-or-nothing approach and broke into the low 70s for the first time in his life. And the amazing thing to him was that the quantum leap to a lower score turned out to be much easier than he ever dreamed.

Lesson #43

TAKE YOUR GAME
TO THE NEXT LEVEL

A**LL GOLFERS WOULD LIKE** to ratchet their games up a notch. Beginners would love to just break 100. Veterans long to shoot in the 70s. Top amateurs covet the professional ranks, and journeymen pros dream about the big dance—the PGA Tour.

Whatever your present level of play, if you want to take it to the next level, you will have to become a P-A-R golfer. Consider the steps below to find out what this involves.

The 'P' in Par Is for Patience

To reach a new level in anything—a building under construction, a 1,000-point move in the stock market, a 20-pound weight loss or improvement in one's golf game—you will need time and patience. To help maintain patience in taking your golf game to the next level, try the following:

1. Look for Gradual Improvement—First of all, keep a record of your scores and stroke averages every 10 rounds. If you are a beginner, try to reduce the average score by five to 10 strokes per year. If you currently shoot in the low 80s, a reduction of two strokes per year would get you into the mid-70s within a relatively short period of time.

On the PGA Tour, a fraction of a stroke off a player's scoring average could mean the difference between being at home on the weekends vs. making cuts, winning tournaments and collecting large sums of money. In other words, small amounts of progress can add up to sizable gains if you are patient.

An important thing to remember in this regard is that lower averages result just as much from keeping bad rounds from getting worse as they do from making good rounds even better. So, don't give up and carelessly let high scores become five strokes worse than necessary. Your effort in doing the best you can, even in a momentary losing battle, will pay dividends with your stroke averages later on.

2. Let Victories Happen—Victories might be defined in various ways: (a) scores toward the lower end of your scoring range, (b) best-ever rounds, (c) matches won or (d) finishing first in a golf tournament.

However you define victories, don't try to force them. Instead, be persistent in practicing and doing the things that are contributing to your lower scoring average, and let the victories happen in due time. Indeed, as your average score decreases, victories eventually will come your way.

3. Defocus from Outcome—Ironically, neither victories nor a low scoring average comes from focusing directly on those specific outcomes. Instead, those outcomes follow from focusing on technique and game plan.

The only thing a golfer can control is what to do in interaction with the ball. Precisely where the ball goes, what score it leads to or whether victory follows are matters that are increasingly beyond your control.

So, patiently focus on what you can control—your technique for swinging the club and your game plan for placing the ball around the course. The scoring average and the victories will gradually take care of themselves.

The 'A' In Par Is for Attitude

Many players trying to move to the next level run into an attitude roadblock. Negativity, pessimism, tension, giving up, etc., often become emotional hurdles that have to be conquered if you are to succeed. Consider the following attitude adjustments:

1. Focus on the Positive—Don't get down on yourself. Find value in everything you do and everything that happens to you. Now, I don't mean phony, Pollyannaish, positive thinking such as, "I am the greatest golfer who ever lived, and nothing can ever go wrong for me." Such a thought is worthless because it is untrue and your psyche can't be fooled that easily.

What is true, however, is that hidden value exists in everything. Examples include what was done well in a match despite a losing effort, how much improvement is evident even though progress may be temporarily stalled, how straight a shot was even though it was hit a little thin, or how aggressive you were on your first putt even though it led to a three-putt. Your improving strengths, straight shots and aggressiveness may be more important for your development than any momentary setbacks you are encountering.

As comedian George Burns once said, "It doesn't hurt to have a positive attitude. Even if you are going to fail, be positive about it. That way, you'll be a successful failure." Good joke, but looking for the hidden value in situations is no joke and can be of considerable value in keeping your attitude in check while your game improves.

2. Cultivate an Unemotional Demeanor—Riding the highs and lows of feelings may be exhilarating, but it doesn't seem to be one of the ingredients for becoming an expert golfer. If you want to join the stars, you may have to become somewhat of a golfing machine.

Consider players like Phil Mickelson, Fred Couples and Ernie Els. When they walk off a green, it is hard to tell whether they just made birdie or bogey because they refrain from getting too high when something good happens or too low when something bad happens. Even the high-strung Tiger Woods seems to be cultivating more of this demeanor of late. Such emotional control reduces distraction when it comes to concentrating on the continuing task that lies ahead, which is essential in taking your game to the next level.

3. Learn to Relax—Being physically relaxed is of absolute importance for the smooth, fluid flow of the golf swing. Fortunately, relaxation is a skill that can be learned, but it will probably take more than tapes or music to teach you how to relax on the golf course.

A sport psychologist can provide a variety of simple techniques in a short period of time that can then be employed in the heat of the action on the golf course. It will take a little practice, but learning the skill of relaxation is essential for your move to the next level.

The 'R' in Par Is
for Responsibility

OK, here comes the hard part. Nobody said it would be easy to excel. Work is involved, and you have no one to blame but yourself if you don't do it and subsequently succeed.

1. Set Realistic Goals—Consider your current station in life and golf, objectively assess your raw potential and be honest about your level of commitment and ambition. Then, based on these considerations, establish a time frame and sequence of realistic goals that build in small steps to the ultimate long-term result you desire.

Emotional control reduces distraction when it comes to concentrating on the continuing task that lies ahead, which is essential in taking your game to the next level.

2. Establish a Plan for Improvement—A plan is a package of strategies for achieving each of your goals. Your plan for improvement will undoubtedly include both physical and mental coaching, an efficient and effective practice schedule, and a strategy for maintaining your motivation over the time period required for achieving your goals.

3. No Blaming—Make sure you are ready to commit to the time and work required to improve. Otherwise, you may set yourself up for failure or give in to convenient excuses.

For example, make sure that you have the necessary time and resources available, that other duties and distractions are taken care of, and that you aren't depending on anyone else (a teaching pro, mental coach, playing companion) who can't be counted on to follow through with their part in your plan for improvement. The commitment and the planning must be such that if you don't succeed, you have no one to blame but yourself. Indeed, it would be better to wait until you are absolutely ready, than to make a half-hearted commitment to the challenge before you.

4. Openness to Change—One unassailable rule for making progress is: If what you are doing isn't working, try something different. Applied to your golf game, if you are stuck at some current level and want to move to a higher level, then you may have to change the way you are doing some things.

Our old ways can become comfortable, even if non-productive, and change is sometimes difficult. But openness to change is a responsibility if you are to succeed in taking your game to the next level.

Comedian Bob Hope may have summed it up best when he said, "If you watch a game, it's fun. If you play it, it's recreation. If you work at it, it's golf." That may be true, but professional golfer Cy Manier would have added that, "Golf is the worst damn fun anybody ever had."

Lesson #44

WIN TOURNAMENTS

Think Like a Champ

H ISTORICALLY, IT'S BEN, BYRON, Arnie and Jack. Now, it's Tiger, Vijay, Ernie and Phil. There's no need for last names for these past and present perennial champions. We know who they are. What we don't know, however, is what makes them tick—what makes them so different from their less-accomplished peers. Unfortunately, they're not going to tell us. Why? Because they probably don't know themselves. If they did know and told us, it would blow their cover and replace their invincibility with vulnerability. Our only recourse is to speculate about the ingredients that go into the making of a champion.

Becoming a Champion

In a 1994 article in *American Psychologist*, K. A. Ericsson and N. Charness detailed the development of an elite performer. The first thing they noted was that you don't have to be born a child prodigy to become a star. That's the good news. The bad news is you do have to work your fingers to the bone in order to succeed. That is, you have to devote yourself to the activity full-time for 10 years. It is also necessary to specialize, since jacks-of-all-trades aren't going to cut it.

Growing up in the southern region of Ohio, lagging Jack Nicklaus by about six years, I heard no shortage of stories about the Herculean feats and activities of the young Bear. One tale told of how he would hit balls for a couple of hours each morning, play 18 holes, go home for lunch and then come back and hit balls for another two hours before playing another 18 in the afternoon. Evenings would often find him back at the course working on some part of his game before turning in for the night.

Nicklaus had no off-season either. His dad reportedly had a circus tent erected on Ohio State's campus so Jack could practice all winter despite the snow and ice that blanketed the Ohio landscape.

Of course, Nicklaus started building his game at an early age, which is another ingredient mentioned by Ericsson and Charness, and completed at least 10 years of preparation before winning his first professional major—the 1962 U.S. Open.

Incidentally, those 10 years of preparation have to involve thousands of hours of what Ericsson and Charness call "deliberate practice." What this means is that you can't go out and simply play the game as most recreational athletes do. Simply playing does not afford one the experience necessary for mastering the many details and subtleties of the game.

For example, in multiple rounds of golf, how often do you get a ball that is sitting dead center in a divot? While you do get them, thankfully it's not that often. With deliberate practice, however, you go to the range and seek out that undesirable situation by dropping balls in every divot you can find. In this way, you learn how to reliably execute a subtle skill that might make the difference between being a journeyman versus a champion at the end of the day.

The Move to the Winner's Circle

Now that you have an idea of the effort and sacrifice necessary for achieving championship caliber golf, what exactly is it that you do to take the final step—to actually make the move into the winner's circle? How do you transition yourself from journeyman status to bona fide champion after you've done all the preparation and are ready to go? Consider the following prescription for success.

1. Immerse Yourself In Pressure—Take every opportunity to play competitive, pressure-packed golf. Play real tournaments and matches that mean something. Playing for a few coins can also get your attention. It's actually not the money itself that is so important. Think of the wager as merely the price you have to pay for gaining experience with pressure.

So forget the Saturday morning socials. You haven't got time for that if you intend to be a champion. You've got to sweat under the gun and feel the heat of real competition. Welcome every opportunity for a do-or-die shot as optimal practice for moving into the winner's circle. After all, that's the situation you will likely face when your date with destiny arrives.

2. Set Intermediate Goals—On your way to the winner's circle, set your sights on top-10 finishes and then top fives. If you are having a bad day or mediocre tournament, don't just throw in the towel to come back and fight another day. Fight that day! Scratch and claw your way up the leaderboard even if your ultimate standing is still likely to be some distance from the top. In effect, what you are doing is practicing scratching and clawing, which are the very behaviors necessary when you have to stretch a little to make it to the winner's circle.

3. Game Plan—Always have a game plan and stick to it. This will aid you in preventing your emotions from taking over and leading you to irrational decisions. While the emotional side of sport is fun, the cognitive (or mental) side is what often leads to success. So use your head while enjoying your heart, and both parts of your anatomy will come out on the winning side.

4. Concentrate On the Task and Not the Outcome—Ted Purdy, a recent first-time winner at the 2005 Byron Nelson Championship, said in a post-round interview: "I let go of my desire to win and just let it happen."

In other words, he resisted his usual focus on needing his first victory and instead took care of the task at hand (e.g., hitting 17 greens in regulation and making five birdie putts), letting the victory happen rather than forcing it.

You can't directly create an outcome. All you have control over is producing the components of what might lead to a favorable outcome. Whether or not victory occurs depends on, among other things, your allotment of luck on that given day and on how others play—things that are quite beyond your control. Take care of business, what you have control over, and let the victories come to you.

5. Cultivate A Killer Instinct—Don't let anyone persuade you into taking it easy on them. To do so is to allow yourself to be manipulated. If you are ever going to reach the winner's circle on a regular basis, you have to get used to beating opponents soundly. Earl Woods referred to his son as "an assassin on the golf course." This was to suggest that Tiger was a nice fellow, in general, but he would beat you to a pulp when the game was on.

6. *Be Patient and Keep Yourself in Position to Win*—While a killer instinct is desirable, you are not always in a position where you can create mayhem. Sometimes you have to be patient, keep yourself in position to win and wait for the opportunity to make your move. If you keep yourself in sight of the winner's circle, the possibility always exists that players ahead of you will fail and fall back. Persevere and, by the end, you may be the only one left standing—in the winner's circle.

7. *Play to Your Strengths*—Play your own game, not your opponent's. If you try to match your opponent's long game when you are a short hitter, you will be drawn into a losing battle.

Recall how Chris DiMarco laid up on the 15th hole at Augusta in the final round of the 2005 Masters, even though he was one shot behind Tiger at the time. The TV announcers went crazy, implying that DiMarco was a wimp and had made a weak decision. To the contrary, DiMarco was appealing to one of his strengths (a wedge shot to the pin for birdie) as opposed to trying one of Tiger's strengths (a long iron into the stratosphere that lands softly and holds the treacherous 15th green). If DiMarco had tried to match Woods' long-game strength, he might have found himself in the water or facing a pitch shot more treacherous than the straightforward one he left himself by laying up short of the lake.

8. *Depend On Your Routine*—To rise above the emotions that arise when you catch sight of the winner's circle, become a veritable machine. That is, put your game on automatic by simply executing your well-practiced pre-shot routine. It is no longer you that strikes the ball, but your routine that does the job for you. The automatic, routine machine has no nerves. It always runs at a deliberate pace, does the same thing every time and unemotionally accepts whatever its mechanism produces.

9. *Slow Down*—You need to slow down everything you are doing when the winner's circle is on the horizon. The high state of motivation produced by potential victory is like a giant battery speeding up everything you do. You not only swing faster, but also walk faster, talk faster and are quicker to respond to any distractions. When under pressure, Nicklaus used to focus on a slow backswing, knowing it would naturally

be quickened by the motivation of the moment. Johnny Miller slowed down his pace of walking, resisting the tendency to run to the ball and quickly hit it again. Others have talked about eye control, the need to stay focused on the task at hand, rather than letting your eyes dart from distraction to distraction as you traverse the final fairways to victory. The realization that everything will tend to be quicker when you get anxious or excited can serve as a reminder to slow everything down to what, in effect, will be a normal pace. That normal pace, however, might seem like slow motion under the circumstances.

10. Endurance—The final nine holes of a golf tournament are like the final three outs in baseball, the final round in a boxing match and the two-minute drill in football. The ultimate questions are: Can you stay on your feet? Can you execute your game plan? Can you stare down your opponent and complete the contest?

A point comes in every game, in every career, in every life, when you simply have to gut it out. A conscious act of the will is required to push you through into new territory, as opposed to just peeking in, only to back away one more time. Indeed, you've been here before, but this time you're going to get the job done.

Venus Williams, as an 18-year-old preparing for her first victory at Wimbledon, said: "I want to have every point . . . all the points . . . I think that I should deserve every point, and not the other person." That's the attitude of a champion—invincibility, inevitability and entitlement.

Lesson #45

Stay Sharp During the Off-season

I N DEFENSE OF GOLF courses closing on Mondays, Donald Ross once said that golfers may not need a rest, but the golf course does. Ben Hogan certainly agreed with the part about golfers not needing a rest. Hogan said he was hesitant to take even one day off for fear he would forget everything he'd ever learned. Imagine how Hogan might have felt if he had been forced to take the entire winter off, as many golfers in our northern climes are required to do annually.

What can golfers do over the winter months to keep from losing all that has been learned from the previous summer? Gary Player, during his winter school days in England, said he would simply swing a club every day, be it indoors or outdoors, just to retain the feel and stay in touch with the game.

Staying in touch—that's what it's all about. Just a little time every day to remind you of what you were thinking and doing when you were in mid-summer form. Following are some considerations for working on your game while coping with limited playing time in the off-season.

1. Forget About Score
Assuming that your area of the country is not blanketed by snow and that you can occasionally play a round during the off-season, don't worry

about the score. In fact, under winter conditions, the USGA suspends the requirement for turning in scores for handicap purposes because it does not want players running up their handicaps with inflated scores that are unrepresentative of their true level of play. This scoring reprieve can actually be enjoyable, allowing time for practice and skill development in contrast to the summer's focus on shooting a good score.

Of course, competition is still feasible under these circumstances. Just base the interaction on something other than score in relation to par. Match play is a good choice, since the outcome of a match is totally relative in the sense that a 7 beating an 8 in the wintertime is just as good as a birdie beating a par in the summertime. Both scores simply win the hole.

Another wintertime alternative might be matching shots involving some particular skill. This type of game might be particularly useful in developing the short game during the colder months when feel for the longer shots is lacking.

2. The 45-minute Round

If the weather in your area is chilly and rainy and not particularly conducive to playing complete rounds, consider stopping at the course on the way home before darkness sets in and playing just a few holes. Joggers get in their 45-minute run each day. Why can't dedicated golfers do the same with a 45-minute round?

Even though it's only 45 minutes, take your time with those precious few holes. This is not a race to see how many holes you can get in. You are out there to play just two or three quality holes. Take shots over until you get them right. Remember, score is not an issue. The intent of the 45-minute round is to work on something, focus on one swing key and repeat it until you get it right, even if it's only for a few holes.

If you happen to be a jogger as well as a golfer, carry just one or two clubs and a few balls, and jog between shots. You'll kill two birds with one stone—getting in your exercise and practicing your swing at the same time. Indeed, if you do it on the hoof, you might even comfortably manage four or five holes in 45 minutes. But still, there's no rush. Better to have fewer quality holes than a greater number of unfocused holes and you just going through the motions.

3. Driving-range Drills

If time or course conditions are not conducive to even the 45-minute round, stop by the driving range every day or so and hit a few balls. It doesn't have to be a lot of balls. Again, it's better to take your time and focus on the task at hand. Hogan reportedly took about 45 minutes to hit just 20 balls. He thought about each shot just as he would do if he were playing an actual round.

Alternate your practice days between the range and the chipping/putting green. Motivate yourself to practice by keeping records of your improvement. It might be the number of shots to the target, the number of chips to within 5 feet or the number of one-putts vs. three-putts. All of the above should enhance your motivation and focus, thereby aiding in your overall development.

4. Indoor Practice

Back in my college years in the snowy north where outdoor golf was virtually impossible during the harsh winters, the golf coach rigged up a net in an old handball court, threw down a couple of driving-range mats and hung up a sign-in sheet to make sure the golf team practiced during the off-season. The effort must have been worthwhile, because one of those years the team finished an amazing fourth in the NCAAs after only about six weeks of outdoor spring practice.

My personal experience with that indoor torture chamber was revealing. One winter I spent all my time on a single swing change that was suggested to me late the previous autumn. It was a pretty big change, but the curious thing was that after a winter of hitting a couple of thousand balls that flew only about 25 feet into a net, I still didn't know for sure whether my swing change was taking or not. I couldn't really tell where the ball was going. I just had to proceed on faith that I was making progress, and then go out in spring to see what had actually happened. Well, when the new season rolled around and I finally got to hit those first few balls out on the range, lo and behold, there it was—a brand new swing, a good ball trajectory and validation for all that indoor winter practice.

Modern technology now allows golfers to do much better than a net in a handball court. At the World Golf Hall of Fame in St. Augustine, Fla., you can hit full shots into a screen that presents a life-sized picture of a hole. Feedback is provided by sensors on the screen that show you where the ball would have gone if you had actually been playing the hole. Information is provided as to the conditions of your next shot so you can select another club and attempt a different shot, just as if you were playing the hole. Other options in the system include a virtual driving range and opportunities to hit putts, chips and pitch shots.

This is quite an improvement over the old net-in-a-handball-court routine, and the apparatus doesn't even require as much space as a handball court. A portion of a basement with a reasonably high ceiling (enough to swing a club) could handle it. Of course, I'm sure it's expensive, but if golf means enough to you, it might be money better spent than the same amount on another new set of clubs or on a brief winter golf vacation.

5. Videotape the Perfect Round

Another innovative way to stay in touch during the off-season involves a video camera and a little work during the preceding summer. While you are in mid-summer form, videotape yourself shooting a perfect round.

To accomplish this perfection, enlist a friend or family member to serve as a camera technician. If you can't find a cohort who is as devoted to your game as you are, then just do the camerawork yourself by rigging up the video camera on a golf cart so as to capture your shots from each point on the course during an 18-hole round. Perfection will result as you take each shot over—from drives to short putts—until you hit each one properly. That's right, unlimited mulligans!

Once the tape is filled with all of these shots (good ones as well as bad ones), edit out the bad shots, leaving you with a classic video of nothing but properly struck shots over an 18-hole round. You'll also have a great score that can be anything you want it to be, based on how demanding you are of yourself in taking shots over.

Imagine an off-season with you periodically reviewing this wonderful round and its fantastic score, along with the knowledge that all those marvelous shots were struck by none other than you. This provides a positive image, a wonderful review of good swing mechanics and a great memory to ingrain in your head over the winter months and into the next summer as you proceed to take your game to the next level.

6. Review Swing Keys

If time or resources do not allow for the more exotic approaches to navigating the off-season, at least stay in touch with your swing keys for a few minutes each day. For example, you might keep a few clubs handy by the garage door to swing in the yard before you go in the house. Or a short, weighted exercise club might offer the same daily review indoors, as you swing it in front of a full-length mirror for a few minutes each day. If you don't do anything else, at least mentally review a note card that contains your swing keys and imagine hitting a few successful shots.

> *Gary Player, during his winter school days in England, said he would simply swing a club every day, be it indoors or outdoors, just to retain the feel and stay in touch with the game.*

Remember, rotate your swing review through various clubs and shots. Staying in touch with the full swing is one thing, but it may take other special reminders to maintain your skill with pitches, chips and putts.

7. Physical and Mental Conditioning

Establish a program of stretching and strengthening exercises supervised by a physical therapist who understands the mechanics of the golf swing. You might also seek assistance from a sport psychologist in the areas of relaxation, visualization, concentration and confidence building. Specific exercises and guidance are necessary for physical and mental conditioning, and the off-season is a great time to focus on both.

Reading books or watching videos about golf might also be useful. However, stay away from material that proposes new swing mechanics, lest you frustrate yourself by not being able to go out to the course to try what is being suggested. Save those books for spring. Instead, during the winter, cozy up around the fire with a book that challenges the way you think and feel about the game, or a biography of some great golfer that inspires you to greater heights as you look forward to becoming a new you in the new season.

Part V

THE STRANGE GAME OF GOLF

GOLF'S MENTAL MYSTERIES

Golf is a game of many mysteries. Take slumps, for example. How can one go from playing so well to playing so poorly—overnight? Lesson #46 tells you about "Breaking a Slump," offering "Six Ways to Get Your Game Back On Track."

Another mystery is how golf can be so easy and yet so difficult at the same time. The general concept of the game, for example, is quite simple—yet the rules of golf can be very complicated. Scorekeeping is basically simple until you encounter one of those situations where an obscure ruling applies. Same for the swing and the strategy—simple until we make them complicated. Lesson #47 offers advice on coping with "Golf's Best and Worst—Simultaneously!"

"The Mental Gymnastics of Putting" (Lesson #48) will forever be a mystery, but help is on the way in this lesson with such topics as the best putter for you, staying with the same putter vs. periodically changing putters, and dealing with the fear of putting. Also included is the best way to practice the mental side of putting.

Lesson #49 is an attempt at "Solving Golf's Mental Mysteries" in four specific situations: (1) illusions in the break of a putt, (2) why birdie putts are harder to make than par or bogey putts, (3) why a short par 5 seems easier than a long par 4 and (4) why approach shots tend to fall short more than they go long.

Lastly, PGA Tour pros are mysterious and amazing specimens. While we may never be able to play quite like them, we can at least learn from the pros and apply that knowledge toward reaching our own potential. Lesson #50, "How the Pros Do It—Make the Most Out of Attending a PGA Tournament," slips you some secrets that will make your learning more efficient the next time you make a Tour stop.

BREAKING A SLUMP

Six Ways to Get Your Game Back on Track

A SLUMP IS WHEN you have temporarily taken leave of your skills. You still possess the skills—you just can't presently locate them. Having your game go AWOL is to be differentiated from someone who has never had the skills in the first place. That person is a novice, rather than a skilled player who is simply in a slump.

So, how do solid players recapture their skills when those skills have mysteriously disappeared? Consider the following suggestions for getting your game back on track.

1. Take a Break—It doesn't have to be a long hiatus—just long enough to clear the current confusion and relieve your frustration. Go fishing, plan a vacation, finish a household project. A few days of yard work can even go a long way toward re-igniting your enthusiasm for golf.

The time away will enhance your motivation and give you a chance to forget some of the faulty tendencies that have crept into your swing. That is, a little absence will not only make the heart grow fonder, but also clear your head for a fresh start in rebuilding a solid game.

2. Consider What You Are Saying to Yourself—Before you even begin tackling the game again, start talking nicer to yourself. Instead of calling yourself a "worthless duffer who couldn't make a double-bogey to save his life," start referring to yourself as a skilled golfer who is simply in a slump. Think about all the accomplished golfers on the PGA and LPGA tours who have disappeared from the leaderboards for extended periods of time, only to return again to stardom after having dealt with their slumps. Remember the ebbs and flows of your own golf career, recalling how you have been down before and have made a comeback before. Tell yourself that you are a capable golfer, and all that's required is some intense practice to get back to the playing level that your skill should support.

3. Return to the Fundamentals—Once you have taken a break and started talking respectfully to yourself, the time has come to head out to the course and rediscover the basics of the game. Indeed, the surest way to emerge from a slump is by returning to the fundamentals.

You can probably remember a time in the not-so-distant past when you were playing quite well. Maybe you were playing so well that you believed you could do even better by leaving your safety zone and experimenting with some new moves to create greater distance. Unfortunately, since experimenting often involves overdoing what you are already doing well, you may have overdone it and lost what was once fundamentally sound about your swing.

For example, if a wide stance was working well, you may have experimentally widened it more until gradually it became something other than the beneficial wide stance you started with. Furthermore, not realizing you had excessively widened your stance, you may have begun experimenting with other things in an attempt to correct the mess your overly widened stance created. As you kept adding more experimental techniques to compensate for other experimental techniques, the fundamentals of your previously solid swing successively dropped by the wayside.

At this point, a complete inventory of your game must be done. Start with the grip, stance, body posture and alignment to make sure you have not varied too much from the standard recommendations in each of these categories. An accomplished golfer with many years of experience might do this fundamental check-up by going off by himself and quietly reviewing all aspects of his game. This can be a peaceful, contemplative experience—to get away from all distractions and put the pieces back together again.

If you are a player with less understanding of the fundamentals of golf, get with a teaching professional and let the expert review your swing.

The more accomplished player should also take this route if the solo review technique described previously doesn't produce results quickly.

Returning your game to the fundamentals is comparable to resetting your computer to the manufacturer's defaults after the machine has rebelled and locked up on you. The fundamentals, or default settings, are good starting points for rebuilding any malfunctioning system.

4. Focus on Swing Keys Rather Than Outcome—Worrying about results when hitting the ball poorly will only create more pressure and make it harder for you to emerge from a slump. If you can just start hitting the ball well again, favorable results will quickly follow.

> *Instead of calling yourself a "worthless duffer who couldn't make a double-bogey to save his life," start referring to yourself as a skilled golfer who is simply in a slump.*

The first step in hitting the ball well again is to identify faulty swing mechanics and replace them via constructive swing keys. Reacquainting yourself with proper swing keys might seem a little foreign at first, so you may have to force yourself initially to perform the new swing keys no matter what the result. As long as you know what you are doing is correct, you can proceed with the confidence that progress is being made every time you repeat the swing keys, even if positive feedback is not immediate.

Focus on nothing but the helpful new swing keys. Execution of these swing keys is your measure of success for the moment, rather than precisely where the ball ends up or what the score is. Indeed, perfect ball flight and low scores may lag behind your efforts to put the proper swing keys back in place.

For example, say you are currently plagued with missed short putts and determine that you are moving your head at impact. To correct this situation, you decide to keep your head overly still, so much so that you are not even looking to see the result but rather just listening for the ball to drop.

With this strategy established, the focus becomes the number of putts where you successfully keep your head overly still, rather than the previous concern over how many putts you were actually making. Indeed, you may still miss some early attempts with this new strategy, but in those cases you won't even see the ball slide past the cup because you will be looking at the place on the green that the ball just vacated—good evidence of your exclusive focus on the swing key of keeping your head overly still.

Furthermore, you can consider yourself a success each time you listen and don't look because you are successfully doing exactly what your new swing key demands. The ultimate reward will come shortly when you start hearing more putts drop as a result of continuing to successfully execute the proper swing key of keeping your head still.

5. Look for Gradual Gains vs. Immediate Full Recovery—If you are a 7-handicap golfer who has slumped to a handicap in the upper teens, don't expect to return to single digits overnight. Those who dig themselves deep enough into a hole aren't going to immediately spring out into the sunlight. Instead, they are going to have to stop the downward momentum first and then start the long, laborious climb back to the surface. The climb will take lots of time and considerable scratching and clawing, but at least there's always the assurance that progress is being made.

As the climb continues, it may help to remember where you were in relation to where you are in the journey. That is, scoring in the mid-80s may not yet measure up to your goal of the high 70s, but it sure is better than the low 90s you were posting in the depths of your slump. You're making progress, and the 70s aren't that far away.

6. Keep Records of Your Play—A graph showing the trend of your scores along with 5- or 10-round averages of various game statistics (fairways hit, greens in regulation, number of putts, etc.) will help you see your progress despite day-to-day fluctuations that might otherwise tend to disappoint you.

Setting intermediate goals along the way to your ultimate goal is another method of enhancing motivation and rewarding yourself on your way back to top form. For example, reward yourself with a green fee for a special course in your area once you have averaged a certain number of fairways hit or greens in regulation, no matter what your scores might have been during this initial period of recovery.

Gradual gains are the key. So get back on the right track, stay with the program and your persistence will eventually pay off with a return to the level of play you once enjoyed.

GOLF'S BEST
AND WORST—
SIMULTANEOUSLY

I N MANY WAYS, GOLF is easy. The concept of propelling a ball around a course into a series of holes couldn't be simpler. Keeping score is rather straightforward. Strategy isn't too hard either. Even the swing can be quite natural.

Yet golf can be so difficult at the same time. Ever read *The Rules of Golf*? Or better yet, the decisions book? Understanding these documents will test the most ardent scholar. Then there's a slump when the golf swing seems anything but natural. And how about addressing the first tee shot of the day or standing over a 3-foot putt on the 18th green for the match? All of a sudden, golf is very difficult.

Let's consider this easy vs. difficult comparison for several parts of the game and see if a psychological perspective can reduce the discrepancy.

The Game and Its Rules

Non-golfers observe the game and conclude that it should be relatively easy to hit a ball around some nicely groomed grass and into a hole. With no awareness of par nor any concept of a good score, non-golfers tend to think of golf like hockey. That is, it doesn't matter how many times you hit the intended object as long as it ultimately reaches its goal.

Besides having to count all your strokes, what the casual viewer fails to realize are important little things like the ball can't be moved before you hit it without counting additional strokes. The ball also needs to go certain distances using certain clubs designed to produce precise results. And short putts need to be holed out on the first try, because it counts just as much for each putt as for the long shots it took to get to the green.

When the novice attempts to play this easy game, some of his initial reactions might include: "This grass (i.e., the rough) is too thick." "What do you mean I can't move it from between these roots without counting a stroke?" "Surely you're not going to make me count that little putt I just missed!" What seemed easy in concept becomes quite difficult in practice.

Add to this even the mere basics of the rules of golf (e.g., tee it up between the markers, don't ground your club in the sand trap and be sure to properly mark your ball on the green), and golf becomes downright tedious.

The coup de grace comes when the beginner is introduced to etiquette. While already subjected to all of the previously mentioned considerations, the unsuspecting newcomer is now prompted to keep moving so as not to slow down play, reminded to rake the traps and repair divots, and cautioned to be quiet and watch where his footsteps and shadows fall so as not to interfere with the play of other golfers in the group.

Nothing to it, this golf. Just get up there and knock the ball around all that nicely groomed terrain.

Psychological Advice: Be realistic and patient. While easy in concept, golf is difficult and involves a considerable amount of learning. From the swing to the rules, develop your game in small steps. If you try to do too much too fast, you'll just frustrate yourself as well as try the patience of your playing companions.

Ben Hogan once said that, in an ideal world, he wouldn't let a beginner tackle the whole game out on the course until he had completed two years of practice at a training facility. That two-year period would involve starting with the putter, then the short game and only much later the full shots, concluding with the driver. So take it easy on yourself. There's a lot to learn and lots of time to enjoy learning it.

Score

Scorekeeping, on the surface, looks pretty straightforward. All you do is count each time the ball is hit and add up the strokes at the end for a total score. Numbers of points do not vary for different ways of executing a play or shot, as is the case in football and basketball. Retroactive scoring isn't involved either, as is the case in bowling when a number of strikes occurs in a row. All that's done in golf is to count each instance of one thing (i.e., striking the ball) and total the score when 18 holes are completed.

Well, it's not quite that simple, is it? What about scoring for balls out of bounds or for water hazards. What about unplayable lies? And then there are all those varying numbers of strokes for obscure penalties that can go as high as four strokes, assuming you don't get disqualified.

Psychological Advice: Since scoring is done by the rules and the rules are here to stay, learn *The Rules of Golf* of the United States Golf Association. Otherwise, you will be at the mercy of the haphazard judgments of other golfers. You may as well become the authority, and then you can be assured that what is going on during a round is fair and accurate, at least for you. You don't have to become obnoxious with your knowledge of the rules. You just want to make sure you are in control of your own destiny. Furthermore, the rules can be interesting and can help you as much as they can hurt you.

Strategy

The strategy for a round of golf is actually quite simple: 1) Drive the ball a reasonable distance somewhere in the fairway. 2) Hit an approach shot to the middle of the green. 3) Knock the first putt close to the hole. 4) Tap the short putt into the hole.

The difficulty arises when this simple plan goes awry. If you don't drive the ball far enough, you may get into trouble by overswinging on the next shot or by selecting the wrong club in an effort to make up for the short drive.

If you miss the fairway and roll into the rough, you may try to come back to the fairway at too risky of an angle and leave yourself in the rough. Miss the green on your approach and the delicate chipping game comes into play. Upon finally reaching the green two strokes later than originally intended, you may get too aggressive on the long putt and require a couple of short putts before you finally finish the hole.

GOLF: THE MENTAL GAME

Psychological advice: Many of the above difficulties are inevitable but can be buffered by having a game plan along with a readiness to engage in smart course management when the game plan goes awry. When you miss a drive on a long par 4, just play the rest of the hole conservatively as if the remaining part were a short par 4. Hit four reasonable shots from the spot of your drive and you'll walk away with a solid bogey. Indeed, you might even "birdie" the "short par 4" and leave the green with the actual par you intended from the beginning.

Practice chipping and pitching endlessly because you know missed greens are going to occur. Phil Mickelson was recently acknowledged for practicing his chipping and pitching more than any other part of his game. It shows every time he makes a spectacular recovery.

When it comes to long putts, just get them close, whether for birdie, par or double bogey. Remember that every hole you three-putt requires a future one-putt to make up for it. While not minimizing the challenge of two-putting, it does seem easier to bear down and avoid a three-putt from 40 feet than to make a one-putt from 15 feet later in the round to compensate for the previous three-putt.

The Swing

The swing, according to revered instructor Ernest Jones, is as natural as swinging a heavy weight at the end of a stick or rope, similar to the old-fashioned sling-shot David used to slay Goliath. In the case of golf, it's a heavy clubhead at the end of a flexible shaft. You just get it swinging rhythmically, and the ball simply gets in the way.

However, golfers never seem to approach the swing quite that simply. They insist on contorting their bodies before the swing, forcing the club into strange angles along multiple planes and ultimately giving the clubhead little chance of returning to the ball in any effective manner. Even the recent teaching of Natural Golf seems a bit complicated compared to Jones' suggestion of simply swinging the clubhead.

Psychological Advice: Science has always abided by the economy principle. That is, in interpreting data, the simplest (or least complex) explanation is preferable to some unnecessarily complicated alternative. Applied to golf, this would suggest that a simpler swing is to be preferred over a complex one.

You may have heard TV analysts refer to a "swing with a lot of moving parts." Such a swing is complex with many things that can go wrong, particularly under the pressure that can arise over a lengthy round of golf. In contrast, a simple swing is a compact, one-piece movement that is more likely to hang together and sustain itself over the course of 18 holes.

Striving for simplicity goes beyond the swing to the swing keys that precede the action. The things you say to yourself before or during the swing should be kept as simple as possible. Better to say one or two things (e.g. back and through), than five or six (e.g. head down, slow back, stop at top, turn hips, follow through high, stay down). The same applies for images entertained during the swing—simpler ones are preferred over more complex ones.

One Last Contrast

Learning to play golf is a bit like learning to play the guitar. What seems relatively easy at first becomes more difficult later, and what seems difficult initially becomes a bit easier later.

When a novice picks up the guitar, strumming the strings over the opening in the base of the instrument seems relatively easy. All you do is just run your fingers over the strings. What seems so difficult is creating chords with your fingers on the neck of the instrument. How are you ever going to get your hand into such contortions, switch your fingers quickly to new chords and remember all the formations and sequences for all the songs you want to play?

Strangely enough, after you have practiced for awhile and learned more about what goes into playing the guitar, the chords become quite automatic. Your hand learns the strange contortions and snaps into each one fairly quickly. What becomes difficult as you progress with the guitar is the variety of strums and finger picks that are necessary to play the instrument with style.

Golf presents a similar contrast. The beginner looks at putting as quite easy. At least the basics of the task can be readily accomplished (i.e., making contact with the ball and rolling it across the green). What seems so difficult is to make a big swing with a club that consistently makes contact with the ball and propels it a reasonable distance straight down the fairway.

Curiously, after years of playing, most golfers develop a fairly reliable long game, enabling them to move the ball from tee to green with less difficulty than they ever dreamed possible. The overwhelming challenge becomes the short game, the epitome of which are those dreaded short putts that seemed so easy back before the sobering realization as to just how difficult golf can be.

Lesson #48

THE MENTAL GYMNASTICS OF PUTTING

ACCORDING TO PGA TOUR records, six players have had rounds totaling 18 putts since 1979. That is truly amazing, but I doubt that any of those rounds involved one-putting all 18 greens. Surely those spectacular rounds included some shots holed from off the green that were offset by two-putts on other greens to reach the total of 18 putts. The point is that you want to become so good at putting that you don't even have to rely on miracle shots from off the green to achieve your 18-putt round. Indeed, if you get some miracle shots, you'll have fewer than 18 putts.

Consider what 18 one-putts could do for your score. If a good putting round is 30 putts and produces a score of 78, then knock off another 12 strokes (down to 18 putts) and you shoot 66. Or imagine you're having one of those days when you're off your game, putting 40 times, and threatening to double- or triple-bogey every hole. If you could do some damage control for that round by having 18 one-putt greens, a score well over 100 could be held to the low 80s.

Therefore, forget about monster drives. Don't even worry about hitting every green in regulation. Even if you did both of those things, the putting game would still determine whether all those great shots ulti-mately paid off. The only sure way to lower your score is to knock in as many putts as possible. Every time a putt drops, a stroke definitely comes off your score that wouldn't have otherwise.

The Best Putter Model

Putters come in all shapes and sizes. There is no need to describe all the various head options, shaft lengths, grips, face compositions and more that are on the market. If you have played at all lately, you probably have seen most of them.

The important psychological consideration is finding the type of putter that not only looks and feels good to you, but is also easy to line up and hit squarely. If a putter for some reason does not give you confi-dence in your alignment, you are unlikely to make a solid stroke. Instead, you'll constantly be trying to adjust or compensate for what you think might be faulty alignment. Any style of putter is fine, as long as it gives you confidence in your alignment and the likelihood of striking the ball squarely.

Staying with the Same Putter
vs. Changing Periodically

If you have a putter that is working well for you, it would be ludicrous to change putters just for the sake of changing. A good, reliable putter is about as hard to come by as a good, reliable spouse. So don't be too quick to exchange either for the latest hot product.

Spouses aside, putters can become balky and ineffective at times. They are still good putters—they are just not cooperating at the moment. It might be the result of stimulus satiation. That is, if you look at the same thing over and over again, eventually it starts to lose its effect. It's like too much ice cream—it just stops appealing to you after a while. The ice cream and the putter are still perfectly good things, but you're just not responding to either of them at the present time because they have become too familiar. Stimulus satiation might justify a temporary change to a different putter.

Consider what happens now when you change putters. First of all, welcome the "Hawthorne Effect," which says that whenever anything changes, a temporary increase in productivity can be expected simply because of something new having been put into place. This happens when it comes to industrial production, and it can also happen with putting. The beneficial effect won't last long, but you may as well enjoy it while you can.

Secondly, since you don't know exactly how to deploy this new putter, you may just allow it do more of the work for you than is customarily the case. Perhaps you'll swing it more smoothly, or you might visualize more positive results. This effect, too, will be temporary, because it won't take long for you to start thinking again and trying to do all the work for the putter instead of just swinging it.

> *To conquer your fear of putting, you have to change your attitude so you think of putting as an opportunity rather than a liability. No shortcut exists on the way to this attitude change.*

Lastly, an unfamiliar putter might direct you back to the fundamentals of putting. Again, since you don't know precisely what to do with this new contraption, your only hope may be to line it up, keep your head still and stroke the ball down the line—good ideas for any type of putting.

Take advantage of all the benefits that derive from changing putters. But I predict that the desire for your old putter will eventually return, and Old Faithful will be ready to cooperate again, particularly after being banished to the trunk of your car for a couple of weeks in the blazing summer sun.

Using Judgments from
Others When Reading Putts

While it is often wise to consider the opinions of others before taking important actions, when it comes to putting, you have to remember that there truly are different strokes for different folks. For example, a player with a lot firmer stroke may read less break into a putt than would a player with a smoother stroke. So, the firm putter's read may be of little use to the smooth putter. Nonetheless, I would still entertain the opinions of as many folks as could legally give them to me, and then make my own decision based on all the input.

The Mental Putting Game

To test yourself in a pressure situation, play 18 holes on the practice green. Practicing 18 realistic long-and-short putt combinations, just like you would find on the course, should be helpful in developing the confidence that you'll never have to three-putt again.

Designing 18 realistic holes on a practice green presents a problem and will require some structure and imagination on your part. That is, you will need to design practice putts that vary in slope, break and length, just like the differences from green to green on the course. One way to create this variability is with the aid of a wristwatch.

For slope, divide the face of the watch into three sectors—1 to 20 seconds, 21 to 40 seconds and 41 to 60 seconds. The first sector will represent a flat putt, the second will indicate an uphill putt and the third sector will require a downhill putt. Now glance at the watch and see where the second hand falls. Then find a part of the green that shares that characteristic.

Do the same process for break, dividing the three sectors into straight, left to right and right to left.

Once you have found a place on the green that meets both the slope and break requirements, look down again. The number of seconds will determine the length of the putt (i.e., 27 seconds on the watch equals a 27-foot putt). Repeat this process of randomization of slope, break and length for each of the 18 practice holes.

To provide an example of one such hole, consider a first glance in the 21-to-40-second range, a second glance in the 1-to-20 range and a third glance with a reading of 48 seconds. These would all combine to indicate an uphill, straight putt of 48 feet, or as close as you can find on the practice green.

Now this technique may sound a bit cumbersome at first, but it will move along faster once you get the system down. Furthermore, a little time between putts will only add to a realistic simulation of the time between putts on the course, time that encourages you to focus more seriously on the next putt.

Lastly, since you put all this effort into creating a pressure-filled putt, be sure to line it up carefully, get a feel for the distance and make a meaningful stroke worthy of an important putt. In addition, always take the little pins on the practice green out of the holes. They won't be there when you are out on the course, so don't get used to them in practice either.

Remember, the goal is no three-putts, as well as running in a few one-putts. If additional pressure is desired, start the string over again if you three-putt any in the sequence of 18 holes.

THE SLOPE   THE BREAK   THE LENGTH

The Line Appears One Way
but Feels Another Way

The conflict here is between the objective line and the subjective line. That is, objectively the putt looks like it is going to break right, yet subjectively something makes you feel that it is going to roll straight. Which assessment do you go with?

First of all, consider the origins of the subjective line. The feeling you have about a putt may come in part from a past experience you have had with that particular green. Intimate knowledge of your putting stroke may contribute to a particular feeling about a putt, even more so if your stroke has some idiosyncrasies that tend to manifest themselves in particular situations (e.g., pulling the ball under pressure).

The source of the feeling about a putt may also be purely emotional. Your adrenaline is flowing, and you just know you are going to hit this ball harder than you usually would, thereby taking some of the break out of the putt.

Whatever the case, your actual putting performance is more likely to follow your emotions than your intellect. Despite the potential validity of the objective line, you'll still probably hit the ball down the subjective line that corresponds to your gut feeling. So why fight it? Follow your intuition and commit yourself to a solid stroke down the subjective line. That solid, committed stroke may actually turn out to be the most important factor when you are retrieving the ball from the hole.

Getting the Most
Out of Putting Practice

Practice drills will be most effective and efficient if they simulate the actual putting demands of the course. In other words, practice the types of putts you actually experience during a round. Hit them under some kind of simulated pressure and do so with serious concentration.

In addition, each practice drill should involve a series of 18 repetitions. If you can successfully repeat something 18 times in practice, there should be no reason why you can't do the same thing during an 18-hole round.

The simplest of drills is to make 18 putts in a row, starting over with every miss. This helps to simulate the pressure on the 17th and 18th greens of an actual round, when a great score is within your grasp. Regular, successful completion of this drill will increase your confidence in making short putts to the extent that you will become more aggressive on lag putts, as well as on attacking chips and pitches.

Fear of Putting

Fear of putting is a curious phenomenon. After all, putting is the scoring opportunity in golf, just like shooting is the scoring opportunity in basketball. Tee shots, approach shots, pitching and chipping only serve to set up the potential scoring putt, just like dribbling and passing do in basketball for the jump shot or slam dunk. Yet in basketball, players can't wait to take a shot. In golf, players often dread the fact that they will ultimately have to putt when the ball gets on the green.

To conquer your fear of putting, you have to change your attitude so you think of putting as an opportunity rather than a liability. No shortcut exists on the way to this attitude change. You have to earn your confidence through practice drills such as those described previously. Only then will you relish the thought of getting on the green and taking a stab at a score. When you're able to achieve this, you will join that enviable group of golfers who can't wait to reach the green and have another opportunity to slam-dunk one.

Solving Golf's Mental Mysteries

NYONE WHO HAS PLAYED golf for a number of years has noticed that there are some strange psychic phenomena that occur on the golf course. They may not be of the same magnitude as UFOs or out-of-body experiences, but they might at least qualify as mental mysteries. The following are just a few examples.

Why Do Putts Sometimes Appear to Break Differently from Opposite Sides of the Hole?—Take a 30-foot putt, for example. Lined up from behind the ball—that is, with the ball between you and the hole—the putt appears to have a slight right-to-left break. However, when you walk around to the other side of the hole and line up the same putt with the hole between you and the ball, lo and behold the putt now seems to break the same amount in the opposite direction.

You also might have a right-to-left bias when looking at the line of any putt. This tendency might be due to something in your putting stroke or way of setting up to the ball that encourages hooking putts ever so slightly. Whatever the reason, after seeing putts regularly move from right to left, it is understandable that anyone might begin to read this tendency into all putts.

The curious thing is that when this right-to-left tendency is applied to opposite sides of the hole, the result is the appearance of the putt breaking in opposite directions. From behind the ball, the putt will appear to go left as the line approaches the hole. But when you turn your eyes around by standing on the opposite side of the hole, the right-to-left bias now turns the putt in the opposite direction.

The long-term remedy for this phenomenon would be to work on your setup and putting stroke so as to develop a stroke that rolls the ball straight down the line. Then, the existing bias would gradually extinguish itself, and a tendency to see the true line of a putt would be achieved over time.

A quick fix might involve making a quick read of the line of the putt strictly from behind the ball, making allowances for the idiosyncrasies of your particular setup and putting stroke. Extensive surveying and viewing from other angles might be avoided, lest they introduce confusion.

Another possible explanation for why putts appear to break differently from opposite sides of the hole may involve a human tendency to look at a distant point on the line of a putt from whatever vantage point the line is being surveyed. That is, when viewing a putt with the ball between you and the hole, the tendency may be to look at the area of the green that is closest to the hole. If the putt is being viewed with the hole between you and the ball, the tendency may be to look at the area of the green that is closest to the ball.

Now, let's assume that the putt is a double breaker—moving from left to right in front of the ball and from right to left near the hole. If you are positioned behind the ball looking toward the hole, you may notice only the right-to-left break near the hole and miss the left-to-right break in front of the ball. On the other hand, if you are on the other side of the hole looking back at the ball, then the focus may be only on the left-to-right break in front of the ball, while missing the right-to-left break near the hole. The contrasting conclusions of these two assessments would be that from behind the ball the putt would be considered to have an exclusively right-to-left break, while from the other side of the hole, the impression would be that the putt breaks only from left to right.

A concerted effort must be made to combine information gathered from various vantage points in lining up a putt. Check out the putt from behind the ball, from across the hole and from the lowest point of the green. These three vantage points should give you the best chance of seeing the various undulations of the putting surface.

Dave Stockton's suggestion might also be employed. He recommends dividing the line into thirds and then reading each individual segment independently of the others. Whatever way the information is gathered, the final job of the golfer is to combine all the data objectively into an overall line for the given putt.

> *Putts that appear to break differently from opposite sides of the hole can cause lots of confusion and frustration on the putting green.*

Why Is a 4-foot Putt for Birdie So Much Harder to Make Than a 4-foot Putt for Par or Bogey?—Not all 4-footers are created equal. You might have made 4-foot putts for par or bogey all day long, but when a 4-footer for birdie suddenly presents itself, you choke.

Remember, any given putt is more than traversing just a few feet of real estate. They are all different, despite having some elements in common, such as length.

For example, putts each have their own context. Obviously, a sidehill or downhill putt from 4 feet is considerably different than one that is straight uphill. Not quite so obvious is the difference between a 4-footer on the 18th green for a best-ever score and a routine 4-footer in the middle of the round. In a similar vein, a 4-foot putt for birdie differs considerably from a 4-footer for either par or bogey. All these putts are different according to their varying contexts.

To compound the difficulty, 4-footers for birdies don't present themselves as often as do 4-footers for pars and bogeys. So, golfers don't get to practice 4-foot putts in the birdie context as often as they do in the par/bogey situation. A further complication due to the rarity of short birdie putts is that the player might get overexcited looking at a birdie putt, creating yet another factor (an emotional one) that has to be contended with in the birdie context.

Since opportunities to practice pressure putts do not occur in sufficient numbers during normal play, it is imperative to create practice situations that simulate having to make the pressure-packed 4-foot putt.

This will give you a chance to get accustomed to routinely handling them.

Perhaps the best simulation is to make 18 4-footers in a row on the practice green, starting the sequence over if one is missed and not quitting until all 18 are made in a row. When the 16th, 17th and 18th putts of this series are reached and the prospect of starting over is imminent, your hands will become clammy and your heart will begin to race, just as if the situation were a putt for birdie during a normal round.

Another well-established technique for creating pressure is that of putting a little money on the line. For example, while taking turns on the practice green, you and a friend could wager on who will be the first to miss a 4-footer. The pot could even be increased with each pair of putts that are made until it gets big enough so that the first person who misses has lost an uncomfortable amount. The latter putts in this series are again sure to create a feeling similar to that which is experienced on the course when standing over a short birdie putt.

Why Do Golfers Think They Should Hit a 480-yard Par 5 in Two Shots, While a 440-yard Par 4 Seems Impossible to Hit in Regulation?—"This is an easy par 5—only 480 yards. If I don't make birdie here, I may as well quit."

Contrast that statement with another golfer's lament: "Oh no, this par 4 is a monster—440 yards—the No. 1 handicap hole. I can count on one hand the number of times I've made par on this hole. I'll be happy just to get a bogey."

Something is radically wrong with this picture. The longer hole is thought to be easier to score on than the shorter one. A birdie is granted higher expectation than a par. Two shots are expected to cover a longer distance more easily than a shorter distance.

This strange phenomenon even evidenced itself at the British Open at Troon. In 1989 the 11th hole was played as a par 5 and had a respectable stroke average of 4.5. However, in 1997 the same hole was shortened by 20 yards, played as a par 4 and produced a stroke average of 4.8, as reported during the first round of the tournament. Apparently, even the best players in the world can fall victim to this mental mystery.

The par value assigned to holes establishes certain expectations in golfers' minds, and those expectations demand a certain level of performance. When facing a short par 5, the only absolute demand is that a score of 5 is made on the hole. That seems easy enough, so the tendency is to relax and get into a favorable physical and mental state for making a birdie.

On the other hand, when the same or shorter hole is a par 4, the demand now is to make a score of 4. This is viewed as being more difficult. Therefore, tension is created along with a tendency to blow the hole.

Similarly, if the green is missed in two on the par 5, that's OK. It's a three-shot hole anyway, and a birdie is still in reach with a good chip and a putt. But miss the par 4 in two, and a feeling of doom prevails because that green was supposed to be hit in two shots and scrambling for the expected par seems a lot more difficult than the opportunity to nestle one up there for birdie on a par 5.

Since expectations are the cause of this paradox, those same expectations must be challenged in correcting the situation. For starters, it might help to reverse the thinking in the two situations. What if you were to think of long par 4s as being short par 5s? In other words, make sure to at least get a 5 on the difficult hole, with the bonus that getting the ball up around the green in two will leave some chance of getting up and down for a 4. In contrast, thinking of the short par 5 as a long par 4 may provide a little extra motivation to actually make the birdie on the hole instead of settling for the par 5.

The ideal would be to forget about the different par values of the holes altogether and just try to get the ball in the hole in the fewest strokes possible by the most strategic method available. Strategy may dictate to lay up on both holes and take your chances with chipping and putting. This strategy might avert a lot of trouble that could come from trying to overpower either of the holes.

Smooth, relaxed shots are always going to be the best. So, focus on your pre-shot routine, which serves to relax and provides a frame of mind of simply advancing the ball in the direction of the green, no matter what the length of the hole or the assigned par value.

Why Do Approach Shots into Greens Seem to Fall Short of the Greens More Often Than Going Long Over the Greens?—This mystery may separate the pros from the amateurs. When pros miss a green, they often seem to be chipping back from behind the green. Contrast this with amateurs who often seem to leave themselves with a chip or a pitch shot from somewhere short of the putting surface. In other words, the pros seem to err on the long side, while amateurs seem to insist on falling short.

One explanation is that the pros know the precise yardages their clubs produce and consistently hit their clubs those prescribed distances. Therefore, when they determine the yardage to the flagstick, they can select the best club and hit it correctly to get the ball to that destination. Amateurs, on the other hand, are not as well informed or consistent regarding the yardages of their clubs. When in doubt they tend to think they can hit the ball farther than they actually can, which may result in their taking less club than is actually necessary. Combine this under-clubbing with the probability that the amateur will not strike the ball as crisply as the pro, and it is little wonder that the shot falls short of the green more often than not.

A shot over water can be much harder than the same shot over dry terrain if you don't control your focus.

The pros also tend to hit the ball past the pin and spin it back to the hole, while amateurs try to land the ball short of the pin and bounce it forward. When pros err, it may be that they have hit the ball a little longer than they intended in trying to allow for their usual backspin. Amateurs, on the other hand, may err on the side of hitting the shot a little shorter than they intended because they are worried about getting a bigger bounce forward than they actually want.

Another factor to consider is that the pros realize that the green is, say, 30 yards deep and focus not just on the green, but also where the flagstick is located within that 30-yard expanse. If the pin is toward the back of the green, they adjust by selecting more club. Amateurs, in contrast, tend to focus on the green in general, and more often than not simply on the front of the green. They are mistakenly thinking about "just getting it to the green." This limited focus can lead to choosing just enough club to, indeed, get the ball to the front of the green but well short of the location of the flagstick.

Therefore, plan your approach shots by taking into account not just the location of the green, but also the location of the flagstick on the green. After all, the objective is to get the ball to the hole—not just on the green. If the flagstick is on the back of the green, select at least one stronger club in making the shot. If the green is elevated, yet one more club may be needed.

Yardages of each club in a player's bag must be determined so that when a club is selected, it can be swung with confidence that it should go only the necessary distance. A tentative swing, or letting up on a shot, is another reason why shots may end up short of the green.

When ultimately addressing the ball, consider focusing on the back edge of the green rather than on the front edge. Focusing on the back edge may get the ball at least to the middle of the green, while focusing on the front may not even get the ball to the green at all.

Why Is a Shot Over Water Harder to Execute Than the Same Shot Over Dry Terrain?—Drive after drive can be launched successfully off the tee until you reach the 13th hole, the one with the little stream in front of the tee. At this point, even though a normal drive will clear the stream by 150 yards, you can be relied upon to dribble the tee shot into the stream.

The same thing happens with the little pond that fronts the 17th green. All that's required is a simple pitch shot of about 50 yards, the kind the golfer has successfully executed all day long. But now the ball is deposited directly into the pond instead of following its usual trajectory safely onto the green.

Once again the culprit is focus. When the water isn't present, the focus is on the intended target—the middle of the fairway or a landing spot on the green. But when water comes into play, the focus invariably shifts to the feared intruder. This shouldn't be much of a surprise, since it is usually in your best interest to focus on intruders. But in this case, such a focus will only lead to the undesirable result of hitting shots at the intruder.

The remedy is to control your focus. Since it is natural to pay attention to intruders, don't fight this tendency. When confronting a water hazard, go ahead and look at it in the planning of your shot. Assess it carefully. Indeed, appreciate the beauty it contributes to the design of the hole. Once you have directed sufficient attention to that feature of the hole, you must now turn your full attention to the target—the intended landing spot for the ball in the fairway or on the green. Maintain focus on that favorable landing spot and resist the temptation to return attention even minimally to any obstacles or hazards.

Ultimately, address the ball with precise alignment, execute the shot with intense focus on seeing the club strike the ball and refuse to look up until you achieve a vivid mental image of the perfect shot going directly at the intended target.

Lesson #50

How the Pros Do It

Make the Most Out of Attending a PGA Tournament

I F YOU'RE A GOLF junkie who's glued to the television every weekend but who has never attended a PGA Tour event, you're missing out on something. Golf in person is quite different from golf on the tube.

For example, television attempts to spice up the action with a lot of jumping between holes and endless analysis regarding every move the golfers make. In contrast, golf at the event is peaceful and silent with a focus on limited action and analysis happening only in the minds of the players and spectators. Indeed, polite applause follows great shots, and cheers resound for periodic heroics, but in general the setting is serene with well-behaved, appreciative fans and beautiful surroundings.

Other benefits accrue from live golf, some of which are included in the following sampler of observations. Consider these suggestions and psychological tips as you rub elbows with the pros.

1. Go Early—Careful planning will optimize your learning and enjoyment. Thursday and Friday are the best days to attend, as you'll find more golfers and fewer spectators. The 36-hole cut has yet to occur, so all the competitors are still in the field. An additional bonus is that the workweek will keep the crowds at bay until the weekend.

2. Go Backward—Start at the 18th green and walk the course backward. If you happen to catch the first group of the day on No. 18, there's a chance you will see every player in the field as you proceed around to the first hole. You also will beat the crowds to some of the best vantage points, as the players come to you rather than you running after them. When you encounter a player of interest, follow the player in the direction of play for a few shots or holes before resuming your backward trek. Such retracing of your steps will extend your day and slow you down so you can fully appreciate the action and the surroundings. In addition, building variety into the situation will decrease your boredom and enhance your motivation to learn. Seeing a variety of players also will provide more examples for the learning process.

3. Get in Shape—Good physical conditioning eliminates fatigue when you are trying to concentrate, learn and enjoy over a long period of time. Keep in mind that golf is perhaps the only sport that involves exercise on the part of the spectator. Indeed, a healthy exhaustion may set in after a day of walking, standing, stretching and exposure to the elements over five or six miles of golfing real estate. An added benefit of the exertion is that you can skip any other exercise that may be part of your daily routine.

4. Skip the Putting—When viewing golf on TV, putting is the component that's most readily appreciated because the viewer can witness the entire shot on the television monitor and can actually see the hole in the green. These two phenomena are made possible, of course, by the aerial perspective that elevated television cameras provide.

However, when it comes to live golf, it's difficult to see the hole from ground level, which makes it hard to appreciate a close putt that doesn't actually drop out of sight into the cup. An additional drawback in viewing putting on site is that the crowds tend to gather around the greens, making the action harder to see.

At the event, you may find the long game more interesting to view, including everything from tee shots to pitch shots. You can see the entirety of towering shots that television has difficulty capturing. Furthermore, with the flag in the hole for the longer shots, the results can be observed from a reasonable, unobstructed distance.

No situation can provide you with everything. So, recognize what each situation has to offer and take full advantage of those aspects.

5. Position Yourself Wisely—Smart viewing wins out over following the crowd and chasing nothing but the thrills and excitement. When observing tee shots, the best place to stand is at a point along the ropes about 5 yards in front of the tee markers. From this position, you are not likely to be blocked by caddies and scorers. You'll be standing at a reasonable angle to the golfer, allowing you to view the mechanics of the swing, and you can still get a nice view of the flight of the ball.

> *You can learn a lot by watching the pros in person if you know what to look for.*

Another option is to position yourself at a point down the fairway near the landing area of the drives that will afford a close-up of the golfers' approach shots to the green. Remember to take cover behind a tree until all the balls have landed, lest you become an unintended backboard for an errant shot.

6. Right-handers Follow Left-handers—A right-handed spectator facing a lefty like Phil Mickelson as he swings obtains a more direct impression of the pro's swing mechanics because he or she can mirror the swing, which is hard to accomplish in observing a fellow right-hander. Keep in mind that Mickelson learned golf by mirroring his dad, who was a right-handed player. Unfortunately, right-handers have only a few southpaws to follow, while left-handers have a multitude of right-handed players to choose from as models.

7. Follow Players Similar to You—There are two ways a player can be similar to you: 1) in stature, build or body type; and 2) in looking the way you feel during the swing.

If you are a player who is vertically challenged, consider following one of the successful shorter players on tour, such as Jeff Sluman. On the other hand, if you are tall and lanky, look for Ernie Els. Players who have a stature that's similar to yours battle the same difficulties you have to contend with. Since they have surmounted those difficulties, it may be instructive to observe them and study just how they continue to do it. It helps to position yourself in relation to the player so as to internalize the feelings and image of the swing.

To enhance this effect, choose a player of your build and body type who also looks the way you feel during the swing. Now, we don't know exactly how we look in swinging a golf club, but occasionally we make a pass at the ball that feels something like the visual impression made by the swing of a given pro. For example, I sometimes put a strong, linear, forward move on the ball that feels a bit like Ben Crenshaw looks when he moves through the ball. At other times, I feel one-piece and compact as Nick Price appears. On rare occasions I feel like the club is simply dropping on the ball, reminiscent of the unforgettable swing of Fred Couples.

8. Take Dead Aim, but Note the Struggle—The pros don't just hit the ball on the green; they get it close to the pin. If amateurs regularly had putts for birdie from 10 to 20 feet, they would make a lot of pars and birdies, too. On the other hand, when the pros misfire and find themselves with 50-foot putts, putts through the fringe or wicked downhill chips from greenside rough, they struggle like everyone else.

However, when the pros struggle, they do it a bit better than the rest of us. They are good chippers, great from the sand and quite accomplished with the 5-foot putt. Still, despite their skill, it's a struggle when they put themselves in less than perfect positions around the green.

You can learn from the pros in this regard. "Take dead aim," as Harvey Penick said, but be prepared to back up your mistakes with a heavily practiced short game. Also, don't be too hard on yourself when you fail to get up and down from a difficult position. Remember, the pros struggle with these challenging situations, too.

9. Observe the Deliberateness, Rhythm and Patience—The pros play a methodical game, with a gentle deliberateness pervading the action. They never rush a shot, are seldom off balance and rarely overswing. Physical exertion appears foreign to them, with rhythm being the key.

The methodical nature of the pros' games is particularly evident on chip shots where they seem to stay down forever, just watching the action between the clubhead, the ball and the turf. Outcome appears to be of secondary concern. It's as if each player is saying, "All I have to do is my job over the ball, and everything will work out as planned. I don't have to see it. I know what's happening even before I look at the result."

You should adopt this mindset as well. Simply do your job over the ball, keep your head down long enough to make sure you have done it and allow for the outcome to take care of itself.

10. Enjoy the Silent, Slow Motion—Television coverage involves strategically placed microphones picking up the crack of the ball off the clubface while cameras jump from one spot on the course to another. In contrast, live golf is relatively silent, with a strange sense of slow motion embodied in the gentle swings, the ball hanging tantalizingly in flight and the ultimate soft landing on the green. Even the players and spectators seem to glide slowly down the fairways, quietly making their appointed rounds. Combine this peaceful flow with the reverent solitude and natural beauty of the golf course, and you will have captured the unparalleled feeling of live, spectator golf.

CONCLUSION

THERE YOU HAVE IT: a journey through the recesses of the collective golfing mind. It's complex, mysterious at times, but now a little more manageable, at least, since you have an organizational framework for making sense of it all.

In closing, here are a few general points that I hope came through loud and clear:

1. *Practice* is not a four-letter word. Therefore, don't avoid it. Do everything you can to make practice fun and interesting so you will engage in it on a regular basis. It's the only way to improvement.

2. Avail yourself eagerly to the pressures of golf. Frequent exposure to the demands of the game is the only way to achieve *mental toughness*.

3. Keep things as *simple* as possible—be it swing keys, mental images or even the games you play. For example, nothing is better than straight medal-play golf if you want to learn how to shoot low scores. (

4. Strive for *control* during your rounds, attempting to calmly place the ball around the course as in a chess game. Knowing you have control over your swing, ball flight and your emotions will bring you success and peace of mind in all places and stages of your golfing life.

I could go on and on, but let me leave you with just two additional thoughts: *Golf is a difficult game.* Don't expect it to be otherwise. For as long as you play, it will be a challenge and try your patience, which only adds to the interest and the lifelong desire to pursue golfing excellence.

Lastly, don't let the difficulty keep you from *playing the game the way it's supposed to be played.* Play by the rules, count all your strokes and be the golfer you really are. Indeed, handling yourself in this manner should make you proud to be a member of a select group of dedicated golfers who *play it straight* in their quest to conquer this grand old game in the fashion that the Scots intended.

INDEX

Index

Index